INQUIRING AND DISCERNING HEARTS

Scholars Press

General Series

Number 7

INQUIRING AND DISCERNING HEARTS
Vocation and Ministry with Young Adults on Campus

Sam Portaro and Gary Peluso

INQUIRING
AND
DISCERNING
HEARTS

Sam Portaro   Gary Peluso

INQUIRING AND DISCERNING HEARTS

by
Sam Portaro and Gary Peluso

© 1993
Scholars Press

Cover Photograph: University of Chicago

Library of Congress Cataloging in Publication Data
Portaro, Sam Anthony.
  Inquiring and discerning hearts: vocation and ministry with
young adults on campus/ by Sam Portaro and Gary Peluso.
    p. cm. — (Scholars Press General series; no. 7)
  Includes bibliographical references.
  ISBN 1-55540-892-3. —ISBN 1-55540-893-1 (pbk.)
  1. Church work with students. 2. College students—Religious life.
I. Peluso, Gary.   II. Title.
BV1610.P67 1993
259'.24'0973—dc20

                                                    93-5720
                                                    CIP

Printed in the United States of America
on acid-free paper

Heavenly Father, we thank you that by water and the Holy Spirit
you have bestowed upon these your servants the forgiveness of sin,
and have raised them to the new life of grace.
Sustain them, O Lord, in your Holy Spirit
Give them an inquiring and discerning heart,
the courage to will and to persevere,
a spirit to know and to love you,
and the gift of joy and wonder in all your works.
AMEN

from The Baptismal Liturgy,
The Book of Common Prayer

TABLE OF CONTENTS

─❧ Acknowledgements ☙─

This project owes much to the commitment, energies, and imaginations of many people. Craig Dykstra and James Wind of The Lilly Endowment encouraged and guided. Laurie Patton and David Rehm, while pursuing their own doctoral studies and sharing responsibilities as Co-Chairs of the Episcopal Church Council at The University of Chicago, devoted many hours to the proposal that framed this undertaking. Patricia Beckman was the efficient and thoughtful administrator who labored over the several drafts and prepared the manuscript for publication. Maria Scott oversaw the financial aspects of the project with sound stewardship and firm compassion. Jennifer Browne, Robert Heath, Christopher and Patricia Beckman, and the Episcopal Church Council supported the project in giving generously of their own ministries that the program and life of the Episcopal Campus Ministry at Brent House continued unabated.

We are especially indebted to those colleagues who read our draft and shared their insights, shaping this study and making it a genuinely collaborative offering: Giles Asbury, Fred Borsch, Paula Brownlee, Jim Carr, Sydney Condray, Charles Doak, Casaundra Williams Franker, Barbara Heck, Richard Hicks, Will Hinson, Barbara Isaacs, Doug King, W. Fred Lamar, James Lewis, Odette Lockwood-Stewart, Robert Lynn, Martin Marty, Alda Marsh Morgan, Alistair Nevius, Jim Nielsen, Michael Paley, Sharon Parks, David Perry, Nathaniel Porter, Clyde Robinson, Wade Clark Roof, Donald Shockley, John Worrell, and Manuel Wortman.

We are grateful, too, for Harry Gilmer, Gina M. Tansley, and their colleagues at Scholars Press, whose encouragement and skill brings our work to fruition by placing it in your hands, adding you to this conversation.

Finally, we give thanks for the students and former students who offered their perspectives and challenged our analyses, for our partners—lay and ordained—who share our passion for this ministry, and for our families and friends who suffer that passion with grace and affection.

—⊰ PREFACE ⊱—

Without counsel purposes are disappointed:
but in the multitude of counsellors they are established.
Proverbs 15:22 (KJV)

How are we to explain the distance between the church and the academy in our present experience? This question arose in one of the many conversations that contributed to this study. Robert Coles suggests one possible answer in the observation that for some in our culture the pursuit of knowledge has itself become a religion.[1] If this observation is correct, then the antipathies and apathies generated between church and academy are those of rivals.

This rivalry is only one of a growing number of competitive relationships in American society. Yet this rivalry is of particular interest because it is a competition between institutions that were once collegial partners. Moreover, it is in the intersection of this rivalry between church and academy that many individuals in our American culture find their own patterns of relationship modelled and formed, for good or for ill.

This study examines the relationship of church and academy on campus in the period just after World War II. It was a time of great optimism and expansion, as succeeding chapters detail. It was also a time, as is our own, over which the shadow of that shattering experience called the Holocaust lengthened. The Holocaust, only fully revealed after

---

[1] Robert Coles, *Times of Surrender* (Iowa City: University of Iowa Press, 1988), 23.

the close of the war, reminds church, academy, and any other individual or institution of the untrustworthiness of human endeavors.

But World War II, the Holocaust, and the destructions of Hiroshima and Nagasaki also teach the profound depths of human responsibility. They reveal that to an alarming extent God entrusts humanity with ultimacy. By revealing the degree to which human endeavor can destroy, these shadows also reveal the invitation to a level of partnership with the Creator that is not welcomed by all. The implications of this revelation are that rivalries—and the exclusive claims by which rivalries are made and sustained—must give way to *collegiality and conversation.*

Some would have used the word "community," but we have chosen other words to describe the characteristics of partnership. For the time being, we remain suspicious of community if only because it has tended toward the formation of rivalries and not the healing of them. We are also suspicious of those notions of community that discourage honest conversation and a genuine respect for difference. If, as Coles suggested, those within both church and academy live poised between rivals, the way to reconciliation demands a courageous examination of the true state of things and honest conversation that acknowledges realities. This entails not only the pride of accomplishments and the promise of potentials, but the candid confession of disappointment.

Disappointment may seem a strange beginning to any work. Yet the richness of this word in its several meanings aptly captures the state of mainline Protestant young adult ministries on American campuses. The venerable Oxford English Dictionary recalls the several dimensions of disappointment:

- to undo the appointment of; to deprive of an appointment, an office or possession; to dispossess, deprive
- to frustrate the expectation or desire of (person); to defeat, balk, or deceive in fulfillment of desire
- to break off (what has been appointed or fixed), to fail to keep or comply by (an engagement); to fail to fulfill an appointment
- to undo or frustrate anything appointed or determined; to defeat the realization or fulfillment of (plans purposes, intentions); to balk, fail, thwart (anticipations, hopes, etc.)
- to appoint, equip, or accoutre improperly[2]

---

[2] *Oxford English Dictionary,* 2nd. ed., prepared by J. A. Simpson & E. S. C. Weiner., vol. IV (Oxford: Clarendon Press, 1989), 720.

Young adult ministries on campus, once a prominent component of the educational and evangelical work of mainline Protestant churches, no longer enjoy priority status. Their "appointment" to bear witness to Christ Jesus and to nurture disciples on campus has in many places been rescinded. In some cases, these ministries have been recalled from active service; in many more, they have simply been deprived of the resources necessary to fulfill their appointment.

Frustration and defeat are well known to all associated with campus ministries. Denominations, unable to equip America's burgeoning system of higher education, are frustrated in attempts to mount effective ministries on campuses that grow more numerous and diverse. Campus ministers are frequently frustrated by the seeming lack of interest or assistance directed toward what they believe to be an important work of the church. But campus ministries have also been a frustration and disappointment to the churches, whose quantitative and qualitative expectations of young adult ministries are seldom met.

Estrangement has been the common response to frustration, each side failing to comply with the expectations of the other and each thus failing to make or sustain a satisfactory relationship. In some instances ministries have been foiled or thwarted by outright deception: by miscommunication and political maneuver. In others, disappointment has been the inevitable result of poor deployment of resources, human and financial—by demanding too much or too little, by granting too much or too little, by sending the wrong message or the wrong messenger.

But the history of mainline Protestant campus ministry does not culminate in a disappointing present, nor is it condemned to a disappointing future. There are signs of hope for campus ministry. In *A Second Chance for American Protestants*, Martin Marty wrote: "I shall argue that the first chance for evangelical witness in culture is spent, but this is no cause for despair. The second chance, which leaves behind the assumptions of Christendom, of 'placed' Christianity, permits more freedom and more mobility in the world."[3] A similar judgment might well be made of young adult ministries on campus.

Beyond Marty's assessment more is demanded: The second chance not only demands the surrender of 'placed' or 'fixed' ministries—ministries strictly bounded and even walled off from the culture around them, the second chance also requires abandoning institutional and

---

[3] Martin E. Marty, *A Second Chance for American Protestants* (New York: Harper & Row, 1963), ix.

organizational assumptions that frustrate conversation. The wisdom of Proverbs is proven in modern experience: insufficient communication and conversation—that is to say, counsel—have disappointed the purposes of young adult ministry on campus. The way out of that disappointment demands deliberate counsel among all concerned for this ministry and for the ministry of the church of which it is a part.

This study grew out of concern for campus ministry and a desire to engage conversation on this work. The project was initiated by the Episcopal Church Council at the University of Chicago whose ministry on that campus is centered at Brent House.[4] The centerpiece of life at

---

[4] This facility, erected as a private home in 1905 and purchased by the Women's Auxiliary of the Episcopal Church in 1929, has been the center of a ministry whose history parallels that of the larger Protestant community. With strong affinity for the World Student Christian Federation, Edna Biller founded the work at Brent House to serve international students. "Mother" Biller and the two women who succeeded her—Elizabeth Williamson and Madge Sanmann—hosted many ecumenical occasions that brought students from diverse cultures into conversation. After World War II, the Reverend Bernard Iddings Bell retired to Chicago's Hyde Park neighborhood, home of the University of Chicago. He brought with him an enthusiasm for faith and learning, and a determination to expand the work of the church in the academic setting. In 1946, the Episcopal Church Council at the University of Chicago was formed and opened the governance of the ministry to this board composed of laity and clergy. With the Reverend Messrs. Phill Lewis and William Baar, who followed Madge Sanmann—herself a Presbyterian laywoman—the international student work continued, but with the addition of a denominational ministry conforming to the then-popular model and adopting the familiar name of the Canterbury Club.

The Reverend John Pyle followed Baar in 1960, by which time the international component was equalled and perhaps in some instances eclipsed by a strong denominational ministry that offered student counselling and bridged the traditional and somewhat formal liturgies of worship with an experimental community called "The Underground Church." This congregation met in a basement chapel and initiated liturgical experimentation. Over dinners in the living room students met such figures as the controversial Bishop James Pike and Malcolm Boyd, author of the best-selling prayerbook, *Are You Running With Me, Jesus?* Upstairs, former bedrooms became the offices of several Protestant campus ministries and an institute for religion and psychotherapy.

By 1975, when Pyle retired, the times had changed again. The national Episcopal Church, which had owned and maintained the building and largely funded the international student ministry, sold Brent House to the Episcopal Diocese of Chicago. The spent energies of student unrest eventuated in apathy toward traditional ministries, though the work continued under the leadership of the Episcopal Church Council and of the Reverend Donald Judson, who served as interim director of the ministry while pursuing his own doctoral studies at the University. In 1978 the Reverend Charles H. D. Brown became chaplain and director of Brent House, by which time many of the ministries that had previously shared the building were

Brent House is vocational formation. Programs in varied disciplines address issues and questions essential to the integration of professional and personal life. Their aim is to encourage conversation between young adults and their mentors—faculty, administrators and professional practitioners in the medical, legal, and business disciplines, and in the scholarly disciplines of teaching and research.

The experience of these conversational programs and the process that shaped them have led to a ministry that embraces theological education and spiritual formation of church members with young adults in a campus setting. The Episcopal Church Council at the University of Chicago defines its purpose in its mission: to interpret the Church to the University and to interpret the University to the Church. Affirming and enlarging Marty's theory of the Protestant second chance, this work of interpretation involves mediation and dialogue between these two worlds and encompasses three basic principles:

This ministry recognizes existing community

Students gathered by pursuit of a particular discipline, either as an undergraduate college or in the concentrated manner of graduate study, form a community whose common center is the discipline itself. This is a natural, even holy, community in as much as study and preparation for service is a godly calling. Any theology that takes seriously the vocation of the laity must accord to professional study and formation in lay disciplines the same respect expected of and accorded to the education and preparation of ordained disciplines.

This ministry recognizes lay authority

Lay leadership is essential to the life and work of the Christian church. Nearly all Brent House programs are conceived, organized and executed by lay people—a living embodiment of what

---

diminished or had separated themselves as each returned to a more denominational base. Student interest in campus ministry ebbed. Brown left in 1980 and the work was overseen by the Episcopal Church Council until 1982 when the Reverend Sam Portaro accepted the chaplaincy. By 1985 work began on a restoration of the property, interest in and response to creative programming increased, and the Episcopal Church Council was renewed.

the Gallup Organizations' studies of American churches report is
the young person's vision for the church.[5] Experience in the
planning and administration of ministry needs to be shared

In their *Ministry of the Laity*, James D. Anderson and Ezra Earl
Jones suggest that "lay ministry be properly defined as the
outward active expressive life and activity of those persons who
through baptism regard themselves as belonging to the people of
God.... The fact that the definition...implies that this ministry is
largely carried out in a non-Christian context (namely the pluralistic modern world) means that another set of worldly assumptions must be invoked for the definition to be intelligible in the
usual settings of modern society."[6] Medical students and physicians, for instance, are best equipped to articulate the questions
and issues affecting the medical discipline. The same assumption
applies to lawyers, business professionals and the like.

Real estate developer Robert McLean puts it most succinctly:
"As lay persons we have a responsibility to write theology in the
language of the particular discipline in which we are engaged."[7]
Brent House—indeed, any campus ministry—is uniquely
equipped with the resources both of theology and of the professional disciplines necessary to their enterprise.

This ministry serves
The foregoing principles are requisite to a ministry that takes
seriously the commission of the Church to serve. This commission
is not to be self-serving. We welcome and respect the participation of a variety of individuals in the work of these programs.

---

[5] "Future decline or growth [of the mainline denominations] depends on the
success of churches in responding to the insistence of young and well-educated
Americans for greater involvement in their churches. A recent Gallup survey shows
70% of adults under 30 believe that the laity rather than clergy should have greater
influence in determining the future of religion in America. The comparable figure for
college graduates is 65%." George Gallup, Jr. and Jim Castelli, *The People's Religion*
(New York: MacMillan Publishing Co., in press), quoted in "The Spiritual Health of
the Episcopal Church," (New York: Office of the Presiding Bishop, The Episcopal
Church Center, n.d.), 17.

[6] James D. Anderson and Ezra Earl Jones, *Ministry of the Laity* (San Francisco:
Harper & Row, 1986), xii.

[7] Robert McLean, "Responsibility to Write Theology" *Cathedral College of the Laity
Newsletter* 4, No. 2 (June 1983): 1.

The Episcopal Church Council, overseeing and participating in the ministry of Brent House, has also gained new energy and focus in recent years. As Brent House has grown, Council leadership has become increasingly involved in and committed to its programs. This group of twelve men and women from both the university community and from the diocese at large is involved in a number of areas of the life of Brent House, from liturgy to programming. Brent House's present experience comes at a time when campus ministry as a whole is struggling to recover a sense of its own mission. The experience of the Episcopal Church Council has been integral to its own self-discernment—its own vocation to campus ministry. The kind of reflection encouraged of other vocations became the instrument by which to discern more clearly its own vocation. Discernment in both instances involves intentional study of one's own ministry from theological, biblical, and psycho-social perspectives.

From the study of one's own vocation clear implications emerge for the avoidance of repetitious error and for the intentional replication of success. One perceives which energies serve one's intention and which are detrimental or counterproductive. This is vocational discernment consonant with the Christian doctrine of the Incarnation, which theology posits the sacredness of human life and experience as integral, even essential, to on-going Revelation. In a larger context, the process of discernment distinguishes all thoughtful "professional" ministry, using professional in its full religious connotation of action taken as both confession and proclamation of faith.

The Council understands its vocational responsibility both to be open to critique and to share its learning more widely. The Council has grown to its present position of strength by doing one-half of its mission well: it has interpreted the Church to the University in the form of vocational reflection. The Council now must work to realize the second half of its mission: to interpret the University to the Church. To this end the Council commissioned Sam Portaro to direct this study to stimulate and clarify the Church's vocation on campus, its mission in higher education.

Ordained an Episcopal priest in 1975, Sam Portaro has served in campus ministry since 1976, when he became Episcopal Chaplain to the College of William & Mary in Virginia and Associate to the Rector of Bruton Parish Church. In 1982 he completed the Doctor of Ministry at Princeton Theological Seminary and assumed his current post at Brent House at the University of Chicago. As project director and primary author of the study he was assisted by research associate and co-author

Gary Peluso, an ordained elder of the United Methodist Church who earned a Ph.D. in Practical Theology at the University of Chicago in 1991.

The purpose of the following essay is to offer an understanding of where mainline Protestant campus ministry has been situated within the national agendas of denominational ministries since World War II. This task is prerequisite to assess campus ministry's current status, as well as to discern a vocation for campus ministry and suggest resources necessary to re-appointment. The exploration has been one of vocation: How have national denominational officials, and other relevant parties, understood the vocation of campus ministry? With what resources have these ministries been equipped by the national churches to fulfill their vocations? These questions and the history revealed in their answers are fundamental to the ultimate concern: What is the vocation of campus ministry and how might this ministry be equipped for the coming years?

In order to answer these questions, we consulted denominational mission statements, position papers, and program budgets for campus ministry. Our attention was centered on documents generated at the national level of denominations. We are aware of the philosophical limitations imposed by this perspective, given the present distance between national leadership and the field of ministry on campus. We are also aware that much can be learned from examining the processes that intervened to create this distance. We are painfully aware of the practical limitations, too. We are very grateful to a number of persons with long memories; none of the denominations we studied have kept consistent or readily available historical records of their life and work on campus.

Some information was also gathered on private funding of campus ministry for the period under consideration (1948-present), with emphasis upon the Lilly Endowment and the Danforth Foundation. Both foundations perceived religious commitment as important to their own philanthropy, and higher education ministry a component of that philanthropic commitment. How did they historically justify that philanthropy, and how did they justify its curtailment? Where and how might the private philanthropic sector be engaged and involved in young adult ministry on campus?

The study is limited to three mainline denominations: The Protestant Episcopal Church, The United Methodist Church, The Presbyterian Church U.S.A.[8] But it is further limited in that its primary focus is over-

---

[8] Catholicism and Lutheranism, though possessed of strong campus ministries, were excluded from this study because both have nationally organized offices of campus ministry that at least until recently have been more or less sequestered both

whelmingly white and of the middle class or higher in the economic sector. The campus work of the denominations under study does extend to African-American campuses, but largely in the retention of historically-Black colleges and universities within the fold of denominational institutions of higher education. Because there is a distinct difference between church-related higher education and campus ministry on private and public campuses, the former occupy a lesser place in this study. Also, minority enrollments have increased most markedly on commuter campuses, that portion of the higher education community least served by traditional denominational campus ministry. This is not to assent to discrimination nor to insinuate inferiority, but rather to acknowledge the biases and limitations of this project.

We are further biased by several important factors. Sam Portaro has been a campus minister at William and Mary and the University of Chicago a total of the last seventeen years. He had heard stories of the bloody demise of campus ministry funding in the late 1960s, of how parental denominations cut off the allowance of their rebellious children, and of the Pied-Piper campus ministers who often led them in rebellion. We wanted to discover whether or not this remembered history was accurate. Moreover, we both believe the present restructuring of our denominations, in spite of present pain, holds great promise for a recovery of a missional mindset and for a fruitful discussion of ecclesiology at every level of our respective denominations.

This book is shaped by the outline of the research. The first six chapters are historical and attempt a story of the interplay between forces at work in American society, in the university, in the churches, and in campus ministry itself.

---

from the politics of the congregational/lay process and from budget determinations. In addition, Catholicism has retained most of its campuses and has thus integrated academy and church in a manner now largely lost to historically mainline Protestant campuses. To include either denomination would skew the study. We were more interested in those denominations that historically have experienced parallel theology and polity. Of course, our findings may have implications for Catholicism and other denominations, especially as the tension of maintaining the academic and religious functions of their institutions of higher education grows more strained and a dichotomy of functions increases, thus approximating the situation we know in the mainstream Protestant culture. It should be further understood that Methodist in this study includes the United Methodist Church and the former Methodist Church; Presbyterian includes the Presbyterian Church USA and its predecessor bodies in the northern United States.

Chapter One, covering 1948-1957, introduces the expansive culture of post-World War II America. It was a time of extensive and rapid growth. Amid the swift changes and enlarged perspectives demanded of the time, institutions and individuals hastened to establish a standard of normalcy and with that standard attempted to contain and order the change. By 1958-1963, chronicled in Chapter Two, expansion at all levels of American life and a growing realization of the nation's diversity fostered more oversight and gave rise to institutional bureaucracy. American government, churches, and higher education grew more complex in organization. Amid diversity, people who shared common interest or cause found organization essential to be heard and to effect response from agencies and institutions. Special purpose groups arose to meet this need, giving voice and visible presence to individuals and issues previously unknown. These groups articulated and demonstrated the discontent of their constituencies, arousing among the established groups and institutions a reciprocal disaffection.

The potential for conversation among the disparate voices of the culture and its institutions began to disintegrate into confusion and chaos from 1963 to 1968, presented in Chapter Three. Bureaucratic structures reached and exceeded the point of maximum efficiency and began to strain as increased demands clogged their machinery. Radical changes were called for, but process was insufficient to respond easily. Disappointment in the structures of institutional leadership and governance gradually grew to distrust, until all authority withered under the heat of protest. Violence ensued. From 1969 to 1973, as indicated in Chapter Four, all American institutions—and the culture itself—were thrown into turmoil. The failure of church, university, or government to lead effectively resulted in the literal disappointment of each. Church memberships dropped as religion and spirituality became less communal, more individual. Universities retreated from the historic leadership of teaching to embrace a market-driven commitment to research. Government lost much of its authority to order or inspire as cynicism and disaffection displaced commitment to democratic process.

With the nation reeling from so much upheaval, the years 1973 to 1980 which form the fifth chapter represented a reasonable retreat into privatism, a time for regathering and restructuring. From 1981 to 1990, treated in Chapter Six, a search for renewed forms of social life, creativity and freedom animated many of those individuals and communities previously on the margins of established American life and institutions, while a genuine fear of displacement and disestablishment filled many of those who occupied the center.

Chapters Seven through Eleven approach a prognosis for young adult ministry on campus through a reconsideration of ideas laid out by Kenneth Underwood in the Danforth study of campus ministry of 1963-69. Underwood argued that clergy fulfilled priestly, pastoral, prophetic and governing roles. Rather than focusing on the clergyperson or professional campus minister as Underwood did, the ministry of the whole church is examined. Underwood's modes of ministry stimulate and suggest a new paradigm for a community of ministry.

In Chapter Seven the priestly role is reinterpreted as the communal task of nurturing vocation. The pastoral role of the community is examined in Chapters Eight and Nine and treated as stewardship, interpreted not only in financial terms, but in the fullness of stewardship's dimensions. Underwood's category of governance is, in Chapter Ten, abandoned in favor of a politics of inclusion and partnership. Chapter Eleven turns to the community's prophetic mode, reinterpreted as reconciling leadership incarnate in active ministry.

All involved in this project—the Episcopal Church Council at the University of Chicago and the co-authors they commissioned—share a love for the church and the university and for the ministries of each. That love undoubtedly biases this work, sometimes sharpening critique and at other times tempering it. This is also the work of reformers who appreciate their place in that historic company of Protestants whose life and faith they share. Thus they do not shy from change but understand it as an essential component of an active Christian faith.

Finally, they acknowledge that Protestant mainline ministry to young adults on campus is in need of reforming. For social, theological, and financial reasons the church and its ministries must change. But the wisdom of Proverbs cautions, perhaps all the more clearly in modern rendering, "Without counsel, plans go wrong, but with many advisors they succeed." (NRSV) The purposes of campus ministry demand counsel—conversation—among the many who bear and share responsibility for this and other ministries of the church. Thoughtful counsel is important lest we abandon or destroy something of value needlessly. Despite the haste or confusion of intention that attended the Protestant presence on campus, these ministries have made and continue to make valuable contributions to God's work in the world. And despite the pain and consternation that accompany the present status of campus and other ministries, traces of God's design may be glimpsed within. We can be proud of many accomplishments. We can find hope in much of our tribulation. But before we abandon our history or jettison our future, can we take counsel, share a conversation? As incentive and impetus to that conversation this book is offered, with this prefatory note from G. K. Chesterton:

> The more modern type of reformer goes up to it and says, "I don't see the use of this; let us clear it away." To which the more intelligent type of reformer will do well to answer: "If you don't see the use of it, I certainly won't let you clear it away. Go away and think. Then, when you can come back and tell me that you *do* see the use of it, I may allow you to destroy it."[9]

---

[9] G. K. Chesterton, *The Thing: Why I Am a Catholic* (New York: Dodd, Mead and Co., 1946), 27, quoted in *The Quotable Chesterton*, eds. Marlin, Swan & Rabatin (San Francisco: Ignatius Press, 1986), 294.

—⚜ 1 ⚜—

THE CENTER THAT WOULD NOT HOLD:
THE POST-WAR YEARS 1948–1957

INTRODUCTION
CENTRIPETAL AND CENTRIFUGAL TENSIONS

Citizens of the United States emerged from World War II as a people grown accustomed to doing without. During the Depression, many did without because material goods were beyond their means. During the war, goods were rationed and lives sacrificed in order to defeat the enemy. Experiences of deprivation and personal sacrifice for a common good shaped a whole generation.

Such experiences, especially the experience of union against common enemies of poverty, then Nazism, created a sense of unity for the always diverse American people. They were strong centripetal forces that drew people to a common center, fostering an environment that favored sameness, homogenization, and a definable "norm."

But memories of a defeated enemy fade. Affluence, such as that many Americans enjoyed in the post-war years, makes remembrances of deprivation recede.

Moreover, rapidly expanding knowledge, technological developments, mushrooming suburbs, and churches that legitimated secular success all contributed to growing centrifugal forces. University disciplines differentiated; few educators could be found to agree on what a person needed to know in order to be considered "educated." Advances in communications media and automobiles allowed people simultaneously to transmit a message to wider areas and to cross geographical boundaries while the message had meaning for a smaller share of the market. The structure of suburbs as "bedroom communities" fostered the growing split between the private and the public. Booming suburban churches tried to be full-service religious supermarkets in order to meet the diverse needs of their busy, upwardly mobile clientele.

The institutional response to these trends was to try to contain rapid growth. Government, academy, and church all practiced a strategy of containment, although a notable counter-culture was active in the latter two—perhaps especially where the church and campus met. This decade is characterized by the regimentation of society, and the philosophies of *in loco parentis* on campus and "home away from home" in campus ministry. But privatization and affluence undercut regimentation, GIs who had faced death resisted being parented, and ecumenical contacts and social justice concerns influenced students to reach for the worlds beyond their home.

SOCIETY:
MILITARIZATION AND SUBURBAN SPRAWL

Americans experienced an unprecedented burst of accomplishment and achievement in the years immediately following World War II. The economy was recovering from the Great Depression, production was moving apace, better jobs and educational opportunities not only made mobility more possible, but made movement far more swift. Those who had gone to high school with only vague, or limited, career notions prior to World War II had been whipped into a disciplined military corps, had seen much of the world and contributed significantly (and even personally) to the life of it. In less than a decade after their homecoming, many had completed a college degree, established families, discovered exciting new career opportunities, and settled into a life that would literally have been beyond their imagining prior to it all. By 1950 much had been accomplished on the domestic scene not merely to absorb the veterans back into the fabric of the country, but even to parlay their returning, and war's technological residuals, into a whole new way of life for this country.

When the Korean conflict began in 1950 there were ample armaments and armies to mobilize quickly and act swiftly. Of the many things Korea may have taught the American people, the two learnings most readily appropriated into the culture were these: that American power was still sufficient to dispatch any enemy swiftly, but vigilance was a necessary discipline to the achievement of victory and maintenance of power. While postwar experience with former ally Russia certainly introduced the fearsome menace of communism, it was the war in Korea that helped shape America's response to such threats.

Nor was vigilance confined to a distant front; new threats were perceived on the domestic scene, as well. In 1949, prior to the Korean engagement, the House Unamerican Activities Committee began checking textbooks for potentially subversive, communist teachings. Some states, including Massachusetts, California, and Illinois, required loyalty oaths of their faculty.[1] Such measures seem a strong incursion into the sanctuary of ideas, the academy. It is as if all the enthusiasm of the post World War II era suddenly stood at attention. To be again at war so soon after armistice, and then so quickly out of war again, only reinforced the military model that would influence the rest of the decade. The attempt to standardize, to regiment the life of the nation seems, from a perspective over four decades removed, consonant with America's experience of war. The nation had been galvanized by World War II and all its citizens mobilized for the war effort. The nation had likely come to think of itself as a military community. Its governance during and just after the war in Europe was shaped by its participation in the military effort. During the World War every citizen and institution had been enlisted and deployed in service. After the wars in Europe and Korea a new generation of political leadership emerged from the ranks of those who had served in the military. Military service, and combat experience in particular, become valuable assets to those seeking elective office or other positions of public leadership.

In 1953 Dwight D. Eisenhower became President of the United States. The General was Commander in Chief to a nation ready for regimentation. Suburban America, which in the early 1950s began its ascendancy, bore remarkable resemblance to the military base. Uniform housing, proximity of workplace and schools, shopping on-base at the strip shopping centers that would neatly contain life to a given geographical

---

[1] David D. Henry, *Challenges Past, Challenges Present* (San Francisco: Jossey-Bass, 1975), 95–97.

area, even the provision of on-site churches to serve what would be a largely homogeneous constituency were all themes redolent of the neatly-contained, disciplined life of a military base.

The military-like rationalizing of life extended to children at school. Socialization was an important part of the curriculum, especially the concept of the "normal." Children in school were shown films on every aspect of life, including the proper way to relate to siblings and the polite manner of occupying one's place at table with the family. Advances in telecommunications made Americans a more private people even as these advances reinforced their fears of being different. Radio and, increasingly, television made them instantly aware of consumer products and, perhaps more importantly, consumer preferences. As products proliferated and choice became more difficult, brand-name loyalties became important distinctions. Consumers were exhorted to lead, to "be the first on the block" to procure new products. The concept of normalcy was the bedrock of marketing as the distinctions between products decreased in the flood of production. How was one to choose the best breakfast cereal, the best automobile, or the best television show when there were so many choices and so little difference among them? Market share became a determining index: the brand that sold the most products was perceived to be superior, though paradoxically, it would simultaneously become the most common.

As the nation more fully recovered from World War and returned home from Korea, the issue of pluralism became all the more apparent. Many cultural and technological forces conspired to break down the walls by which pre-war America had been subdivided. Radio and the automobile had opened the greater possibility of mobility, and the consequent exposure to difference, before the Second World War. Economic well-being became, to the survivors of the Great Depression, the greatest security—transcending ethnic boundaries. Television and cars, a growing interstate highway system, an expanded telephone system, mass marketing of consumer products, were but a few of the many dynamic changes that came to a society and to institutions long accustomed to other ways. McCarthyism was an understandable, if somewhat convulsive, response in this new environment. It was, at least at one level, a futile (and some might argue, fatal) grasp at control.

The overwhelming images of the period from Korea to near the end of the 1950s were images of containment and control. Even the phrase "nuclear family," while denoting a cohesive unit was still an irony in an era of nuclear explosions. Meant to convey the fundamental indivisible unit of family structure, it was a dominant image of containment, suggesting a space and relationships which could not be broken. But, as the atom could be split, so could a family.

THE ACADEMY'S NEW STATUS:
GIS AND IN LOCO PARENTIS

Americans—those who had gone off to fight and those who had stayed home—now faced a rebuilding job of massive proportions. When the war had begun many of the institutions of American society had still not recovered from the Depression's devastation. Nor had there been time, energy or material in wartime to address already-deferred repair and restoration. Despite the tremendous energies required to fight the war, the fact of winning was like a tonic, a shot of adrenalin. War had been an interruption that, as diversions sometimes will, refreshed a nation dispirited by the economic reversals of the Great Depression. War had fired up a weary nation. The returning forces—and those who greeted them at home—were far from exhausted by the effort war had demanded of them. They were exhilarated and refreshed. Having "cleaned up" the war, Americans now turned to cleaning up at home.[2] With God, and technology, on their side, they had won a war. Now they would put their household back in order, too.

But American institutions at every level were suddenly faced at war's end with a multitude of pressing decisions to make. Compared to the nation that had lately entered the war, recovering as it was from its own domestic economic crises, post-war America was a veritable land of opportunity again. War had rejuvenated the economy and created jobs. Still, the transition would not be an easy or painless one. Crisis was still the operative mode. While the crises facing the nation and its institutions were largely positive in nature, they were no less pivotal as points of decision. Even as crises of difficulty call for quick decision and a later sorting of consequences, so also do fortuitous crises force expedient solution without the luxury of deep consideration. Many of those decisions were made reasonably and pragmatically. Some were quite creative and perhaps even brilliant. Some would prove enduring, while some were deemed even at the time to be only temporary in nature. But the consequences of some were lasting.

---

[2] Robert Wuthnow, *The Restructuring of American Religion* (Princeton: Princeton University Press, 1988), 26.

This rapid growth and combination of pragmatic and only partly-reflective decisions is seen in what happened to higher education. Between the academic years 1939-40 and 1943-44 civilian enrollments at American colleges and universities dropped 41%. As the war effort escalated, the United States' Government and its attendant agencies became significant employers of personnel and deployers of resources. The government began contracting with universities and colleges for the use of classroom, dormitory and recreational facilities for the training of military reservists. By autumn of 1941 a wartime program was in place; some 660 institutions of higher education received contracts for training military personnel.

The role of American academic research and development, deployed by the U. S. government and its military forces, brought the academy to a new place in the fabric of American life. Rosie the Riveter had joined forces with Robert (Oppenheimer) the Researcher and Enrico (Fermi) the Engineer to bring the war to conclusion. The academy had done its part to win the war and had thus secured a place for itself in the society that would emerge thereafter.

In November of 1942, President Roosevelt lowered the draft age to eighteen and promised that those whose education was disrupted would receive government help to resume it after the war.[3] Fearing massive post-war unemployment as veterans streamed back into the workforce, Congress passed the G. I. Bill in 1944, but did so with the expectation that few would utilize higher education provisions offering a minimum of one year's training, with one additional month of education for each month of military service, up to a maximum of forty-eight months.[4] In February of 1946 returning veterans comprised 125,000 of the 2,078,095 enrolled in American colleges and universities. By fall of that year that number had swelled to over one million veterans.[5] In 1947 the number of veterans enrolled on campus peaked. Their explosive entry into the

---

[3] The percentage of state and federal funding of college and university budgets in the period 1939–40 to 1943–44 increased. At the beginning of that period student fees represented 35.7% of the academic institutions' funding, government funding representing only 5.4%. By the end of the period—1943–44—the proportion of academic institutional budgets derived from student fees had dropped by half, to 17.9%, while government funding had increased more than six-fold to 35.7%. Henry, *Challenges*, 38–59.

[4] Ibid., 71–72.

[5] U.S. Bureau of the Census. *Statistical Abstract of the United States* 110 edition (Washington, D.C.: U.S. Bureau of the Census), 122.

American system of higher education opened the way for an increasing population to follow.

Indeed, the academy figured importantly in a post-war America. Evidently unaware of the essential and expansive role education would enjoy as spoils of war, the government defined higher education as a "benefit" and offered it to returning veterans as reward for services rendered. The result was a "tremendous psychological lift"[6] to the educational system. A college education was deemed an asset to career choices in an increasingly mobile society. In 1947-48 the President's Commission on Higher Education published a six-volume report, *Higher Education for American Democracy* concluding that all barriers to equal opportunity in education must fall. Education must respond to new social needs: for a trained workforce, especially in the sciences; to create unity in diversity; to expand knowledge of the world; and to explore peaceful uses for atomic energy.[7]

It was a daunting and humbling agenda. But in the wake of war's accomplishments and enthusiasms, the academy was enticed by new-found admiration and the promise of social and political assistance. It was a promising partnership that was based upon the foundation of wartime cooperation, and the success of academic research and technology, not the least of which was the Manhattan Project and its military application. Those who had harnessed the power of the atom could surely harness the explosive energies of the post-war society. These energies, contained by the country's natural desire to resume a disrupted and deferred domestic agenda, were used to fire a great internal combustion engine. As each partner had fueled the engine with resources to bring the great war to conclusion momentum had built. Tuned by mutual admiration, the partners revved the engine of American society as the forces of learning, government, and technological production moved America into a new era of prosperity.

In the years immediately following World War II many Americans became connected in one way or another to the academy. Returning veterans joined with youths of college age to fill the campuses. A large number of those veterans had trained for military service on campus grounds, sat in those classrooms, lived in those dorms—and had thus experienced a taste of the academic environment. In one respect it was something of a homecoming, and perhaps even a form of debriefing, as

---

6 Henry, *Challenges*, 95–97.

7 Ibid., 72.

those trained on campus returned to civilian life through the same door-way that had opened for them the world at war. Among those who returned to campus to collect their earned educational "benefit" were a significant number who might not otherwise have been there. These were those who, before the war, would likely not have thought of higher education as an option. The role of the academy as preparation for specific professional vocations, and the different labor culture that had prevailed prior to the war, would simply not have included college for them. Prior to the war they might have farmed, worked at a variety of manufacturing jobs, or taken up established or entrepreneurial business. After the war all these changed. Science and technology made possible, and an expanding populace made necessary, a culture of increased pro-ductivity. Higher education was integral to this change, transferring technological advances from war-time research to these domestic activi-ties. New technologies, too, came from cross-disciplinary work in the universities that preceded, and remained integral to, the growing phenomenon of "research and development." Ideas and principles dis-covered in one lab often found application elsewhere. For instance, the same technology that created the mushroom cloud and its destruction would eventually become a major source of electrical power and promise healing in nuclear medicine.

The GI Bill of Rights and the growing alliance between government, industry, and the academy created a welcoming environment for these newcomers to the college and university experience. By the time the last of them moved through the system, 2,232,000 GIs passed through America's colleges and universities on their post-war entitlements. Proportionally, their influence was staggering.[8]

These newcomers were different, so different from the traditional student culture that they constituted a company to themselves. They were "outsiders."[9] Unlike the pre-war college student, many of those who came to campus after the war brought wives, and even families, with them. But they brought much more, as well. They brought a differ-ent set of experiences, expectations and goals. In some respects they were

---

[8] For example, the undergraduate enrollment of the University of Michigan in 1948 was 20,000. Fully 11,000 of them were veterans. At Lehigh University 940 of the 1,336 students enrolled in 1948 were returning GIs. In the peak years of 1946–48 vet-erans comprised the majority of all males enrolled in college. Helen Lefkowitz Horowitz, *Campus Life: Undergraduate Cultures from the End of the Eighteenth Century to the Present* (Chicago: University of Chicago Press, 1987), 184–87.

[9] Ibid., 184.

more single-minded and task-oriented. That is to say that their needs and purposes were both generationally and experientially different from students who had attended school before the war or who came to it now without that experience. The veterans of war brought a gravity and intensity appropriate to war's experience. They had seen death and brought to campus a sense of their own mortality that stood in marked contrast to the limitless horizons of collegiate youth. Those structures and activities that shaped the undergraduate culture of the pre-war college and were so much a part of the campus ethos were of little importance to veterans of an American Depression and a World War.

The habits and disciplines forged in military training and actual warfare shaped the manners and mindset of the campus-bound veterans. Their approach to the academic experience and its routines could not help but be shaped by their military training. The communal lessons to be learned of dorm living had been learned in barracks. The affiliative socialization of fraternity and sorority and voluntary organizations was of little use to those who had known combat experience and its deep bonds. The social diversions of a single, young adult community were inappropriate to students bearing responsibility for a wife and maybe even children. Thus their status as outsiders would continue to distinguish them from the younger students with whom they shared campus.[10] *And, in time, their distinctive experience of higher education would color their expectations of their children's campus experience.*

The colleges and universities suddenly knew an unprecedented prominence in the American culture. The veterans and their families on campus, added to those of the usual college age pursuing their studies alongside them, made campus life an important experience to more families in the larger culture. Americans were suddenly on campus or had children on campus—and many were experiencing this phenomenon for the first time. The veterans especially were enjoying it, for they were succeeding—even excelling—in this new experience. Studies of the period indicate that veterans consistently made higher grades than nonveterans. The combination of their motivation and their focused discipline conspired to bring them gratifying reward.[11]

The cycle of influence that ensued would have lasting effect. The veterans introduced into the academy a goal-orientation that gradually challenged the working philosophy of higher education that pursued

---

[10] Ibid., 185.
[11] Ibid., 185–87.

learning for the sake of learning. It may be more fair to say that the veterans only reawakened this tension, since American higher education had been born of functionalism—introduced on these shores for the purpose of training ministers, and later teachers, physicians and lawyers. At any rate, the introduction of generational and experiential differences in the student body had a lasting effect upon the academy.[12]

This is not to say that the student culture of the 1950s was quiescent. Horowitz illustrates the experience of many students in one named Willie Morris who "came to the University of Texas from Yazoo City, Mississippi" expecting the campus to be "like his hometown, only 'bigger and better.'" Willie, like many of his generation of students, joined several of the campus organizations, taking an active role in fraternity, student government, band and others. In time, however, Willie grew "more lonely, more contemptuous of this organized anarchy, more despairing of the ritualized childishness and grasping narcissism of the fraternity life."[13] The experience of this student is important for what it reveals of the student reaction to those structures presumably designed to carry over into the college experience at least some of the familiar structures of home. After all, the fraternities and sororities for all their self-governance, were still households presided over by housemothers. Dormitories, too, were still in this era attempting, often feebly against the tide of increased enrollments, to retain something of the residential quality of home and parental oversight. Even in the large state universities where coeducational structures were quickly eroding the gender-specific traditions of higher education, women's dorms retained housemothers and enforced curfews.

The irony of Willie Morris's experience is in the word "loneliness." For at the very least the extension of home's nurture to campus was meant to minimize such pain. Sororities, fraternities, and the denominational campus religious groups all sought to create and cultivate communities of belonging, identifiable structures of affiliation. They were intended to be safe and manageable environments where loneliness could not intrude. But the expanding campus walls that had been conceived as protective quickly were perceived to be restrictive. Thus, the student saw through the agenda of leadership which cast the mantle of family nurture and care over designs of control and containment in a rapidly deteriorating, highly competitive culture of increased options

---

[12] Ibid., 187.
[13] Ibid., 170.

and opinion. The inward focus of any organization or structure grew less attractive in the realm of expanding possibilities and exciting difference.

Neither was Willie the only student chafing under restriction. Those veterans who had faced their own mortality had little use for the philosophy of *in loco parentis* – that university officials were legally and morally responsible for the behavior of their students, that the university acted in the place of the parents. Those who had experienced war's culture could not help but suffer restrictions on drinking, dating, and the like as prudish nonsense.

The presence of more women on campus, as students or as wives, also chipped away at *in loco parentis* rules. Women students, for whom war actually provided greater educational and career opportunity, were displaced by the returning veterans after the war. Also, the presence of wives who accompanied their veteran husbands to campus, and perhaps just the sheer availability of men, heightened interest in marriage.[14] Education, after all, was not the only aspect of human experience that war had interrupted. Expectations, reinforced by the general cultural tendencies toward conformity in regimentation, tended toward the home as the center of American life, and the wife at the heart of that center.

The trend was not long-lived. Women had in large measure kept the nation together and functional throughout the war. They had certainly done their part in the great effort. After the initial shock and jubilation of war's end wore off, they gradually remembered that achievement. While war may have interrupted the educations and careers of their brothers and husbands, peacetime was proving an increasingly burdensome interruption of their own educational and career ambitions. By the mid-1950s diversity on American campuses meant the presence of women in a province once largely dominated by men.

Indeed, barriers long held in American society were challenged. The integration of the armed forces from 1940 to 1950 had set in motion yet another change that would continue to collide with American sentiments and structures as racial integration confronted the institutions of national life. Education figured prominently in the mix. The racial barriers that had long separated African-Americans from their neighbors in the public education system were brought to the fore in Little Rock, Arkansas, in 1954. There quickly followed a rapid and escalating succession of similar challenges in Montgomery, Alabama, and elsewhere.

---

[14] Ibid., 217–18.

Even higher education itself went mobile as the residential campus met the relatively new phenomenon of the commuter campus which, despite attempts to gather its diversity in names like "community college" or "city college," was dominated by mobility itself. Lawns and dorms were replaced by parking lots filled with automobiles, and the ordered routine of collegiate days gave way to classes at all hours of the day and the night.[15]

The changes came too rapidly, and the educational system expanded too quickly to be assimilated by America's institutions or their constituent citizens. The growing diversity in all parts of life encouraged increased specialization as institutions attempted to keep pace.

For these reasons—increased numbers and increased focus—campus formed the center of a new community in American society. If only for a brief while in the early years at war's end, campus was certainly where numerous people were. Furthermore, if the focus of the church was the people, and if the people were in larger measure on campus, an inevitable meeting was in the making. The church would have to deal with the modern university in the throes of expansion and at a time when its own growth was posing profound demand. Crisis was inevitable.

MINISTRY ON CAMPUS:
HOME AWAY FROM HOME AND ECUMENICAL HORIZONS

In quite a real sense the church went back to school and the school went back to church as the two institutions joined forces in the massive attempt to respond to post-war conditions. The needs and the motives of each institution were so mixed, however, as to make any analysis of the time complex.

The church certainly had compelling reason to go where the people were, if only to follow the basic mandate to serve. Moreover, the church had little choice but to go to campus if it were to survive economically. The location of churches and universities is tied to the locus of populations and resources. The church can and often has responded to population shifts with relative ease. The decayed condition of post-Depression, post-war church facilities sometimes made relocation and rebuilding a popular option, especially for congregations who stood to

---

[15] In 1956 the Presbyterians were among the first to recognize and attempt experimental ministry with commuter students in Chicago, Philadelphia, and Los Angeles. *Minutes of the Presbyterian Church* (1956), part 2, 50.

gain by selling real estate that lay in the path of commercial expansion. Too, responding to the need on campus was for the church more a matter of deployment than of building. Ordained pastoral leadership to orga- nize and staff campus ministries was a priority. This "solution" to the growing need on campus was, however, part of the "problem" posed for the church in the midst of post-war expansion. The parochial church also needed clergy; and the primary candidates, at least for the denomina- tions included in this study (all three of which relied increasingly upon an educated clergy), were likely to be found on campus.[16]

The churches went to the schools, expanding their denominational ministries in hopes of increasing the pool of clergy candidates and to minister to their own members and constituents who were utilizing higher education in record numbers. Among the returning veterans of the war were a number of military chaplains who had been posted out of domestic assignments and pressed into wartime service. The Committee on Chaplains and Service Personnel of the Presbyterian Church reported in 1948 that twenty-one demobilized chaplains had been placed in three- year appointments "at strategic centers where large numbers of former service men and women are completing their college work," a project undertaken jointly with the Westminster Foundation under the auspices of the Board of Christian Education of that denomination. The Board report noted that a pre-war (1939) census of 62 "university pastors" at 53 colleges and universities had now grown to 128 workers at 101 campus sites, although spending per student had decreased.[17]

A sense of urgency was clearly heard in the report of the Division of College Work to the General Convention of the Episcopal Church in

---

[16] During World War II seminary enrollments, understandably, had fallen off. Of the 40,000 Methodist congregations (of the 8-million member denomination) in America in 1946, only 15,000 of the congregations had full-time ministers. Fully twenty-five percent of the 12,000 Presbyterian pulpits serving 2.7 million members were vacant, and twenty percent more were filled only by temporary "stated supply" pastors. The Episcopal Church showed a twenty-percent deficiency in full-time parochial clergy serving its membership of 2.1 million. With the older clergy retiring and no younger ones waiting in the wings, the churches would have had some catch- ing up to do in any case. Moreover, the churches began to grow. From 1944–1948 the membership of the Methodist Church increased faster than any time since 1925, and leaders in that denomination projected they would need 3,000 more clergy by 1953. Wuthnow, *Restructuring*, 29.

[17] *Minutes of the General Assembly of the Presbyterian Church in the United States of America* (Philadelphia: 1948) part 1, *Journal and Statistics*, p. 75 and part 2, *Board Reports*, 66.
Hereafter cited as *Minutes of the Presbyterian Church* with date and part number.

1949. That document identified the American campus as "one of the most vital missionary fields in American life. A sound program for the campus community involves a continuing ministry to the boys and girls of the Church who are away from home and an aggressive effort to leaven the demands of the intellectual life with the leaven of Christian thought and life....No field is more important." Moreover, "No field is more neglected by this Church."[18] Campus work leaders asked for a $25,000 increase over the $60,000 amount budgeted by the national church. The tone conveys the sense of immediacy and the magnitude of the demand, while the paternal vocabulary ("boys and girls") indicates the generational difference between the existing church leadership and the constituency it sought to missionize. In the Methodist Church a similar urgency was measured in the more tangible language of budget appropriations to student work at the national level that grew from $97,574 in 1944 to $151,590 in 1947.[19]

But the university also benefitted from the presence and work of the church. State-supported schools and the growing pluralism of once-denominationally centered private schools increased with the demands of larger enrollments. As an adjunct to a growing complex of student services, campus ministries and near-campus churches provided a place where married students and their children could be accommodated in established programs that offered intergenerational activities and education. Student centers and the array of student organizations and activities on campus had been equipped largely to serve the needs of the younger, single student. Churches were a natural locus for the social, emotional, and developmental needs of the older and often married student. In the immediate postwar period it was widely assumed by religionists that socialization was the "most effective means of reinforcing values."[20] Campus ministries often served just that purpose. To that end, their purpose was contextually defined.

That context became much more diverse than it had been prior to the war. Changes in the student body (GIs, families, women), in the curriculum, and the rise of technology over the humanities strained the sense of a university. Consistent with the prevailing mood of the culture, the

---

[18] Home Department, Division of College Work, *Journal of the General Convention* (Hammond: W.B. Conkey Company, 1949), 460–61. Hereafter cited as *Journal of the General Convention* with date.

[19] *Yearbook. Board of Education, The Methodist Church* (1948), 731.

[20] Wuthnow, *Restructuring*, 63.

churches began to trumpet campus ministry as an integrating center in a shifting and fragmenting world.

This need for an integrating center may be one reason why denominations expanded their campus ministries in the decade following the war.[21] Prior to the war the most extensive ministry on campus had been the work of the Young Men's Christian Associations and, following World War I, the Student Christian Movement—both ministries shaped not only for students but largely by students as well. Moreover, these organizations represented non-denominational initiatives and, as parachurch bodies, were sometimes highly critical of the institutional church. It is clear that, so far as the churches were concerned, campus was an alien culture.

But in the post-war period, the denominations decided either to make peace with or to conquer the campus. In 1948 the Westminster Fellowship voted to unite youth and student work and, at the initiative of high school graduates, the Westminster Fellowships were extended to 105 student centers.[22] Graduates of high school programs made the transition to denominational programs on campus, often providing leadership and momentum, as well as continuity.[23]

Presbyterians defined the task on campus as missionary and evangelical and distributed $183,202 for work at university centers.[24] In 1949 the Presbyterians prefaced a Board of Education Report with a Preamble, the cadences of which were unmistakably derivative:

> We, the People of the Presbyterian Church in the United States of America, in order to form a more perfect expression of the Christian Faith and Life, advance the Kingdom of God on earth, insure domestic responsibility, provide for the discipleship of youth, promote the educational welfare of the Church, and secure the blessings of leadership to ourselves and our posterity, do ordain and establish Christian Education to the glory of His name in whom old things pass away and all things become new. We pledge our-

---

[21] A rather consistent pattern is for denominations to fold interdenominational co-operative ministries into denominational structures. Sunday schools would be another prominent example.

[22] As this example suggests, campus ministries in this period were the beneficiaries of strong youth programs in local churches.

[23] John B. Linder, Alva I. Cox, Jr., and Linda-Marie Deloff, *By Faith: Christian Students Among the Cloud of Witnesses* (New York: Friendship Press, 1991), 29.

[24] *Minutes of the Presbyterian Church* (1949) part 2, 47–48, 134.

selves to this Cause that Christ shall see in his Church "the manifestation of the sons of God."[25]

The tone is both patriotic and provocative. Adopting the shape of the Preamble to the American Constitution, its drafters seemed intent upon a new course, diverging from what may have been perceived as growing secularism. A Gallup survey commissioned by *The Ladies Home Journal* in 1947 revealed "a 'profound gulf' between America's avowed ethical standards and the observable realities of national life."[26] Tensions between sacred and profane sectors of American life grew.

In the Journal of General Convention of the Episcopal Church of 1952, College Work is still listed under the budgetary jurisdiction of the Home Department, whose responsibility extends to "all missionary work in the U.S." The same journal lists as areas of emphasis for the succeeding triennium, "Negroes, Indians, urban population shifts, colleges, armed forces." The stated goal of the department for College Work was a college worker on every campus. In reality the Episcopal Church could only boast 13 full-time workers at 25 of the largest colleges or universities, and a full-time presence at only 24 of 48 state universities. A budget of $106,520—an increase of $38,140 over the previous triennium—was approved and the report's goals adopted. The scope of the priority grows in the realization that such increase was granted by a General Convention whose previous triennium had operated at a half million dollar deficit per year. Still, of the General Program Budget of 1953, which amounted to $5,929,043, the College Work proportion was modest. But its stated mission was not: "College work is an important field, both of missionary extension and of leadership training. It is noteworthy that the program of the Episcopal Church is far more than student work. It includes faculty as well, and is designed to undergird secular education with the compelling motive and philosophy of the Christian Faith."[27]

It is the Journal of the General Conference of the Methodist Church in 1952 that best reveals, albeit subtly, a shift in posture—and a growing debate—on the role, and relationship, of campus ministry to a denomi-

---

[25] Ibid., 3.

[26] "This survey, one of the first scientific efforts to explore the religious views of Americans in depth, drew the conclusion that, while the religious potential in the United States was very great, the quality of religion and its influence on American life were not so apparent." George Gallup and Jim Castelli, *The People's Religion: American Faith in the 90's* (New York: Macmillan Publishing Co., 1989), 7.

[27] *Journal of the General Convention*, (1952), 262.

nation. In the Bishops' Address[28] of that year pleasure was expressed that so many young men were answering the call to ordained ministry. But the note of parental pride and responsibility sounds more clearly in the reminder to boards entrusted with trusteeship of campus work. These trustees "are the guardians of the free spirit and the Christian idealism that should prevail in our colleges." The bishops warmly acknowledge that Wesley Foundations and colleges are again "drawing closer to the Church which gave them birth." The cozy, familial image continues in the parental acknowledgment that the church ought also to draw closer to these Wesley Foundations and colleges, shouldering more financial responsibility. But the guardianship is depicted even more sharply, and the image of containment introduced, in the assertion that the church ought to retain not only the privilege to choose trustees, but should also encourage their students to enroll in Methodist schools in order to halt a perceived "drift toward materialism and nihilism."[29]

The debate over the mission and role of campus ministry began to polarize in this atmosphere. The language of missiology receded and new notions moved to the fore. A national report on Methodism and Higher Education in 1952 described the Wesley Foundation as "the Church at work on the university campus. A center of Christian training and recruitment, where study, fellowship, and worship are primary means to Christian ends, a Wesley Foundation is a 'a home away from home.'"[30] The report numbers 160 Wesley Foundations and 22 interdenominational units, with 22 new structures built and 22 existing structures reconstructed in the previous four-year period. The prevailing concern in reports of Methodists, Episcopalians, and Presbyterians in this post-Korean War period is the growing secularism and practical atheism that was becoming the dominant national philosophy.[31]

The antidote prescribed was one, essentially, of containment. The primary role of campus ministries in the denominations here under study was suggested by their operational names: The Wesley Foundation, of the Methodists; The Westminster Fellowship, of the Presbyterians; and

---

[28] This address is actually known as "the Episcopal Address," but is here designated as the "Bishops' Address" in order to avoid confusion with the Episcopal Church. The address is composed and delivered by a single bishop but with substantial input and potential revision by colleagues. The bishops speak for the bishops, not the whole church; but the address gives insight into the way these leaders framed problems and shaped solutions.

[29] *Journal of the Methodist Church* (1952), 169–71.

[30] Ibid., 1187–89.

[31] Ibid.

The Canterbury Club, of the Episcopalians. The warmth of affiliation and the coziness of companionship are intentionally evoked.

The parental role extended toward all educational oversight. And while their own children were not yet on campus, the recent alumni/ae of campus ministries would likely have warmed to those philosophies of campus ministry that accorded not just with their own experience, but with what they desired for their own offspring. Additionally, leaders in the major denominations tended then, as they do now, to be older adults and thus older parents, whose own children were likely at college age. An interest in all educational matters, including Sunday School or Church School programs, flourished in this period. Presbyterians had introduced their curriculum, *Christian Faith and Life, A Program for Church and Home*, in 1948 and were still praising it in 1951.[32] The first *Seabury Series* published as an educational resource by the Episcopal Church was only one of many such initiatives undertaken by denominations to meet the educational needs of the churches' growing population.

It is hardly surprising then that campus ministry gradually came to be seen, at least by some, as an extension of the parish Christian education program. When it became impossible, as it did in the mid-1950s, to locate a parish on or even near every campus, denominational centers became the logical answer to providing nurture in a controlled environment. Governance, in many cases, was seen as a kind of guardianship. Student activity was programmed much as it might have been in the parish high school youth group, and overseen by adult leadership in the form of ordained chaplains. At least this is how it was to have been from the perspective of those in denominational leadership.

The General Conference of the Methodist Church in 1956 defined the Wesley Foundation as "the organized educational ministry of the Methodist Church at a state or independent college or university."[33] The same conference also noted the higher rate of divorce in the culture, counting 3 million divorced persons in the United States and, interestingly, factoring and citing the additional statistical observation that the net effect of this number was four and one half million women and children who had been deserted—and, presumably, in need of nurturing structures, which is a concern of guardianship.[34]

The Journal of the General Convention of the Episcopal Church in 1955 maintained that "As college students go away from home, the

---

[32] *Minutes of the Presbyterian Church* (1951) part 2, 9.
[33] *Journal of the Methodist Church* (1956), 1450.
[34] Ibid., 205.

Church should go with them, providing a positive and stable influence in their new lives."[35] It was further reported that almost every diocese had in place a commission for college work, and the national church provided a College Work Consultant to give guidance to them. The agenda for College Work was "to integrate college students and other academic personnel into the life of the parish church."[36]

The Presbyterians indicated mounting concern in their annual General Assembly Minutes. In 1951 Westminster Fellowships began to experience inadequate support for established centers and insufficient resources to undertake any new work on the state campuses that were growing not only in size but in number.[37] The portion of the report devoted to campus work was revealingly titled "On the Threshold of Life," and reminded Presbyterians that of all U. S. church bodies, theirs sent the highest percentage of its youth to college.[38] By 1952 the priority was more sharply articulated: "One major issue faces the Church—either it will undertake its educational task with more seriousness or pay the penalty of its neglect."[39] In token of that seriousness it was determined to evaluate the work of the Department of Student Work with the purpose of recommending expansion or retraction of program. The decreased enrollments created by the Korean War and the lowered birth rates of the 1930s naturally brought such questions of stewardship to the fore. But by 1953 the educational task was more closely and intentionally tied to the life of the home: "The Church has the responsibility of building a strong religious bridge over the college years, connecting the Christian homes from which our youth come to their own homes which they in turn must build."[40] In the Board of Christian Education report, the Student Work Survey Committee returned its judgment that the church "must take steps immediately to make funds sufficient to provide (1) a more adequate ministry to Presbyterian-preference students in all institutions; (2) a systematic ministry to graduate and professional students and faculty; and (3) an increased impact on all areas of university life."[41]

In 1954 Presbyterians changed the name of their national campus entity from "Student Work Department" to the "Department of Campus

35 *Journal of the General Convention*, (1955), 388.
36 Ibid.
37 *Minutes of the Presbyterian Church* (1951) part 1, 117.
38 Ibid., part 2, 45.
39 *Minutes of the Presbyterian Church* (1952) part 2, 6.
40 *Minutes of the Presbyterian Church* (1953) part 1, 101.
41 *Minutes of the Presbyterian Church* (1953) part 2, 24.

Religious Life."[42] The name evokes an enlarged conception of the church's purpose on campus, but it also evinces a recasting of the missionary function. If the church could no longer plant itself on the campus, or no longer saw that as its primary objective, then its attention could turn to gathering its own unto itself. Not insignificantly, the pastor to Presbyterian students was more frequently identified as the Presbyterian *chaplain*, circumscribing the defined community of the pastors concerned to a denominational one, a trend that would extend to several denominations and for like reason. Even the language of missiology, though still in use, had come to mean something different. "No group of missionaries in our time faces a more difficult task than these university pastors, set down in the midst of the secular university world."[43] To meet the coming demand of the baby boom, plans were laid for the deployment of student pastors who, as partners with non-denominational staff, would work with colleges and local pastors. Mission language increasingly came to mean recruitment to specific denominational membership, and more particularly, ordained service. The denominational campus Christian fellowships were hothouses of church vocations.[44]

But a strategy of containment was not the only operative one. Some student ministry executives and campus ministers encouraged students to expand their horizons, to venture forth from their childhood home, to look toward the ecumene, the whole inhabited earth, from the perspective of a biblically informed and reflective Gospel. The Board of Education report in the minutes of the Presbyterian General Assembly in 1955 amplified its concept of Campus Christian Life, articulating:

> To bear living witness to the gospel of Jesus Christ in universities and colleges so that there will result…a fellowship of faculty and students in a consciously Christian community in which all questioners and inquirers are welcome and respected….
> Where the credibility of the Christian position will be established by study…and demonstration,

---

[42] *Minutes of the Presbyterian Church* (1954) part 2, 5, 28–32.

[43] Ibid., 25.

[44] Specific goals, established in 1954 and reiterated here, determined to place a Presbyterian pastor at every campus with an enrollment greater than 4000 students if at least 400 students indicated a Presbyterian preference; on campuses of 1000–4000 students, to work in cooperation with the National Council of Churches; and at schools under 1000, to promote Student Christian Fellowships working with pastors of near-by churches. Ibid., 25.

Where the evangelical Christian world view will be made clear against the
background of other world views on the campus,
Where thoughtful, Christian discipleship will be developed and the extension, unity, and renewal of the Church throughout the world will be
sought.[45]

One concrete example of Christian discipleship that transcended
boundaries often honored at home was exercised in race relations.
Denominational student movements were frequently among the pro-in-
tegrationists. On integrated state college campuses, some student
religious organizations and campus ministries quietly integrated their
campus programs and extended the practical awareness of integration to
those on segregated campuses by including African-American students
in their annual conferences and retreats.[46]

All the while these plans were being made, life on the campus itself
was changing, and it is not entirely clear that any of the denominations
here studied had any awareness of those changes in the campus culture.
In this time of considerable change, the denominational containment and
guardianship that marked so many functions of church life aimed to
insulate from forces outside. In the nineteenth century Horace Bushnell,
a leading influence in shaping Christian education, had championed the
concept of Christian Nurture, itself but a Protestant version of a familiar
Catholic perspective. The theory posited that the best means of securing
the gospel lay in rearing children who were so grounded in Christian
teaching and practice that they would never know themselves as other
than Christian. The Catholic saying, "give us a child until the age of six,
and we'll give you a Catholic for life," held to essentially the same
principle. But such restricting notions of nurture are ill-equipped to
survive in a culture of diverse, freely accessible ideas. If, by the mid-
1950s, campus ministry was largely concerned with issues of
containment and guardianship in an increasingly diverse and complex
culture, then the very structure of campus ministry communities would
have tended to insure not only a uniformity of denominational identity,
but also a uniformity of other kinds as well. Such entities would tend to
attract those students, faculty, and others for whom the denominational
agenda and the values of nurturing containment were equally important.
Increasingly in this period the reports of campus ministries and their

---

[45] *Minutes of the Presbyterian Church* (1955) part 2, 24.
[46] Edwin L. Brock, "Methodism's Growing Cleavage," *The Christian Century* 72 (24
August 1955): 972.

boards to their national denominational bodies evince, as does the whole tenor of mainline churches, a growing demarcation between "us" who are identified as those within the churches, and "them" who are that growing number attracted by or loyal to other values and principles.

While the churches were devising more homelike centers hospitable to their own children on campus, the students themselves were growing both in number and perspective. The campus was to play an important role in reshaping modern mission and ministry. The distinctive nature of campus ministry is evidenced in the evolution of denominational rationales. Earlier documents described the church on campus as a sheltering community of denominational family, a sanctuary for the "boys and girls." In the mid-1950s, less and less was the church perceived as the locus of campus life; more and more the university was acknowledged as a community for ministry. The Board of Education Report to the General Assembly of the Presbyterian Church in 1956 offered the lofty vision of the university as the place where "Christian workers can guide a large segment of the state's future citizenry in discovering that God is the central fact in the universe, that men can fulfill their highest possibilities only through obedience to his will, that culture...achieves genuine worth simply to the extent to which it assists human beings toward maturity in the Christian faith."[47]

That ambition was about to feel the stinging effrontery of the gauntlet. On the other side of the world "godless" workers of a different state fulfilled a high ambition with neither obedience to or faith in America's God, an achievement against which all else would pale. The Soviet Union launched Sputnik.

---

[47] *Minutes of the Presbyterian Church* (1957) part 2, 39.

—⚔ **2** ⚔—

CHALLENGING BOUNDARIES:
SEARCHING FOR COMMUNITIES OF IDENTITY
AND INTEGRITY 1958–1963

INTRODUCTION

The immediate post-World War II decade, sketched in the previous chapter, was characterized by mushrooming growth and attempts to contain both that growth and Communist expansion. It was a decade of strict social conformity, epitomized by suburban families in tract houses with well-kept lawns and dutiful, obedient children. A potent hierarchy of values—white over black, father over family, men over women, to name but a few—let everybody know his or her place in an ordered society.

But shifting world patterns and continued domestic growth could not be controlled or contained for long. The centrifugal forces gradually overwhelmed the centripetal. The period from 1958 to 1968, the subject of the next two chapters, saw most established boundaries questioned, removed, and/or changed. The "Superpowers"—America and the Soviet Union—flexed military muscle and stretched intellectual resources in efforts to gain physical and psychological turf. Blacks refused to be the victims of racism and segregation any longer. A better-educated laity pressed for greater voice in religious congregations, while many clergy sought professional "expert" status. By the end of the decade, other boundaries were pushed. Generations clashed over American involvement in Vietnam. Women organized a movement to liberate themselves from patriarchy. A sexual "revolution" challenged long-held values and presumptions.

Campus ministries were affected by all of these boundary shifts. How should the church on campus respond to Communism's varied threats and to the university's increasing role as a military research center? What is the appropriate prophetic stance of Christians on campus regarding racism in the South and the North, or about the Vietnam War? What about the Christian's role in changing attitudes towards the sexes and sexual behaviors? What can campus ministries do to help students prepare themselves not only for a career but for lay vocations as disciples of Christ in their chosen walks of life?

Moreover, campus ministry's position in church and university shifted as these boundaries changed and as new concerns were added to the already full agendas of each. As special purpose groups formed and Americans differentiated themselves from one another, campus ministry moved either to the margins of church and university, or had the opportunity to minister in the interstices—depending on one's perspective. In either case, many campus ministries, as well as many other groups in the academy and the society, pursued a search for a community of identity and integrity. That is, persons sought an integrating center where ideals and practice were consonant. Whether they found such is another matter.

SOCIETY:
FEAR, EDUCATION, AND CONFLICT

World War II officially ended in 1945, but the American people maintained a war mentality for much of the period under study here. Both the Cold War and massive government involvement in culture contributed to this mood. Cold War anxieties were piqued in 1957, in the Russian launching of Sputnik I, the first satellite to orbit the earth successfully. This event threatened America's self-understanding that it was technologically superior to the USSR, a superiority it claimed since the atomic end of World War II. With Sputnik I, the Soviet Union won a major Cold War battle. Their achievement could hardly have been more devastating to American hegemony. It struck America at the point of greatest pride and the foundation of modern security: technology. It launched an extended war fought on a new battlefield. This mission into outer space was not only an important technological breakthrough; it was also a strategic psychological victory for the Soviets.

By placing a satellite in earth orbit, Russia invaded America's new-found sense of security and inflamed the McCarthy-aided suspicion of Communism. New possibilities for surveillance and communication in a device beyond reach of American defenses gave the Russians an edge in the vigilance business. Only three years previously, in 1954, the phrase "under God" had been added to the pledge of allegiance to the American flag. Now, in addition to God, the nation lived beneath another's eye. Concern that Communism, or any other system, might challenge America's rise was aggravated by the little Soviet star circling in the heavens.

The achievement of the Soviet Union was all the more painful, striking as it did just when America's educational system was struggling. When America returned to its domestic agenda after the war, it found an educational infrastructure in need of permanent facilities, stable funding, and the means to accurately estimate student enrollments. Hastily-built campuses and makeshift expansion made of surplus Quonset huts and barracks only temporarily served a growing need for facilities. As America approached the mid-1950s the post-war wave of veterans had swelled and subsided, leaving in its wake many new campuses and vastly-expanded old ones.

The response of the Eisenhower administration to the new Soviet technological threat was a new war effort, a domestic mobilization. Passage of the National Defense Education Act in 1958 made education at all levels a priority and assured federal assistance. The alliances built during previous World Wars between American farms, factories, and government were now extended to schools, colleges and universities. By 1957 the Department of Defense, the Atomic Energy Commission, the National Aeronautical and Space Administration were among the growing number of governmental agencies and organizations actively funding projects on American campuses. The "benefit" of education that assisted the veterans' re-entry into post-war American society had increased in value. Education was now considered an entitlement. Economic progress spurred the creation of prestigious, professional jobs increasing the value of academic achievement. As a college degree trans-lated into higher income, students developed less and less interest in curricular content and greater interest in making the grade. Moreover, the "democratization of higher education" made college more accessible to those who had previously been "outside" its sphere of influence, opening a stairway of social and economic mobility to the middle and lower classes.[1]

But not everyone was happy with the initiative. Among those disaffected by the changing shape of American education were two very different groups. At one extreme were those who held education in suspicion. Among the anti-intellectuals were many whose lives and livelihoods were being displaced by the shift in priorities. Their values of hard work and industry, of native wit and sheer grit were eclipsed by a growing educated class. This suspicious faction was hardly powerless. Indeed, they frequently were represented prominently in government, most notably at the state level. Their influence was evident in the desegregation struggles that locked state and federal governments in contention. Less visibly, they contributed to reshaping the educational system with their insistence upon pragmatism and utility. In their eyes education and its expansion were undertaken not for the sake of learning itself, but for measurable, practical purposes. Education was a commodity; the more practical its application, the greater its value.

At the other end of the spectrum was a generation of youthful rebels who espoused a "bohemian" lifestyle, a freewheeling and poetic experience of life that protested objectified learning. Influenced by the writings of Jack Kerouac and Allen Ginsberg, they were critical of the grade-motivated "grinds," adherents of the new gnosticism taking shape in a world where knowledge itself was quickly becoming a weapon. The beatniks refused to participate in this new militarism. Further, within the colleges and universities were a growing number of graduate students and faculty mentors who objected to the alliance of military, industrial, political and educational forces identified as "the system."[2] This bohemian group was a short-lived phenomenon, but its constituents were important precursors of the anti-military-industrial alliance and paved the way for a generation of students soon to join them.

Conflicts arose not only over the status of higher education. Disunity became increasingly evident in the whole society. A significant number

---

[1] Horowitz, *Campus Life*, 220–21. Higher education was under particularly acute stress. In 1950 student enrollments amounted to 2.6 million but by 1960 had grown to 3.6 million. Looking ahead, the demographics were staggering: the number of persons from age 18 to 24 was to increase from 16.2 million in 1960 to 24.4 million by 1970. Meanwhile, the number of those eligible to enter college was predicted to increase.

[2] Ibid., 221, 224.

of Americans attained middle-class or better status. A whole generation of children had been reared in this comfort. Yet, conversely, the stratification of the larger society was growing. Economic prosperity brought more freedoms for some, but created a revolution of rising expectations for the have-nots. Whole races of citizens had not only been left out of redevelopment, but many had even been relegated to lower status as their role in national production shifted. Occupations and industries that were economic staples were changed by technology. Many who had made their livelihoods in these works, even meagerly, were thus displaced. They were being left out at the table. It is no little irony that when they set out to exercise their own share of freedom's bounty in 1960 four black students of North Carolina A & T did so by taking their place at a lunch counter.

For a time, John F. Kennedy looked as if he might be able to unite the generations and bridge divisions. When Kennedy took office in January 1961 his inauguration speech was well-crafted, calling for a balance of freedom and responsibility, of government activism and citizen volunteerism. But Kennedy's victory was hardly a landslide. Indeed, it was a very close election. While he seemed to some the perfect bridge between the growing divisions, generational and otherwise, that sent hairline cracks through the old structures of American society, his election—and the very closeness of it—were but further evidence of growing divisions.

The American cultural and institutional landscape was changing. Shifts in world and domestic systems led to changed governmental interaction with the culture and prompted the response which generated numerous special purpose groups.[3] The expansionary economy of the 1950s, for example, contributed to a division of labor in society and all its institutions, including government, the church, and higher education. The same expansion contributed to cultural unrest. The have-nots who had fought for their country but were denied the same benefits as whites would no longer remain silent. The haves, especially within the universities, had the leisure and distance to name America's hypocrisies and injustices.

Thus the culture was gradually fragmented into subcultures. Larger constituencies were segmented into smaller and presumably more manageable units. Universities came to be thought of and treated as "multiversities," as the unitive purpose and program of the academy gave way to a variety of diverse departments and disciplines.

---

[3] Wuthnow, *Restructuring*.

ACADEMY:
PREPARING FOR THE BOOMERS AND CIVIL RIGHTS

At the same time that government fortified higher education programs, demographers were imploring the academy to prepare themselves for a tidal-wave of students: the baby boom, due to reach college age by the early 1960s. The baby boom created a new segment of society, a cohort that would radically alter the social landscape. The extension of education beyond the nominal rudimentary level attained by previous generations became the norm and was, increasingly, a practical necessity to even basic employment. This baby boom generation found a common bond in the experience of higher education. Unlike their parents, however, they were freed from many economic strains. Many delayed marriage and its responsibilities. Although they studied, they enjoyed more time for extracurricular experience. They anticipated work and earning, but higher education served not only to prepare for but to defer that experience. In the diverse company of their contemporaries, they learned of many new ways of living and shared a variety of new perspectives. They were free to leave home, sometimes at great distance. All their boundaries were changing.

As the culture ventured beyond the confines of a contained order to new frontiers, another boundary was tested on February 1, 1960. Four Black students from North Carolina Agricultural & Technical College entered a Woolworth's store in Greensboro, North Carolina, and seated themselves at a lunch counter designated for white patrons only. This time the test was intentional, the boundary carefully selected and the strategy planned. This event is frequently included in accounts of this period and cited for its place within the larger civil rights movement of which it was an important episode. But the event has special significance for this study in that its primary players were college students. Students had played other roles in the mounting civil rights movement: children who had bravely walked into the primary and elementary schools where they were not wanted, high school students who registered for classes over violent protests. The Greensboro four were college students and, while they may have been aided and abetted in their demonstration by organizers of the civil rights movement, they were young adults whose example would have a noted effect upon their peers.

But sympathies for the protestors were not geographically limited; others were soon to join. The Greensboro sit-in prompted a quick, sympathetic response from white students, some of whom came from schools in the North to join the mounting public protests and demonstrations. Watching old footage of the television news coverage of high school desegregation battles waged on Southern turf reveals a reality obscured by the violence of the time itself. Reactions to high school desegregation were angry, ugly and violent. Some of that anger, ugliness and violence emanated from white students, but by far the most vehement and violent behavior was that of parents and other adults of the communities involved. When white students, who were to share the hallways and classrooms with newly enrolled black students, were interviewed on camera their reactions were remarkably balanced and, by comparison to the times, irenic. These students represented many on America's campuses from all parts of the country who saw within their black peers in Greensboro, and their Northern contemporaries who quickly joined the struggle, members of their own cohort. This student cohort and their role in the mounting war was growing more defined. Like their parents before them, they were finding common cause in an escalating conflict, and the war they engaged was—in their eyes—a just war.

The alliances forged between students of disparate background out of the Greensboro sit-in, and other events that would follow, were possible in large measure because of certain social and economic forces. The generational cohort, the "baby-boomers," had been targeted by American manufacturers and retailers as a distinctive group. Horowitz cites the emergence of this group as a distinct "youth culture" as elemental to understanding this time. Even the music popularly marketed to them was distinctive. "Popular songs changed their message to the young: whereas before they had expressed inward rebellion against the pressures of conformity, they now insisted on authenticity."[4] It is this "authenticity" that is notable. The clash, the crisis of this confrontation, was more than generational rebellion against authority; it was the active critique of a society whose practices and institutions lacked consonance with its stated, professed ideals. It was a critique of the "fundamental contradiction" between America's high democratic values and its actual practices, a critique noted by Gunnar Myrdal in his assessment of American racism, and by others who exposed similar disparity in other inequities of the society.[5] In this regard, the tenor of these times was uniquely shaped by education itself, for education was a key factor that made such critique possible. Changes in sexual mores, patterns of alco-

---

4 Horowitz, *Campus Life*, 226–28.
5 Wuthnow, *Restructuring*, 147.

hol and drug use, and emergent feminism and related issues of gender challenged adult authority and separated this generation from their parents. "Confronting a hostile world, young people lowered the barriers among themselves."[6]

Student activism from this era has been the subject of much commentary. Much has been written about the role of campus violence and civil disobedience that began in this period and extended a decade into the several subsequent conflicts that rocked the nation. Some link this upheaval to generational rebellion and rites of passage. Others suspect political intrigues by foreign enemies and domestic troublemakers. Some cite the failure of the American family and others the breakdown of established institutions, traditions, values and morals. Few have suggested that the unrest of the students that began in the Greensboro sit-in may have been evidence not of any great failure, but evidence of a particularly American success. It was not simply for what had gone wrong, but for what had actually been done rather well, that students assumed action.

A sociologist found, in a study of the initiators of campus radicalism in the 1960s, that these student leaders were "democratically bred, intelligent children of highly educated parents. As children they had grown up in professional households where the demands of success within the American economic and social system had compromised their parents' youthful idealism....They believed in the intrinsic value of education and came to college with the expectation that in it reposed value and virtue."[7] This profile of campus rebels, and the turmoil of these years, suggests that this generation of America's children came to young adulthood with some specific tools: a sound education in civics and more than a vague notion of the Christian gospel.

College and university students of the 1960s received their primary and secondary educations in the classrooms of a post-war educational system, in schools that taught civic responsibility and American democracy. From early childhood onward, patriotism was interwoven into the fabric of every curriculum. Students learned the biographies of national heroes and memorized the classical documents of American government. Historical and national holidays marked the passage of the school year much as holy days establish the various liturgical calendars of religious communities. The Declaration of Independence, the Preamble to the Constitution, the Bill of Rights were documents handled, read and

---

6 Horowitz, 226–28, 244.
7 Ibid., 223.

studied. The right to vote, and the responsibility to serve the elective system, were ingrained. The Pledge of Allegiance was recited and, to a lesser extent and until 1962, so were prayers.[8]

Education for the children born to the veterans of both a world war and a severe economic depression enjoyed a sacrality in a society that, if only for this generation, revered a trinity of school, church and home. Each of the three possessed its own distinct being, but together they enjoyed a unity that made their separation inconceivable, even unconscionable. Education of children was a singular priority for those whose own educations had been denied by the Depression's hardship and delayed by wars. The gratifications afforded by education only made it the more precious to parents whose lives were literally transformed socially and economically by education's benefits. They wanted those benefits for their children, and more. They wanted their children to learn music and social skills. They wanted their children to learn practical skills and interpersonal relationship through Girls Scouts and Boy Scouts, YMCA/YWCA and Red Cross Swimming programs and Little League sports. They wanted educational benefit in all that their children experienced, including religion.

There was a new sense of hope for many. Higher education was targeted as "one of the most spectacular growth industries;" nearly all of the approximately two thousand American colleges and universities planned expansion and two hundred new campuses were in planning or under construction in 1962.[9] American society was mushrooming still, and a spirit of optimism and idealism prevailed. Change stimulated creativity as institutions embraced the inevitable onslaught of enrollments stimulated by the market for higher education. In the early 1960s, for example, American educator Clark Kerr began laying plans for a new campus of the California university system to be located in Santa Cruz. It would be a collegiate environment made of students and teachers living together in intimate communities.[10] It was hardly a new concept to establish a campus of residential colleges fostering a sense of academic community as the heart of an education that eschewed grades and competition for nurture and conversation. Thomas Jefferson had a similar

---

[8] For some interesting statistics on the percentage of schools opening the day with prayers in the South verses the West and Midwest, see A. James Reichley, *Religion in American Public Life* (Washington, D.C.: Brookings Institution, 1985), 145.

[9] Paul Venable Turner, *Campus: An American Planning Tradition*, The Architectural History Foundation/MIT Press Series vol. 7 (Cambridge: MIT Press, 1984), 249–50.

[10] Ibid., 281–82.

vision for his University of Virginia. But, like President Kennedy who openly admired Jefferson, Kerr managed to appropriate the Jeffersonian ideals for a new generation. It was an idealism grounded in an irrefutably patriotic tradition.

CHURCH ON CAMPUS:
EQUIPPING FOR SPECIALIZED MINISTRY

Denominations

In 1958 church attendance peaked. In that year nearly forty-nine percent of Americans surveyed said they had been to a religious service during the past week.[11] Wuthnow suggests several possible contributors to the subsequent decline of religious involvement. The population growth which expanded the number of young people in the society created a more clearly defined stage in the life cycle during which young adults could experiment with different beliefs and practices. Growth in the economy and leisure time stimulated a restlessness or impatience with traditional other-worldly spirituality while making it possible for new and competing movements to finance themselves. Increased mobility undoubtedly exposed people to new ways of life even as it complicated the churches' ability to follow its population. In some respects, the higher education experience shared in all these factors.

Episcopalians had long held the lead in college-educated membership. By the 1950s only one Methodist in five had been to college, only one Presbyterian in three. Within twenty years the college-educated membership of these denominations increased, to the point of a majority or near-majority in the Episcopal and Presbyterian churches, and a notable increase for Methodists. The ratio would have improved even more spectacularly if the college-educated had not fled the churches in the late 1960s.[12] Those who stayed, returned, or entered the church may have been fewer in number, but they were more educated, and that brought a change of perspective.

Theology of the Laity

These more educated laity were poised for more authority and theologians were laying the groundwork for them. In 1958 Westminster

---

[11] Wuthnow, *Restructuring*, 159.
[12] Ibid., 160.

Press published the work of a Dutch missiologist, Hendrik Kraemer. *A Theology of the Laity* was one of the first indications of a notable theological and ecclesiological shift within the church. While the churches had devoted much time and thought to the role of clergy and related authorities, little had been done to explore the theological significance of the laity themselves.

Kraemer, however, was hardly the first exponent of a new perspective on the role of church members. Roland Allen, a Church of England missionary, devoted much thought to a changing vision of the church shaped less by hierarchical authority and more by respect for ministry at the local level. Allen, who died in 1947, predicted that the themes that had animated his own life and ministry would not likely gain an interested following until 1960.[13] It was a prescient prediction. In 1960 Donald Attwater's English translation of Yves Congar's *Laity, Church and World* was published.[14]

The notion of shared ministries and increased interest of the laity in a larger share of the action and activity of the church surfaced in campus ministries as well. The Commission on Christian Higher Education of the National Council of Churches (NCC) assisted the formation in 1953 of the Faculty Christian Fellowship. It was estimated that local chapters of the fellowship ranged from 200 to 600 in the first five years of its existence. Campus ministers and local pastors with campus responsibilities were the organizing force, calling together the faculty on a regular basis. But denominations were content to affirm the work of the independent organization rather than encourage separate faculty programs.[15]

At the student level a similar movement was underway. For example, Presbyterian students of the Westminster Fellowship decided to meet separately from the Westminster Fellowship National Council. In 1958 the students voted to become part of a newly forming United Campus Christian Fellowship. Noteworthy is the desire of the students to share responsibility for their own governance. Increasingly students objected to the extension of dependency into the young adult years. Such

---

[13] *The Compulsion of the Spirit: A Roland Allen Reader*, ed. David Paton & Charles H. Long (Grand Rapids, MI: William B. Eerdmans Publishing Co. & Cincinnati, OH: Forward Movement Publications, 1983), vii–viii.

[14] Yves Congar, *Laity, Church and World*, trans. by Donald Attwater (Baltimore: Helicon Press, 1960).

[15] Richard N. Bender, *The Faculty Christian Movement and the Methodist Church* (Nashville: Division of Educational Institutions, Board of Education, The Methodist Church, 1958), 3–11.

expressions for greater autonomy were early indications that the status of *in loco parentis*, like other forms of institutional authority, was in transition. Nor were these the only limits being tested.

Equipped for New Challenges?

With so many boundaries being tested and higher education expanding so rapidly, the churches reviewed and re-visioned their ministries in higher education. Denominational officials reflected more rigorously on the ministry of the church with and to higher education. Fine documents were produced. But one notes time and again in denominational reports that funding was never sufficient to realize the visions. For example, the report of the Standing Committee on Christian Education of the newly formed United Presbyterian Church in the USA (UPCUSA) called on the Board of Christian Education to draft a statement on "The Church and Higher Education." The General Council budget recommended appropriations from their first priority funds adequate to sustain operating costs of the Westminster Foundations. They further recommended $515,500 from second priority funds and $307,250 from third priority funds to act on the 1957 goal of expanding their campus work to other university centers and community colleges.[16] The Department of Campus Life of the General Division of Higher Education reported 144 Westminster Foundations, including 16 run jointly by the merging churches. An additional 42 centers were cooperative ventures with other denominations. The total funds appropriated at the national level for campus work from all available resources came to $694, 250.[17] Although vision and interest increased, resources sufficient to enable the vision were not forthcoming.

By 1959 the students' desire to join the United Campus Christian Fellowship was realized. Theirs was, as the name implied, a collegial fellowship. There was no apparent desire or design to effect an institutional merger of campus ministries across denominational lines. The Westminster Foundation boards and the Department of Campus Christian Life would not be merged with analogous bodies in other member denominations.[18] The Board appropriated $734,000 for a fully

---

[16] Second and third priority funds, however, never materialized. *Minutes of the Presbyterian Church* (1958) part 1, 587.

[17] *Minutes of the Presbyterian Church* (1958) part 2, 51. The funds appropriated included grants to each synod with a campus ministry an amount equivalent to the salary of one full-time campus minister.

[18] *Minutes of the Presbyterian Church* (1959) part 1, 167–68.

integrated campus ministry of the new United Presbyterian Church in the U.S.A. in 150 student centers.[19] But a year later, in the report for 1960, the Standing Committee on Christian Education complained of diminishing funds for campus ministry. The enlarged vision of campus ministry championed by the Board of Christian Education was not shared by the General Assembly.

Despite always tight finances, the church on campus did develop. The General Assembly of the United Presbyterian Church USA received in 1961 the report it had commissioned in 1958 and expected to receive in 1959, "The Church and Higher Education." The report reflects the concerns raised by Sputnik and the intensifying Cold War in an introductory assertion that the United States and the communist world are engaged in "a race for the best minds."[20] Within this context of competition, the report notes that the landscape of higher education was changing as the public exerted an unprecedented demand for higher education with a high priority on technical training. The authors of the report decry the divorce of research from teaching and worry that students seem to place priority on grades, skills, jobs, and projected income and security. Conversely, they also note a renewed interest in theology on campus. But this theological interest grows in a religiously and culturally pluralistic context; the Church has not yet made an understanding of the Gospel relevant to this modern world. Practical demographic concerns also call the church to action on campus. Increased enrollments and increased internationalization of education are realities and potentialities that demand the church's attention.[21] But the church, the report asserts, is inadequate to the task.

The church is inadequate because "Protestantism in America failed to develop an adequate theological rationale for the place of higher learning in the life of the Church."[22] The report proposes as essential to an "adequate theological rationale" some basic affirmations: that God is Lord of all life and knowledge; that every Christian is called to a vocation; and that all Christians are called to lives of self-giving service.[23] It is the second of those affirmations, that every Christian is called to a vocation, that remains the most significant. It is significant in its addition

---

[19] *Minutes of the Presbyterian Church* (1959) part 2, 58. This church was created in 1958 from the merger of two Presbyterian denominations.

[20] *Minutes of the Presbyterian Church* (1961) part 1, 152–53.

[21] Ibid., 154–57.

[22] Ibid., 158.

[23] Ibid., 160–61.

of a distinctively different dimension to previous theological affirmations relative to education.

The first affirmation—that God is Lord of all life and knowledge—was certainly a foundational principle in the establishment of colleges and universities as a major component of the church's work in this nation. The third affirmation—that all Christians are called to lives of self-giving service and that that service finds its nurture in an education that is framed by this principle—was also common to the institutional charters of colleges and universities established by the churches prior to World War II. It is the principle of vocation—more commonly applied in limited fashion to ordination and ecclesial orders—that reflects a new, or at least renewed, vision of education as essential to all ministry, ordained and lay.

As the report amplified these essentials, it described a vision of the life of the church in the university. A foundational "mission statement" is set forth in the first assertion: that the Church is a witnessing community. "The central purpose of the Church in the university is to bear living witness to the Gospel of Jesus Christ through an inclusive, consciously Christian community, within the college or university, in which all inquiries are welcome and respected and all may encounter and respond to Jesus Christ and engage in His mission in the world." [24] Extending this focal mission, the church in the university is described as a witnessing church; a community of obedience; an open community where truth ought to be openly pursued; a supportive community; and, lastly, the church in the university is not the fullness of the church, but is a special mission.[25]

In the fulfillment of this special mission, the report concludes, the church can expect its ministry on campus to provide vocational witness that strengthens both the university and church in upholding obedience to God's call. The church can also expect its ministry on campus to provide undergirding concern, and presumably a vocal and critical concern, aimed at challenging the university's own institutional response to its vocation. Such concern and critique is understood to include questioning those forces, alliances, and decisions that contribute to the growing separation of scientific and humanistic disciplines. These include the growing dependence of the university upon government, commercial, and private

---

[24]   Ibid., 164.
[25]   Ibid., 165.

research projects. And, finally, the church can expect its ministry on campus to provide pastoral care.

The Board of Christian Education had for five years used its publishing profits for campus ministry. There were simply no funds for adequate expansion despite the doubling or tripling of the college-age population that was anticipated. Also the board cited the need for adult Christian education as the ministry of the laity was being rediscovered in the biblical tradition. Board appropriations to Westminster Foundations in 1960 totaled $834,798. Nevertheless, the budgetary limitations are evident in a Board of Christian Education request that Westminster Foundations assume financial support of all staff other than "the key person," even as it urged continued outreach. This outreach, it suggested, was the work of local congregations. But the increase in two-year colleges, undergraduate commuters, and multiplying public schools of higher education had outdistanced any reasonable hope of a comprehensive campus ministry.

The churches could not muster and mobilize the massive resources in the same way that the government could—volunteer organizations cannot tax their members. The battle language of mobilization and war peppered ecclesiastical statements of this period, especially in the Methodist Church. The Commission on Christian Higher Education Report to the General Conference of the Methodist Church in 1960 bore the militant title, "To Win the Long Conquest." In the 1956-60 quadrennium the denomination's stated educational priority had been to battle materialistic atheism and Communism by linking knowledge with a vital piety. Meeting in January 1957, the Commission adopted a fifty point *Christian Higher Education Blueprint,* a plan largely realized by the end of the quadrennium in 1960. Bonds between educational institutions and the church were strengthened through Commission-sponsored conferences for college trustees aimed at helping them understand their role as church stewards. Students and denominational colleges were encouraged to commit themselves to thoroughly Christian standards and ideals, and there was throughout the church a deepened appreciation for the necessity of Christian higher education as the field of public educational opportunities expanded. Churches were exhorted to provide adequate moral and financial support for the denomination's colleges. In addition, the General Conference set financial goals with the intent of moving primary funding for colleges and campus ministry to the Annual Conference level. Per member giving for colleges increased from 30 cents per member in 1955-56 to 66 cents per member in 1958-59. Support for

Wesley Foundations moved from 8 cents per member to 19 cents per member in the same period. Total church dollar support for Wesley Foundations went from $777,984 in 1956 to $1,844, 656 in 1959.[26] Working cooperatively with the Division of Educational Institutions, annual conference commissions, and boards of trustees, the Commission promoted the Wesley Foundations as "representatives of the Church on the campuses of state and independent institutions of higher learning...[bearing] witness to Christian faith in a way that will be relevant to the lives of students."[27] Further, they set about interpreting the work of higher education to the church, requesting the annual conferences to set aside a certain percentage of their funds for schools and colleges even as they encouraged the church to send "its best men" to work on campus, where the future culture was being shaped. Standards for campus ministry professionals were articulated and established good preaching as an important means for student evangelism.[28] It was an ambitious program, ambitiously engaged. Even so, American higher education and the American culture were moving rapidly, and in new directions.

By 1960 it was clear that education in America had taken a turn. The Methodist Commission on Christian Higher Education, in its report in 1960, sought a corrective to a growing reliance upon science and technology. The church, the report maintained, has a responsibility to society to show that education means more than the technical. "The strength of Western democracies must be of the Spirit."[29]

The Bishops' Address of the same year indicated awareness of and concern for these changes. They identified the foe as the modern idolatry of what they called "scientism" and technology, and they looked to denominational schools and campus ministries to combat the foe. They expressed gratitude for stronger partnerships of colleges, Wesley Foundations, and local churches made possible by a successful financial campaign, but they saw need for strong relationships well beyond the ties of budget. By 1960 there were 181 Wesley Foundations in the denomination, staffed by those the bishops identified as "some of our most gifted and devoted men and women." The bishops were concerned, however, that the church "often left them to their labors without adequate support or appreciation."[30] Despite such encouraging and sympa-

---

[26] *Journal of the Methodist Church*, ed. Leon T. Moore (1960), 1567.

[27] Ibid., 1569.

[28] Ibid, 1570.

[29] Ibid., 1560.

[30] Ibid., 210.

thetic words, the bishops and their church faced a mounting list of demanding ministries while resources did not keep pace.

The quadrennial emphases of 1960-64 in the Methodist Church shows the place of campus ministry in an enlarged pantheon of concern. The church established spiritual life as its major focus of attention for the quadrennium. Evangelistic outreach was to be emphasized in personal witness, the establishment of new church schools, the organization of new churches, inner city initiatives, small and country church work, in the family, in industrial life, and—lastly—in university and college students. Those who set the agenda recognized that requisite leadership to meet future challenges mandated that young people be trained "in the spiritual disciplines." The conclusion reached, however, was not an endorsement of a more literate laity but the traditional plea for more ordained leadership: "We call upon our educational institutions to bring to the attention of their students the opportunities and privileges of the Christian ministry. They should, along with the church and the home, assume responsibility for enlisting their youth for the Christian ministry."[31] To reach these goals the General Conference recommended increasing per member financial support for denominational higher education from the previous quadrennium's 66¢ per member high to $1.50 per member, and support for Wesley Foundations from 19 cents per member to 50 cents per member. And a goal of $1 million per year was urged for Negro education.

In many respects the Methodist and Episcopal churches shared the concern of the Presbyterians, though the Presbyterians were by far the most thoughtful in struggling through to conclusions. All three denominations were aware of the mounting role of higher education as the generational cohort now called the "baby-boomers" edged toward the campuses. All three denominations noted in varied reports of the time the institutional breach between church and campus and proposed reconciliation of that distance as important work to be done. The bottom line to all such reports was the same: allocations to campus ministry were insufficient and would have to be increased to meet the growing need. In this period of the early 1960s Presbyterian and Episcopalian national church budgets edged campus ministry allocations upward, while Methodists successfully shifted primary funding to the annual conference level, markedly increasing the dollars spent on campus ministry. But at no time, and in no report, were the allocations ever deemed

---

[31] Ibid., 1585–89.

sufficient to the task. Indeed, in every case the charge was made that present funding was inadequate and increasingly so when compared to anticipated need. Included in domestic mission or educational ministry categories, campus ministry took its place alongside a growing number of needs challenging the resources of the church.

Even though higher education ministries did not grow as rapidly as advocates hoped, they did grow. With their expansion—and the churches'—came institutional differentiation. This division of labor was sometimes interpreted positively, but it was often negatively interpreted as fragmentation. Campus ministry, indeed all ministries, began to take on distinct identities as specialized components of a larger whole. The organizational structures of the denominations here under study were arranged and rearranged as each component sought a logical lodging within the particular scheme of the denomination. Wuthnow notes as important the emergence of what he calls "special purpose groups" within the churches.[32] These groups represent, at least in part, the partitioning of ministry and mission into working units or divisions within the church. Social ministries, such as race relations, economics, and pastoral issues, proliferated. The work of education, for example, was parcelled into separate divisions, each overseeing particular work. There were, in many places at both the national and lower judicatory levels, separate offices for denominational colleges, for campus ministry, and for Christian Education—which was further subdivided into divisions for pre-school, elementary, junior high, senior high, and adult.

For example, the Presbyterians maintained campus ministry as one of two foci (the other being their denominational colleges) within a General Division of Higher Education. But the emphasis of the report in 1961 upon campus ministry as a "community" set within the larger entity of the campus was, by 1963, contradicted by a subsequent finding that "every individual is faced with the dilemma of trying to hold on to a center while being a member of any number of communities of interest."[33] Episcopalians in 1961 designated their College Work Program as one facet of their Home Missions, a category that included urban-industrial concerns, inner-city ministry, resettlement of American Indians, and increased chaplains for the armed forces. Any clear sense of unified mission, for the whole or its constituent parts, is difficult to discern.

---

[32] Wuthnow, *Restructuring*.
[33] *Minutes of the Presbyterian Church* (1963) part 2, 15.

The ideal proposed by Kerr, and widely emulated elsewhere, that the expansion of campuses and exploding enrollments be mitigated by the creation of small residence colleges, echoes the churches' conception of campus ministries as communities within the university. The church was encouraged by some not "to dominate educational institutions, but rather enter into dialogue with them in order that, on the university's own terms, it may become what God intended it to be."[34] In addition to conversing with the university, the church was charged to provide communities on campuses in order to help satisfy the human need for relationships and because such communities and relationships can be the contexts of shared experience in which one is grasped by truth.[35] Establishing "little platoons" within American society seemed the only manageable answer to rampant social change and expansion that showed no signs of abating.

Changing Role of the Campus Minister

While the division of labor continued and roles became more specialized, claims to authority weakened. Growing democratization, encouraged at least in part by an educational process that opened opportunity to larger numbers, made distinctions less tenable. As the laity became more educated, both in the quantity who availed themselves of higher education and the quality that set the baccalaureate as a new normative standard, the hierarchy that once set clergy apart by virtue of advanced learning was challenged. With greater numbers of the laity seeking professional and post-baccalaureate degrees, the degree of difference between the clergy's education and the laity's education grew smaller. As the professional class in American society grew, clergy constituted less and less of an elite. As the governance and care of parishes grew more complex, clergy experienced increased demand for what amounted to clinical counselling care, sophisticated oral communications, large-scale property management—all gathered into the complicated financial, personnel, and public relations systems of the non-profit, volunteer organization. These demands challenged the self-perceptions of clergy. The "pastoral" distinction was less satisfactory; clergy sought the status of the "professional" as a distinguishing characteristic.

The professional evolution of clergy to executive function, if not status, was at least in part an extension of the post-war increase of

---

34 Cantelon, 34.
35 Ibid., 88–89.

institutional size and the demand for diversified program. As the institutional church grew in size and ministries were parcelled out, the concept of pastor as "first among equals," and the church as community engaged in unified mission and life, eroded. The collegial relations between clergy also changed as areas of specialized ministry like campus ministry, youth ministry, Christian Education, pastoral counselling, and other appellations introduced distinction and difference. The very "ordering" of ministries into lay and ordained apostolates was for this generation, as it was for the early church, a response to growth in the community. Within a reordered church religious professionals would "bear responsibilities for evolving this lay apostolate, for attacking the privatization of religious interest and for working toward the theological maturity of the laity."[36] But the distinction of apostolates signified further division within the whole, and the possibility for difference—and divisiveness—as each carved out a niche within the institution. Partitioning, compartmentalizing, was not confined to the larger entities of the culture. It was increasingly a mark of the church and its members.

In 1963, the report of the United Presbyterian Church Board of Christian Education repeated the concern that change had unleashed among the people of the land a retreat into "expedient privatism."[37] Gordon Chamberlain, a writer on staff at Riverside Church in New York, for nine years in charge of campus ministries, undertook a study of church-college interaction. He interviewed administrators, faculty and churches connected with five campuses to determine attitudes toward the academy, religion and churches.

Chamberlain's study is evidence for both fragmentation and privatism. The thirty-five teachers interviewed by Chamberlain concluded that "Christian theology seemed to have little significance to contribute to higher education."[38] Administrators, too, divorced the intellectual from the spiritual. Although all but one were church members, they evinced no sense that their work was a Christian vocation.[39] The fifty-two students interviewed evidenced a deep split between spiritual church and intellectual academy.[40] Of the thirty-three clergy interviewed,

---

[36] Gibson Winter, "The New Christendom in the Metropolis," *Christianity and Crisis* Vol. XXII(26 November 1962): 208.

[37] *Minutes of the Presbyterian Church* (1963) part 2, 14–15.

[38] J. Gordon Chamberlain, *Churches and the Campus* (Philadelphia: The Westminster Press, 1963), 70.

[39] Ibid., 78.

[40] Ibid., 80–92.

only three who had not been a campus minister had ever read a book on the church and higher education and, by their own admission, their churches' youth programs poorly prepared their students for higher education's intellectual challenges.[41]

Chamberlain included interviews with thirteen lay people not connected to any campuses. Their interest in the church's involvement in higher education was motivated by fear of Communism and a conviction that the church should undergird the free enterprise system, although how the church was to do this was left unclear. The lay people circumscribed the church to the spiritual realm, although their definition of that realm was vague. And they demonstrated little sense of their work as Christian vocation.[42] The common testimony of all groups interviewed and the conclusions drawn were that the college and the church reported little need for each other, and that a sense of one's work as Christian vocation was lacking in the church and on the campus.[43] Thus lines of partition and personal fragmentation were, in the early 1960s, evident.

Reports like Chamberlain's indicated the growing distance between church and academy, and growing disintegration of individuals, just when massive change was imminent. Work like Chamberlain's indicated cause for attention.

The Danforth Study

In 1963 the Danforth Foundation commissioned a major study of the church, higher education, and social policy. Characterized as a "major Protestant 'experiment' in specialized ministries," the project was described by director Kenneth Underwood as a response to "a crisis of contemporary religious commitment and consciousness."[44] While the findings of the project were not published until 1969, it is significant that the Danforth initiative in 1963 singled out campus ministries as

> the most generally significant and illuminating sector of religious leadership for intensive investigation and analysis ...[because] they symbolize and articulate best the spiritual problems and occasions that grip the nation. The Protestant campus ministry, of all religious leadership in this country, has

---

[41] Ibid., 102, 119.

[42] Ibid., 123–25.

[43] Ibid., 131–45.

[44] *The Church, the University and Social Policy: The Danforth Study on Campus Ministries*, ed. Kenneth Underwood, 2 vols. (Middletown, CT: Wesleyan University Press, 1969), vol. 1, 3. Hereafter abbreviated to Danforth with volume number and page.

been most involved with the intellectual, social, and moral movements of
the best-educated youth in America. The problems and potentialities of faith
and ethics which confront this particular ministry are likely to be those
which most religious leaders will have to face as the questions, doubts, and
hopes voiced by college and university leaders are brought out through the
mass media, primary and secondary schools, and adult and continuing education into the mainstream of the whole society.[45]

The claim is hyperbolic, and reflects an elitism of church, higher education, government and social policy-makers of the time—authorities
whose power subsequently would be called into question. Without
diminishing or inflating the value of the Danforth Study itself, its selection of a single segment for study—the collegiate, "baby-boom" cohort
and its life and role on campus, in church, and in social policy—is a
recognition of campus life, ministry, and influence.

Higher education and religion were, themselves, self-consciously
discrete communities among a growing number of such communities in
the larger society. The partitioning of the society and its organizations
into smaller, more manageable units was possibly the only response
available to the daunting reality of unchecked expansion on every front.
The premise of the Danforth Study that campus ministry is a sociological
microcosm, the study of which can reveal far-reaching implications, is
indication that the institutions under study—higher education, church,
government—were neither integral nor integrated. On the face of it, the
country and its institutions may still have thought of themselves as
whole and unified, but a closer examination reveals that the whole fabric
of the structure was a maze of tiny, hairline cracks defining the varied
communities within the whole.

WARNING SIGNS

In 1963 the Reverend Martin Luther King, Jr., led a march on
Washington, D.C. In that impressive event one segment in the society—
the African-American community—articulated and demonstrated not
only its desire for equal freedom, but its visible presence as one of the
increasing number of communities within the larger community of the
nation.

In November of that year President John F. Kennedy, symbol of
American hope and unity, was assassinated in Dallas, Texas. The stress

---

45 Ibid.

was unbearable. Hairline cracks widened, and the society verged on fracture.

—⚜ **3** ⚜—

THE GATHERING STORM IN SOCIETY AND CHURCH: 1963–1968

INTRODUCTION

What holds a people together? Common values, force, religion, filial piety, heritage, ethnic or racial identity, practices, geography? This question became increasingly difficult for citizens of the United States to answer as the 1960s progressed. Special purpose groups continued to multiply as dispossessed and silenced peoples organized and found voices. Generational conflict increased, or at least became more public. Authority at every level was challenged by students on campus and, increasingly, by college-educated adults in the churches. The church's vocation to society in general and to the campus in particular was questioned from both within the church and without. In addition, and very importantly, the fiscal boom of the post-war years began to weaken; and congregations increased the percentage of their funds they kept at home.

SOCIETY:
DISAPPEARANCE OF THE COMMON GOOD

Kennedy's assassination signalled the disappearance of the common good.[1] The sense of a common good, the notion that there was a public good, long dictated by the values of a dominant white male culture, had managed to hold through Kennedy's election. Indeed, his public persona encouraged those values. Kennedy urged the citizens to extend themselves for the good of the country and appealed to a new patriotism upon which foundation civil rights would be extended and The New Frontier approached. The youthful, charismatic personality of this man who had inherited wealth and power despite an Irish-American, Roman Catholic heritage became the hero of a new and significant proportion of the nation. He was very much a symbol of a new generation of leadership, a contemporary of the World War II veterans who were then coming to leadership in all sectors of American life. Widespread identification with this President made his untimely death the more traumatic for the nation. In the cultivation of a Presidential style Kennedy conveyed a sense of order and control, of ease and grace, amid the growing complexities of the nation's life. The image of a youthful veteran, even hero, of war presiding confidently with an attractive, cultured wife and two children beside him became something of a cultural icon which provided a sense of national unity in diversity.

But with Kennedy's assassination that sense of unity dissipated. The fault lines identified in the previous chapter fractured. Regardless of one's politics, whether one agreed with his policies or not, Kennedy's death touched an entire nation. The violent assassination of this President conveyed the singular message that something was wrong, terribly wrong. It was a cathartic event that revealed a radical brokenness that could no longer be denied. The confident invincibility of authority was revealed to be hollow, the vulnerability of institutions was exposed. The image of unity no longer sufficed to cover the truth that America and its institutions had grown more complex, with ever-expanding distinctions and differences magnified by advancing communications media that only made everyone more aware of the diversity and more quickly.

---

[1] For an extended consideration of the common good see Joseph C. Hough, Jr., "The University and the Common Good," *Theology and the University: Essays in Honor of John B. Cobb, Jr.,* eds. David Ray Griffin and Joseph C. Hough, Jr. (Albany: State University of New York Press, 1991), 97–124.

By the mid-1960s Americans faced a variety of new concerns and changed relationships. Civil rights momentum grew and strategies diversified. Mainline American Protestant dominance declined as Catholic and Jewish leadership emerged. Entitlements and research contracts expanded the role of higher education and reshaped its priorities. Institutions and individuals, too, met the complexity of the time with confusion and a profound longing for order. Special purpose groups grew at an accelerated pace

The special purpose groups asserted in this period a heightened self-interest as each assumed responsibility for its own welfare. The most prominent was the African-American community or caucus—or more specifically, that portion of the African-American community that asserted a specific identity and full enfranchisement for the race in the name of "black power." Ethnic pride and the resurgence of tribal community became the impetus for social and political action. Not all African-American citizens embraced "black power," nor did all agree with the methods advocated for its exercise. But the group that found a life, a *raison d'être* in the willful adoption of the African cultural heritage remains an example of the process of self-identification and self-assertion common to the fragmented, increasingly distinct and frequently separated groups scattered throughout the society and its institutions.

ACADEMY:
RIGHTS AND AUTHORITY

The Greensboro sit-in and similar demonstrations in the early 1960s were student events. A high proportion of the black civil rights activists throughout the decade of the 1960s was of student age. Martin Luther King, Jr. and others captured the attention of the media, but African-Americans in their early twenties were prominent and effective leaders in the movement. They formed, in 1964, the Student Nonviolent Coordinating Committee (SNCC), one of the most prominent of the several groups advocating change.[2] African-American students and their non-African-American supporters worked through SNCC, and through a host of smaller, less-formal local committees and organizations to engage the issues of racism on and off campus. Their example had almost immediate, and lasting, effect on others of their own generation

---

[2] Flowers, 10.

As early as 1960, students revealed their dissatisfaction with the prevailing tenor of American politics and culture. The Berkeley campus of the University of California played a prominent role in this rising unrest and its activist manifestation. In May 1960 students from Berkeley gathered in San Francisco and staged a demonstration, a sit-in, at City Hall protesting the hearings of the House Un-American Activities Committee. The actions of the students, and photographs and film clips of their removal from City Hall, captured the attention of their peers around the country. Students from Harvard, moved by the action of their contemporaries in Berkeley, mounted a more modest show of solidarity in a class on the Cambridge campus.[3]

Students grew more aware of their power, especially when the institutions of which they were a part were characterized as power centers. Shortly after the UC/Berkeley demonstrations, student organizers realized that there were other issues and concerns they could address. Attention from the media had drawn to Berkeley a number of students who shared the convictions of the early organizers and now came to join them. By 1963 students from the Berkeley campus were making regular incursions into the communities around them. They deployed intentional strategies to confront racism in Bay-area businesses and institutions. Targeting the Sheraton Palace Hotel, the students waged demonstrations to protest what they deemed unfair personnel policies. The students did win an agreement with the hotel industry to end discriminatory policies, but the victory was double-edged. Pressure upon the University of California at Berkeley was forthcoming from the surrounding communities, which wanted more discipline exercised over student activism. The university banned off-campus causes or political concerns within the university's gates. A line of demarcation was drawn between campus and community, and students were forbidden to cross it. The university administration, and the community and state governments that backed it, exercised parent-like authority, effectively "grounding" the dissident

---

[3] Stephen Most, Mark Kitchell and Susan Griffin *Berkeley in the Sixties* Mark Kitchell, prod. and dir. (1990), documentary film. Clark Kerr, then President of the University of California at Berkeley, rightly identified the cultural role of the university in his own assessment of American academia. Referring to America's colleges and universities as "the knowledge industry," an industry that represented in 1960 about 29 percent of the nation's gross national product (GNP), he compared the academy of the twentieth century with the railroad of the nineteenth century, each transformative agents in the life of the national economy and culture.

students. The students, hardly compliant and unquestioning, determined to respond.[4]

In the autumn of 1964 students distributing literature at Sather Gate at the University of California in Berkeley were "told by a campus officer that they could not distribute their materials in that location."[5] Angry dissent erupted as the students protested, and they escalated their grievances over several weeks. Page Smith identified this event as the start of the "student rebellion," the "opening gun in a war that would last intermittently for the next eight years."[6] Smith cited three major influences behind student unrest: the progressively disheartening situation of undergraduates, at least at Berkeley; the civil rights movement, which drew young adults, black and white, in common cause against segregation; and the Vietnam War, which, after the alleged attack of American ships in the Tonkin Gulf in 1964 and congressional approval of Executive powers, escalated rapidly.[7] The incidents at Berkeley spread to other campuses as students found a voice and much to protest.

Largely overshadowed by other controversies of the time, including those of race at home and escalating war abroad, these skirmishes were loosely catalogued under the more generic theme of "student unrest." But these little episodes of rebellion touch the nature of institutional establishment and became for the student culture on campus their own point of engagement with the larger civil rights movement. As the civil rights movement progressed, opening more social patterns and institutions to critique, white middle-class students turned their attention to their own situation. From the students' point of view, the student protest at Berkeley had not only to do with the content of the literature being distributed: Students protested the notion that such distribution required permission.

Democracy depends upon participatory constituencies. It is to the benefit of democratic institutions to promote or provide instruction in the exercise of such participatory life. But education that aroused questions about authority, and educational institutions that became seats of

---

4 Ibid.

5 Page Smith, *Killing the Spirit: Higher Education in America* (New York: Viking, 1990), 156.

6 Ibid. It should also be noted that in 1964 the General Division of the Presbyterian Board of Christian Education, at the request of Presbyterian college presidents, convened a conference on the legal and moral requirements for colleges to act *in loco parentis* within the context of a shifting student culture.

7 Ibid., 156–57.

resistance to authority, threatened the delicate equipoise of the very institutions education was believed to serve. Campus unrest revealed that
students actually appropriated the principles they were taught and participated in a political system that encouraged their expression. But confusion ensued when the exercise of political freedoms was met with military resistance and when Christian social conscience aroused not ecclesiastical sympathy but discord. As the war in Vietnam progressed, and the
need for soldiers intruded into dormitories and classrooms, confusion
grew in the minds of all who dared to ask what really was in the best interest of the nation and of its citizens. America's attitudes were changing.
Differences of perspective and opinion became more pronounced.

One significant change was generational. Parents and students experienced college differently and differently valued those experiences. The
parents of the "baby-boom" group, for the most part, attended college as
adults and experienced campus life as war veterans, sometimes married
and even then parents. But for the younger student—entering college at
age 17 or 18—college was an extension of an uninterrupted, formal
educational process. The passage to adulthood for the parents of collegians in the 1960s was a passage through the Great Depression and a
World War that demanded a precocious maturity. Their experience was
framed by the experience of privation; they were deprived of an experience of youth that they did not want to deny their children. Passage to
adulthood for their children—the collegians of the 1960s and early
1970s—was frustrated by a level of parental expectation and relative
affluence that prolonged their passage into adulthood and that, in time,
came to be resented by the collegians as an enforced infantalization. They
were to go to college, in part, to experience what their parents had not.
The post-war veterans attended college on a GI Bill designed to delay
their entry into the workforce; their children attended college right out of
high school, effectively delaying their entry into the workforce by
extending "childhood" by an additional four or more years of financial
dependency within institutions ordered on the custodial model of the
private boarding school.

But *in loco parentis* policies had been strained by veterans who
encountered them after World War II. Still, having experienced military
discipline, veterans adapted to their restraints. Their children, however,
experiencing campus as relatively independent and affluent young
adults, challenged these policies as archaic and intrusive. Students of this
period rebelled against the custodial nature of higher education.
Compulsory "closing hours" for men's and women's dormitories, resi-

dent house mothers, and a host of campus rules governing social and academic life strained relations between students and administrators whose task was the imposition and enforcement of such policies. The appreciation for authority that marked the post-World-War II experience of their parents gave way to the students' questioning of authority.

Many questions arose from these different experiences of and changing relationships to authority. When the people had been united in common cause against economic depression and foreign dictatorship, or united in common mission in the restoration of domestic life, authority related to the larger goal and all relationships were measured against service to that end. But when divided by personal interest and diversity of opinion, in disagreement over racial and economic parity and increasingly dissatisfied with escalating military involvement in Southeast Asia, Americans stood in changed relationship to one another and to the traditional authorities.

In 1965 all students qualified to attend college were accorded access to higher education through federal assistance.[8] In 1964 there were no government matching grants to higher education, but by the end of 1965 the federal government had invested $286,131,306 in matching grants. That investment nearly doubled in 1966 at $528,794,000. This national commitment to higher education, when added to the considerable governmental research investment on campus, yoked the community of higher education with the institutions of federal government in a prominent way. It was not a wholly fortuitous partnership given the growing student suspicion of all institutionalized authority.

While public and governmental support for higher education encouraged a greater egalitarianism on campus,[9] this policy also had ironic consequences, for it opened higher education to larger numbers of people, and from more divergent constituencies. It expanded liberalization to a broader cross-section of society. Studies of the period indicate that the tremendous shifts toward liberalization were linked to the influence of higher education. Differences in levels of education proved to be the "best single predictor of differences in attitudes and values."[10] Unwittingly, the conservative institutions of government and religion, in their support of higher education, were subsidizing a growing liberal dissent on campus and enabling the propagation of that liberalization to a wider population.

---

[8] Robert B. Reich, "The Real Economy," *The Atlantic* (February 1991), 47.

[9] Wuthnow, *Restructuring*, 156.

[10] Ibid., 157.

THE CHURCH AND THE CAMPUS:
VOCATIONAL AND AUTHORITY CRISES

Exploring Vocation

A volume of essays published in 1964 under the title, *The Campus Ministry*,[11] focused intently upon the church as the *laos* of God. The emphasis and importance of campus ministry was "to help Christians discover afresh how 'to be' the laos (the people) of God."[12] The work of campus ministry was to gather the people of God for the purpose of equipping the "saints for the work of ministry" (Ephesians 4:12).[13] This work was itself a work of evangelism, proclaiming as it does not only the good news of Jesus Christ, but the exceedingly good news that the task of ministry extends to all God's people.[14] Campus ministry was to concern itself with vocation in its most basic, biblical meaning: a calling by God into a life of service and community.[15] Campus ministry was also to provide pastorally for God's people in the academic community, and to accept the necessity of experimentation and research. Campus ministry was to be responsibly related to both the church and the university, and must periodically gather to perceive clearly its task of mission.

The authors were concerned not only about the vocation of campus ministry, but the vocation of the university, as well. One essayist, writing on the role of faculty, maintained that the university's vocation is study and that the church had too long neglected that important ministry to the extent that the church had "made itself irrelevant to its primary task" of educational ministry.[16] This essay noted the Faculty Christian Fellowship, which struggled with its own philosophy but also provided its membership with opportunities for research, faith-learning studies, and a national conference. The experience of this fellowship and others like it showed that "...a Christian faculty movement cannot function denominationally,"[17] a point that seemed to accord with the attitude of

---

[11] George L. Earnshaw, ed., *The Campus Ministry* (Valley Forge: Judson Press, 1964).

[12] George L. Earnshaw, preface to *The Campus Ministry*, 9.

[13] George L. Earnshaw, "A General Philosophy for a Relevant Campus Ministry," *The Campus Ministry*, 20.

[14] Ibid., 27.

[15] Ibid., 28.

[16] William B. Rogers, "The Role of a Christian Faculty Movement," *The Campus Ministry*, 141–42.

[17] Ibid., 149.

students of the same period. Verlyn Barker, in an essay on the United Campus Christian Fellowship, suggested that the proper posture of the church on campus was one of humility, a party to the campus conversation, but "a listener and learner, as well as a teacher."[18] The prevailing tone of the leadership in campus ministry, at home and abroad, bespoke sincere regard for the fullness of the church's ministry and urged cooperation and conversation over triumphalism and authoritarianism.

The whole relationship between church and society, especially the vocation of the former in the latter, was called into question in 1965 by Harvey Cox. Cox lambasted the church for its insistence upon establishment precisely when the people of God and the culture at large demanded an alternative. His alternatives for the churches' work on campus were, by the time of their publication, an increasingly common litany, at least among those familiar with the campus and concerned for its religious life:

> It is clear that any work which is not radically ecumenical has no place on the university campus, or indeed anywhere else....It is also clear that the gathered stage of this church's life will occur in small, disciplined groups constituted on a functional basis....What is the role of the church in the university? The 'organizational church' has no role. It should stay out. The church as a reconciling community of servants determined to serve the university even when no one thanks them, praises them, or notices them does have a place in the university. That place will be evident to those who have eyes to see.[19]

Denominational Vocations

When the three denominations under study here each met in 1964, discussion regarding their vocation in American society and in the world was prominent. Mission, global consciousness, and ecumenism were major topics. The Methodist Church declared as its quadrennial emphasis, "One Witness in One World."[20] The Episcopal Church, whose previous triennial emphasis was world mission, received the report of the Anglican Congress of 1963 in Toronto entitled "Mutual Responsibility and Interdependence." The report was endorsed as the basis for a

---

[18] Verlyn L. Barker, "The United Campus Christian Fellowship," *The Campus Ministry*, 284.

[19] Harvey Cox, *The Secular City* (New York: Macmillan Company, 1985), 236.

[20] *Journal of the Methodist Church*, eds. Leon T. Moore and J. Wesley Hole (1964), 2073.

worldwide mission policy.[21] The Presbyterian Church pondered the displacement of American Protestantism and, turning its attention to domestic mission, continued funding to a conference of sociologists and campus chaplains studying the intersection of theology and sociology. Ecumenical interests were devoted to patterns for inter-denominational cooperation in campus ministry.[22]

Changing roles should entail changing structures and leadership, but the machinery of these denominations was made for another time and was ill-equipped to deal with the change. By 1964, membership and religious participation, as noted earlier, had peaked and were level, if not declining, in nearly all mainline denominations. Fiscal resources were not keeping pace with the demands of mission and ministry. For example, in accepting the Canadian report, "Mutual Responsibility and Interdependence," as their world-wide mission policy, the Episcopalians resorted to an interesting form of ecclesiastical bookkeeping. When the matter of funding the program was raised, it was determined that such funding as was needed would be provided outside the normal budget. The program was described as "a spiritual movement within the Church, rather than a program requiring a budget."[23]

Questions about the church's vocation in the world were complicated by authority problems within the church. The authority problem was most prominently indicated in a rising class of thoughtful, articulate, and educated laity eager to assume responsibility for ministry. The North American Conference on the Ministry of the Laity in the World convened in Chicago, in January 1966, and released a message—presumably addressed to the predominantly ordained leadership of the churches— with a twelve-point agenda requesting:

1)   ...new experiments in the expression of Christian ministry in the world....

2)   ...more thorough education and training at various levels of competence and responsibility, for lay people as they minister in the world, of

---

[21] *Journal of the General Convention* (1964), 731–37.

[22] *Minutes of the Presbyterian Church* (1964) part 2, 32–33.

[23] *Journal of the General Convention*, (1964), 732. To be fair, the Episcopal Church did devote over $5 million per year in 1964–67 to overseas mission, compared to just over $3 million per year in the same triennium to home mission. Of the $9.8 million triennium home mission budget, $1.1 million was earmarked for urban missions. Still, the Joint Committee on Program and Budget submitted this report with a complaint that it showed poor stewardship for a church that could support two to three times more for its national budget. Ibid., 735.

both secular and religious educational facilities, including colleges, seminaries, and youth and adult community centers.

3) ...a "sharp" increase of responsibilities of laymen for decision making within the churches.

4) ...that clergy and laymen help each other to discern and face in honesty their mutual problems of radical doubt and their feelings of isolation.

5) ...that the churches help to identify and to assess difficult practical ethical issues by

   a. Working with and through laymen who are directly involved in understanding such issues and in making decisions about them.

   b. Learning to study and to penetrate the power structures in modern society which dehumanize and degrade men and women who work in them.

6) ...that the churches without delay make their membership open to all, regardless of ethnic, racial or economic status, that representatives of all sectors of the population be included in their conferences, committees and official bodies, and that suitable financial provision be made for this....

8) ...study of world needs and opportunities that more effective and peaceful solutions, with possible alternatives to military action, may be found in settling international problems....

9) ...that local churches, too, study ways in which they may free, train and support lay people for service in the world, and implement changes in the deployment of the clergy, in local church education programs, and in the better use of church buildings and facilities.

10) ...that local churches encourage the formation of informal groups to experiment in radically new ways of social concern and action, to respond to injustice and suffering with new and imaginative action,...

11) ...that local churches make a ruthless examination of their structures and budgets, in order to assess how far these help the laymen in their ministry in the world....

12) ...that denominations examine carefully their budgetary policies, their educational curricula, their national programs and their staff allocations, to see whether these help or block the laymen in their ministry in the world.[24]

---

[24] "A Message from the North American Conference on the Ministry of the Laity in the World," (Chicago: January 1966), 1–2.
The denominations involved from the United States included: African Methodist Episcopal Church, African Methodist Episcopal Zion Church, American Baptist Convention, American Lutheran Church, Christian Church (Disciples), Christian Methodist Episcopal Church, Church of the Brethren, Evangelical United Brethren Church, Friends United Meeting, Greek Orthodox Archdiocese of North and South

Questions of authority like those apparent in the foregoing agenda arose within the church as the mission of the church, which had once been conceived as integral to and manageable by the whole, grew larger and was divided into component parts under the authority of an enlarged bureaucracy, often perceived to be removed from, or at least out of touch with, local experience. Campus ministry was but one of those ministerial subdivisions, all of them siblings within a growing—and amid denominational mergers, even a blended—family.

As ecclesial understandings of vocation became less integrated, more diverse, budget problems grew. Fiscal constraints are a recurring theme in denominational reports and budgets often profoundly influence how an institution acts out its vocation. At no time—not even the most prosperous years in the life of the denominations—were resources sufficient to accomplish all that was desired. The Presbyterians in 1964 admitted the ambition of their earlier determination to establish a denominational ministry on every American campus, scaled to the size of the school. American higher education expanded so rapidly and prolifically that by 1964 there was no hope of realizing such a goal.

The realization that came to the Presbyterian Church in 1964, that they could not fulfill their heady dream of comprehensive campus ministry, was an admission of limitation. There were limits to resources, and seemingly limitless claims upon them. And there were ministries in place, ministries dependent in large measure upon the financial support of denominations. The student constituency, unlike the local congregation, can never provide sufficient funding for autonomous support. A few campus ministries had been or eventually became independent congregations. Some small number of independent campus ministry foundations enjoyed modest endowment income as a supplement to annual expenses. But a larger number of free-standing campus ministries—Westminster Fellowships, Wesley Foundations, and Canterbury Clubs—

American, Hungarian Reformed Church, Lutheran Church in America, Methodist Church, National Baptist Convention USA Inc., Philadelphia Yearly Meeting of the Religious Society of Friends, Presbyterian Church USA, Protestant Episcopal Church USA, Reformed Church of America, Salvation Army, Seventh-Day Baptist General Conference, United Church of Christ, United Presbyterian Church USA. Those involved from Canada: Anglican Church of Canada, Church of Christ (Disciples), Lutheran Church in America, Canada Section, Presbyterian Church of Canada, Salvation Army, United Church of Canada. The National Agency Representatives included: National Council of Churches, National Council of Young Men's Christian Associations USA, National Board of Young Women's Christian Associations USA, Young Women's Christian Associations in Canada.

depended upon support from the national and local judicatories to maintain buildings and provide staff and programs.

Ecumenical Ventures

If existing ministries were to be maintained and any new initiatives undertaken, new sources of support were deemed necessary. In 1964 United Ministries in Higher Education (UMHE) was formed by the members of the United Campus Christian Fellowship—the United Presbyterians, Evangelical United Brethren, Disciples of Christ, and the United Church of Christ—as an ecumenical-cooperative effort among these churches to pool their resources for campus ministry.[25] The new organization won praise from the United Presbyterians for "increased effectiveness as well as improved stewardship of funds."[26] Through its membership in UMHE, by 1967 the Presbyterians claimed representation on 350 campuses, a considerable increase over the 155 sites reported in 1963.

In 1965, the four campus minister associations of the UCCF voted to disband to form, along with the American Baptists, a new five-denomination body christened the National Campus Ministers Association [NCMA]. Such collegial efforts had the positive benefit of enlarging the scope of ministry on campus and, if only temporarily, offered relief from financial strain. Campus ministers enjoyed a greater sense of "professionalization" that came of establishing their ministry as an area of specialization, and they benefitted from the collegial exchange of concerns with knowledgeable and sympathetic peers.

But there were negative effects, too. Growing denominational bureaucracies and the departmentalization of ministries separated campus ministry as a specialized guild and removed the work of the church on campus farther from the visible center of denominational concern. When campus ministry, denominational colleges, and Christian education were more or less co-equal components of a church's educational mission and visible elements in national and local denominational bud-

---

[25] McCormick, 56. It should also be noted that these denominations were or became members of the Consultation on Church Union. Motivations for joining included both ecumenical spirit and financial constraints. The amount of each is difficult to determine.

[26] *Minutes of the Presbyterian Church* (1966) part 1, 185. The General Assembly also urged synods to look for ways to expand this ministry. In fact, this is the period during which the Presbyterian Church, which had been giving substantial monies to Westminster Foundations, decided that funding for campus ministry belonged at the synod level.

gets, the educational ministry of the church was regularly deliberated and engaged as integral to the life and work of the church.

One unfortunate consequence of encouraging campus ministry as a specialized area with a professional organization of campus ministers and interdenominational structures is that campus ministers became further distanced from the center of denominational concern, and they rarely contributed to the larger conversation of the church. Indeed, the annual budget requests and reports filed by title became for many the sole communication with the denomination. Denominational leaders and assemblies, for their part, entrusted responsibility for educational ministries to the "specialists" with little or no interest in or mechanisms for accountability. The resulting breakdown in communications frequently meant that success in these ministries was rarely recognized, problems were allowed to fester, and denominational contact came largely at the point of crisis.

Interdenominational cooperation further complicated issues of accountability. The conscientious campus minister who served a multi-denominational ministry, and who desired to be accountable, could multiply the number of meetings, budgets, and reports by the number of sponsoring denominations involved in the cooperative ministry. Even if multiple staff representing the participating denominations were present on site, this ideal eroded in lean times.

As budgets grow tighter, program is the first sacrifice, then personnel, and lastly, property. In many places the only way to salvage ministries savaged by budget cuts is to reduce staff—and ordained staff, in particular, since theirs is the most costly personnel expense. The resulting streamlining is not always a bad thing. In some instances, it led previously distant or disconnected Christian denominations into cooperative conversation and collegial ministry. But expediency is not ecumenism.[27]

---

[27] The forced merger of ministries, while attractive on the ledger, often left much to be desired and may have had lasting effect in the confusions they presented to young adult seekers. One wonders how much of the restructuring of American religion Wuthnow describes was accelerated by generations of American students who left denominational congregations only to find an amalgamated ministry on campus in which denominational identity and tradition were sacrificed for the sake of economy. In addition to the many challenges to their faith students would meet on campus, what were they to make of the dissonance between parental encouragement to commit to a particular denomination in adolescence and campus ministries that eschewed denominational particularities?

For campus ministry, leaner times were on the horizon. Difficulties were not only financial in nature but—as indicated above—were generational and related to authority and to vocation.

Further Study of Campus Ministry

Samuel Gibson, in his study of Methodist ministries in higher education, characterized campus ministry as an entity in "late adolescence." In obvious reference to denominational politics, he observed that "occasional parental threats to cut its allowance (or even, at times, to disinherit it) only serve to increase rebellion and alienation."[28] But the source of the rebellion was more than generational difference. As is frequently the case in families, the source was grounded in cross purposes magnified by ineffectual communications.

"When there is no controlling and cohesive image of an operation—as often seems to be the case today concerning campus ministry," Gibson wrote, "then there is resulting confusion and lack of clarity about its nature, purpose, and methods."[29] The image of campus ministry as youth movement or fellowship, as an extracurricular activity that is part of a well-rounded program, as a home-away-from-home—campus ministry as student work—was not consonant with the Methodist *Discipline*, which defined campus ministry as educational ministry. His own surveys of Methodist campus ministries indicated a clear conflict between church leaders and campus leaders. The church leaders tended to want "production of loyal churchmen and recruitment for church-related vocations," results that reflect expected return on invested dollars. Campus leaders, on the other hand, sought reform of the church and involvement in social issues as priorities.[30] Clergy in general, and campus ministers in particular, lacked any organizing role to order their many functions. Campus ministers were confused over the nature, role, relationships, and strategy of campus ministry.

"The campus ministry has been increasingly defined as a missionary-educational-evangelistic-pastoral-lay training endeavor....It is no longer simply an educational endeavor and therefore ought not be identified simply as a Board of Education activity. It has the full scope of concerns of the local church. The campus ministry unit is a primary unit of the

---

[28] Samuel Norris Gibson, *The Campus Ministry and the Church's Mission in Higher Education* (Nashville: The Division of Higher Education, General Board of Education, The Methodist Church, 1967), iii.

[29] Ibid., 4.

[30] Ibid., 4–5, 27.

Church's mission and ministry, and not a supporting service unit."[31] Gibson concluded that lack of adequate ecclesiology was the most likely cause of confusion. What his study did identify was the disparity between denominational, congregational, and campus ministry goals. Less clear is the role, or responsibility, of campus ministry's contribution to such an ecclesiology. The question of authority is implied: who has the authority to shape that ecclesiology?

The questions raised and implied by Gibson's study were common to the time. They were less frequently articulated than they were demonstrated. Behind the *in loco parentis* controversies on campus were these questions of where authority was lodged, and whose authority would prevail.

Funding and Dissent

The church, like the government, saw growing disparities among its constituencies. In 1964 the UPCUSA elected a black moderator and noted in its reports a growing gap between pulpit and pew. By 1965 the church's involvement in social action at home and abroad disquieted some, signalling tensions between the grassroots and the bureaucracy of the denomination.[32] Financing the church's work was never easy; it was made the more difficult by these tensions.

But these tensions, and later student protests, were not the cause of declining monies for campus ministry at the national level. For example, in 1966 the Presbyterians' Standing Committee on Christian Education reported that the Board had been supplementing general benevolence funds with profits from its publishing arm to finance colleges and campus ministries. Decreasing profits from publishing mandated a change. Funds to church-related colleges were cut $208,000; campus ministry was decreased $260,000; and the Board's general program diminished by $204,000.[33] The Board of Christian Education, consequently, granted $258,000 from its general funds to campus ministry.

The dissatisfaction of the college-age generation with the church was felt and acknowledged in the late 1960s. The Episcopal Church in its General Convention of 1967 adopted a position paper on youth that likened the over-30 generation to immigrants from the old country and the under-30 generation as those for whom the new country is home. The report advocated that the church listen to and include the voices of its

---

[31] Ibid., 208.
[32] *Minutes of the Presbyterian Church* (1966) part 1, 184.
[33] Ibid.

youthful members in decision-making. Recognizing the inter-generational quality of education, the report held that the youthful generation had much to teach the church of how to live in the new era. And the report urged a mission to the youthful generation, a mission to find the words to communicate the Word to this younger generation on their own terms.[34]

In fact, national funds for ministries to higher education were radically dis-appointed by the same convention. In preparation for the General Convention the program and budget agencies of the denomination, as was their custom, drafted extensive reports, including a full budget for the 1967–69 triennium. Just prior to the actual convention, the Executive Council of the denomination met. It was determined in their meeting that the ready budget did not allow sufficient resources to meet the demands of a deteriorating society. Presiding Bishop John Hines proposed an innovative initiative called the General Convention Special Program (GCSP). This program called for financial grants to be made to various groups within and without the church. The allocation of these grants was reserved to an executive committee chaired by an Episcopal layman, Leon Modeste, himself a product of Brooklyn's slums, and a principal architect of the program. The funds themselves were to be derived from the budgeted revenues of the denomination. Because GCSP was not to be funded by a particular fund-drive or campaign, any and all grants it made were to be taken from funds normally used to support the programs and operations of the denomination. The Executive Council at their pre-convention meeting rejected the proposed budget and drafted an entirely new budget that created the GCSP funds.[35] Convention deputies who had come prepared to debate the budget prepared and circulated for advance study found a new document in its place. The amended budget eliminated line items from the budget, substituting larger categorical designations. Monies were allocated to the larger categories, then parcelled by denominational executives in the national office. The last-minute change and the confusion of a completely altered format for budget reports discouraged adequate scrutiny or detailed debate. Given the climate of the times and the stated priorities of the GCSP to address the civil rights agenda the choice was not between one

---

[34] *Journal of the General Convention*, position paper, (1967) v–vi. Despite the report's adoption, subsequent action on a resolution to include youth in decision-making structures of the denomination died in committee.

[35] Robert Prichard, *A History of the Episcopal Church* (Harrisburg, PA: Morehouse Publishing, 1991), 262.

budget or another, but a choice that was, for many, unarguable: it was a choice for or against racism.

It was this amended budget that was presented for vote and passed at the General Convention in 1967. With its passage, the major funding priorities of the denomination changed. The GCSP devoted its largest portion of funding to projects arising from the civil rights agenda, thus the programs of the denomination previously funded by General Convention—of which campus ministry was one—were made to give up a significant portion of their program budget for the sake of GCSP projects. College and university students demonstrated their affection and respect for Presiding Bishop Hines, carrying placards reading, "We love Big John,"[36] and similar sentiments in support of the man who was most prominently identified with the GCSP and its agenda. The students and their chaplains had little idea at the time that this convention and this program would radically alter the shape of Episcopal ministry on campus at the national level.

The drama for the Methodists in 1968 was not budget reallocations but uniting with the Evangelical United Brethren to become The United Methodist Church. Bishops at the General Conference did acknowledge the dissent of their youth, but their address rejected youth's criticism that the church is an impotent, moribund institution led by clergy of the same ilk. The bishops maintained that they shared youth's concern for the welfare of the church. Addressing higher education, the bishops held that the church needed to express more than verbal appreciation for the work of the academy, that it needed to offer "more of that economic oxygen known as financial resources to assure the vital and lively continuance of these institutions." But beyond this point, the address considered only the denomination's seminaries.[37]

The General Conference did, however, reaffirm the church's support for higher education. A decade earlier the church had urged a commitment of 66¢ per member for denominational colleges and 19¢ per member support for Wesley Foundations. The conference of 1968 raised those goals to $1.50 per member for denominational college support, and 50¢ per member for the support of "campus ministry."[38]

---

[36] William F. Maxwell, "The Episcopal 62nd: A Great Convention" *Christian Century* 84 (8 November 1967): 1441–42.

[37] *Journal of the United Methodist Church*, eds. Emerson D. Bragg, J. Welsey Hole, and Charles D. White (1968), part 1, 233–35.

[38] Ibid., part 2, 1340. The new designation, "campus ministry," as distinct from Wesley Foundations, was a product of the merger with the Evangelical United

The new United Methodist Church affirmed its "commitment to an ecumenical approach to campus ministry."[39] This referred primarily to participation in ecumenical student organizations, but also to the actual ministries. This ecumenical affirmation seemed a marked change from the unabashedly denominational stance of the 1950s, but—given United Methodists' subsequent history with UMHE—one wonders how widely this nuanced vision was embraced by the newly-united church.[40] Under the quadrennial theme, "A New Church in a New World," the "new church" ratified the old order as higher education funding goals of the previous quadrennium were continued for the next.[41]

The story of what happened to funding for campus ministry at the national level in the churches under study here has little to do with the common mythology that funding was cut off with an angry parental vehemence. Neither can the picture be painted with a broad brush. The Presbyterian policy had been to give substantial funding for local ministries from the national level. General Assembly funds had long been supplemented by publishing profits from the Board of Christian Education's reserves. Those reserves diminished about the same time that the civil rights agenda caused all the churches to review the ministries they funded and how they funded them. In addition, the expansive years of the 1950s had given way to the leveling-off of national economic inflation and a desire for local governance in the middle 1960s. Episcopal funding for campus ministry at the national level disappeared literally overnight as the GCSP was conceived. Although most local ministries were not directly affected, the connections between ministries—embodied in provincial staff—were severed. Methodist campus ministry, although unable to keep pace with inflation, was not adversely affected in this period by General Conference decisions. Primary funding for local ministries had been shifted almost a decade earlier from the national to the annual conference level.

In no case was funding cut primarily because of student unrest or parental anger. In each case where funding declined, however, level or declining national revenues coupled with much needed attention to the

---

Brethren. The Brethren were members of United Ministries in Higher Education (UMHE); the new United Methodist Church became a member of that organization.

[39] Ibid., 1345.

[40] Ibid., 1346. The United Methodist Church withdrew from UMHE in 1979 when UMHE became United Ministries in Education. As of 1972, less than half of the annual conferences had formal ties with state or regional UMHE commissions.

[41] Ibid., 1820–21.

civil rights movement reduced the monies available on the national level for campus ministry. In addition, campus ministers, often alienated from their denominations, were in no position to advocate either retaining national funding or turning to local judicatories for help. The evidence suggests that the confusion of the time and the reactionary nature of the churches' programming and good intentions in regards to civil rights issues conspired to further distance campus (and other educational) ministry from the center of the churches' concern and significantly diminish support for it.

THE LATE 1960S:
STORM CLOUDS DARKEN

To set campus ministry within the larger context of the culture and to consider the several forces at work within both the church and the academy is to see how the relationship of campus ministry to these institutions was affected by significant changes. The pivotal years, 1967 and 1968, were remarkable for attitudinal shifts that mark a turning point. The political shift from the Democratic presidencies of John Kennedy and Lyndon Johnson to the Republican administration of Richard Nixon marked an ideological divide of enormous proportion. Under Johnson the war in Southeast Asia escalated dramatically, and with it, the need for military personnel. Attempting to establish equality in the Selective Service System, a lottery was instituted and draftees were inducted according to birthdate in a random sequence established by the drawing of 366 dates out of a hopper. The lottery itself was televised. College and university men and their families watched nervously as each date was drawn and, by the end of the program, knew the order and probable likelihood of induction.

As the war reached more deeply into the complexities of Southeast Asia, and more deeply into the homes of American privilege and stability, sentiment toward the war and the government waging it grew antagonistic. The war and the draft did more than any other factor to alter student attitudes and to mobilize student opinion. In 1967, 35% of students surveyed identified themselves as doves; by 1969 that number had almost doubled to 69%.[42] Yet the campus was not united in opposition.

At a signal point of unrest over the war—the bombing of Cambodia—students on nearly half of America's campuses mounted

---

[42] Horowitz, *Campus Life*, 232–33.

some kind of demonstration or protest. A "strike," or refusal to attend classes, was mounted by some students, but only on 350 campuses. The majority of students on the majority of campuses continued to meet their classes and continued to work diligently at their academic pursuits, and their social ones. Even at the peak of anti-war protests in 1969 surveys revealed that "only 28 percent of the college population had taken part in a demonstration of any kind during their four years. Media coverage greatly exaggerated both the degree of radicalism and the extent of engagement."[43]

Still, the Vietnam War did profoundly affect student attitudes. As noted earlier, student attitudes toward authority grew out of questions raised by the civil rights movement even as slavery had created a similar crisis of legitimation one hundred years earlier. It was difficult, if not impossible, to square the precepts of Christianity and American constitutional government with the disenfranchisement of a whole race of people. Such questions eroded deeply embedded trust of church and government and gave way to questions about other established authorities. The prevalent administration of colleges and universities as institutions functioning *in loco parentis* gave rise to student dissatisfaction over what they perceived to be the retardation or abrogation of their status as young adults. The disputes over restrictive, paternalistic administrative policies governing campus life functioned as transition to protest over the war in Vietnam. On the one hand, parents, church and state university trustees, university administrators, and church leadership were telling students they were not sufficiently mature to order their own lives; on the other hand the same authorities determined that students were sufficiently mature to die in a war they did not understand and with which many of them did not agree. "The Vietnam War changed the meaning of authority to many college youth."[44]

The war had no less profound an effect within the church. The churches, like the campuses, were divided in opinion on the war even as they had been, and in many cases remained, divided on the issue of civil rights. The Episcopal Church debated facets of the war in its 1967 General Convention. The House of Bishops drafted a resolution, subsequently approved by the House of Deputies with slight modifications, stating that non-combatant and alternative civilian service are legitimate ways for conscientious objectors to serve their country. They urged that

---

43 Ibid., 223.
44 Ibid., 233.

Congress broaden its conscientious objection category to include those who have non-religiously based moral objections to the war. But realizing that conscientious objection and higher education provided safe haven for a growing class of privileged American youth, they further recommended that Congress examine the selective service process to eliminate racial and economic discrimination, even recommending that the exemption for seminarians be dropped.[45] The Convention considered several resolutions regarding the war itself, eventually adopting one of moderate tone acknowledging that good people may hold divergent positions and affirming support for troops and support personnel. The Convention rejected, though, a clause that would have called upon the United States to raise taxes, if necessary, to put funds equal to war funds into reconstruction of Vietnam.[46] Despite all attempts at moderation, however, the strain was enervating. Tension made it difficult even to pose questions.

On November 12, 1967, President Lyndon Johnson attended morning worship at Bruton Parish Church in Williamsburg, Virginia—a large, even diverse, Episcopal congregation, but one reflective of upper middle-class moderation. The Rector, Cotesworth Pinckney Lewis, preaching on Isaiah 9:2, posed a rhetorical question that under the circumstances was construed to be directed toward the visiting President. Lewis dared to ask *why* the United States was involved in the war. The response of media and public figures reflected the range of opinion at large from enthusiastic gratitude to hateful vilification. As historian John Booty noted of the incident, "When Johnson decided not to seek re-election and reporters asked him why, he responded that his thinking began to change in November of 1967."[47]

The transition from the Democratic administrations of Kennedy and Johnson to the Republican administration of Richard Nixon also marked a change in governmental and public attitudes toward higher education. The post-World War II administrations of Truman and Eisenhower contributed much to establishing education, and higher education in particular, as a national priority and resource and to the rebuilding of America's education infrastructure. The Kennedy and Johnson administrations greatly assisted higher education in the development of a federal plan to carry on university programs "clearly related to the national

---

[45] *Journal of the General Convention* (1967), 375.

[46] Ibid., 510–17.

[47] John Booty, *The Episcopal Church in Crisis*, foreword by Martin E. Marty (Cambridge, MA: Cowley Publications, 1988), 75–77.

interest."[48] These programs included not only government-backed research, especially for the military, but also increased entitlements that opened higher education to a larger proportion of the American citizenry. While it would be unjust to attribute to Nixon's administration changes precipitated by their predecessors, the evidence indicates that federal support for education declined after 1968, and some support was eliminated altogether.[49]

It is possible, in the case of government as in the case of the church, to overestimate or misattribute antagonism as the source of a changed attitude toward and support of higher education. It is fair, however, to suggest that education—and higher education in particular—was accorded a different, lower priority on the agendas of both the church and the government after 1968. The unrest of the period, created of divergent opinion from a variety of coalescing groups grown more confident and vocal through organization, indicates that the agendas of all institutions were crowded. Confidence in authority was at an all-time low, the country severely demoralized by a wave of tragedies.

In the spring of 1968 The Reverend Martin Luther King, Jr., was murdered by sniper fire in Memphis, Tennessee. His assassination unleashed a wave of urban violence that left large portions of the nation's major cities in smouldering rubble and emotional shock. Later, in June 1968, while campaigning for the presidency, Robert Kennedy was assassinated in the back passageway of a hotel just after completing a speech to enthusiastic supporters. The double loss of these two prominent and heroic figures devastated an already fragile nation. Just how volatile the climate, and how short the fuse, was evidenced in the shocking violence of the Democratic National Convention in Chicago in 1968. Student anger and activism escalated into a full-scale military encounter as the Chicago Police in reinforced riot gear engaged and enraged an already seething anger. Many of the protesters were young adults, a good many of them students. How many, and from what kinds of institutions or cultural settings, is unknown. But the image of all youthful protestors as students was a strong one and, after the confrontation in Chicago, a wave of violent protest followed as students vented the shock and outrage of what they considered brutality against peers and contemporaries.

---

[48] Henry, 8.
[49] Ibid., 133.

—⚜ **4** ⚜—

A Profound Dis-Appointment:
1968–1973

INTRODUCTION

By the autumn of 1968 the nation and its campuses were testy and in turmoil. The decade of the 1960s, as sketched in previous chapters, progressed from high optimism to low dudgeon. The rapid and unparalleled growth both within the society and on the campus, by the early 1960s, moved on an ascending curve. But by mid-decade, the seemingly endless benefits of expansion and the exhilaration of growth reached a plateau. With summer's end in 1968, several assassinations and the unexpected violence of poverty and politics left the nation, its institutions and its citizens in confusion and disarray.

The years 1968 through the early 1970s were days of disappointment for many segments of American society. Generations were disappointed with each other: for the ideals held, for the behaviors evidenced, or for a perceived failure of integrity. Furthermore, students who had grown accustomed to thinking of unbounded futures, faced a stagnant economy and rising inflation. Some expressed disappointment with their church, either for acting too publicly while neglecting basic care-giving, or for being too tied to the status quo. Lyndon Johnson's unprecedented expansion of domestic policy and programs did little to quell rising tensions between diverse constituencies and gave rise to apathy or outright cynicism toward participatory democracy. Virtually the whole nation was sickened and disappointed by some aspect of the Vietnam War.

SOCIETY:
OUTER PROTEST AND INNER SEARCH

With Richard Nixon's inauguration in January 1969 a perceptible change came over the land that had important ramifications for dissenting groups. The violence of the closing years of the Johnson administration was scattered over several social issues and the vast territory of America. As the decade moved toward its close, and Nixon shaped Presidential authority to his own style, unrest and violence seemed to achieve a focus. Escalation of the war in Vietnam, and Nixon's "the buck stops here" attitude, tended to galvanize protest around the issue of the war and the office of the Presidency.

In the 1969-70 academic year campus protest peaked. Horowitz records the statistics: 9,408 outbreaks, 731 leading to police intervention and arrests, 410 damaging property, 230 involving physical violence—indicating that over 90 percent of all incidents ended without force. Confined neither to campus nor to *bona fide* students, these protests took place in banks, corporate offices, government buildings, and induction centers. Many of the activists were not students, but only identified as such. Despite the statistics, even this level of student radicalism and political activism was not as great as was student unrest in the 1930s. But the media's—and the public's—indiscriminate perceptions of the campus unrest were greatly inflated.[1]

College and university campuses were not only the sites of broadly based social unrest; they were often actively engaged in internal turmoil. Tension arose between teachers and administrators who disagreed over principles and practicalities. When ideals met realities, trouble ensued. For example, those who supported the cause of civil rights advocated increased enrollments of African-American students. When those students were encouraged to take initiative and exercise their basic freedoms, they assembled to share their experience as African-Americans and they spoke out against the repression of their own history and culture. The result was disagreement between teachers, and between

---

[1] Horowitz, *Campus Life*, 234.

teachers and administrators, over the role of African-American studies in the established academic canon. The tension would be played out again and again as women, gays and lesbians, and Native American students discovered and demanded the recovery of their history, literature and cultural heritage.

The religious landscape also diversified, revealing further dissatisfaction with conventional religion. In Easter week of 1966 the cover of *Time* magazine posed the question, "Is God Dead?"[2] With that simple device, the media managed to distill and distort years of theological inquiry into the difficulty of speaking about God in the modern culture. But by the end of the decade, exploration into the supernatural abounded. New religions flourished. Transcendental Meditation, Zen Buddhism, Yoga groups, Hare Krishna Society, and the Unification Church shared places in the culture alongside the *est* movements, Rolfing, Bioenergetics, and Silva Mind Control.

CAMPUS:
THE BUBBLE BURSTS

Donald Shockley describes the children of the baby boom as a group "socialized in such fashion as to create a generation characterized by extraordinarily high expectations."[3] But the baby boom cohort was not alone in holding high expectations; indeed, they came to those expectations by nurture.

As Horowitz notes, undergraduates of the baby boom cohort were "the first college generation born largely of college-educated parents."[4] Those parents, many of whom had attended college as veterans and thus eschewed campus life for a more utilitarian view of higher education, held high, even rigorous, expectations of their children and of their children's campus experience. "They had entered college to gain professional and vocational skills. Now they insisted that their children follow their lead. They had been in a hurry. Now they hurried their children. Gone was the once-honored moratorium after college that gave youths

---

[2] Flowers, 20.

[3] Donald G. Shockley, *Campus Ministry: The Church Beyond Itself* (Louisville: Westminster/John Knox, 1989), 91.

[4] Horowitz, *Campus Life*, 246.

two years or so to experiment, do good, or find themselves before embarking on a career."[5]

Tensions were palpable among the student population. Pressure upon males to succeed was spurred by the rising certainty that military service in an unpopular war that seemed only to grow larger awaited those who could not maintain the requisite grades to stay in school. In 1961 America suffered 14 casualties in Vietnam, in 1963 the number had risen to 489. In 1966 over half a million American troops were engaged and the death toll that year alone reached 4000.[6] Parental expectations were, then, not wholly pecuniary; as the war ground relentlessly on more and more parents questioned whether this war was worth the life of a son or daughter.

The palliatives to so much anxiety increased as students sought respite from relentless and inescapable realities. Marijuana and new drugs joined the popular consumption of alcohol. Some students resorted to suicide.

As the winter of 1969 gave way to the spring of 1970, campuses across the nation were arrayed against the war in Vietnam. In May 1970 students on some sixty campuses mounted a strike to protest the invasion of Cambodia by United States troops. About two hundred students at Kent State University gathered on May 4 in demonstration against the invasion. A modest 28-person unit of the National Guard stood at the ready about one hundred years away. For no apparent reason shots were fired by the guardsmen into the crowd of unarmed students; four students were killed. Ten days later at Jackson State College a contingent of state and local police fired into an unarmed crowd of demonstrating students and killed two. A number of schools closed early that Spring, their students sent home. The shootings sickened the nation, and administrators determined to pull the plug on protest by design. Campus landscapes and buildings were re-configured to discourage congregation; subsequently buildings were built and campuses laid out to minimize such opportunities as gave rise to these tragedies. By the end of the 1969-1970 academic year whatever had been of the so-called student movement was, for all practical purposes, disbanded.

---

[5] Ibid.

[6] David E. Sumner, *The Episcopal Church's History 1945–1985* (Wilton, CT: Morehouse Publishing, 1987), 61.

CAMPUS MINISTRY

Student Movements

By 1968 a "student movement"—like the civil rights movement before it, the women's movement that was a close contemporary, and the gay liberation movement that would be launched with the 1969 raid of the Stonewall Bar in Greenwich Village—was a fixture of American culture. Like the other "movements," the student movement was hardly unified but rather consisted of students diverse in opinion and allegiance. Under the vast umbrella of the student movement huddled a variety of student organizations espousing different agendas. The movement included anti-war, civil-rights, anti-authoritarian, sexual-liberation, and even religious-reform components.

Among the varied student organizations of the time were a number of campus religious groups, students organized by denominational identity into groups bearing names like Canterbury Club, Westminster Fellowship, and Wesley Foundation. Local groups were often linked to regional and national organizations and enjoyed regular gatherings. As student organizations grew increasingly aware of the political dimensions of their life together and their responsibilities to a larger society they took greater initiative for their own governance. They had been taught democratic process and, given the opportunity to exercise it, students used their organizations not only for their own sustenance and fellowship, but as vehicles of communication and instruments of power. They drafted resolutions, directed statements, deliberated issues. As the decade of the 1960s advanced, many student religious organizations conceived of themselves as part of the larger student movement.

In September 1966 the students of several religious bodies voted to form the University Christian Movement (UCM). Perhaps the most significant aspect of this new organization was that it was more ecumenical than any predecessor. It included the National Newman Student Federation (Catholic), the National Federation of Catholic College Students, the Young Friends of America (Quaker), Campus Commission of the Standing Conference of Orthodox Bishops in America, the National Student Council of the YMCA, the Baptist Student Movement, the Lutheran Student Association of America, the Methodist Student Movement, the National Canterbury Committee (Episcopal), the Westminster Fellowship of the Presbyterian Church, and the United

Campus Christian Federation.[7] Unlike the much earlier Student Volunteer Movement whose evangelical roots and fervor represented a missionary extension of Christianity through students deeply grounded in and committed to their faith traditions, the new UCM more frequently expressed itself in the denial of denominational traditions—loyalties that were deemed expendable hindrances to cooperative action. Like other such movements in American society of the time, the UCM prized autonomy as a student-administered organization beyond the bounds of denominational control.[8]

Encompassing so much diversity, the student movement must be viewed as an umbrella term, something of a convenient fiction. Behind the so-called student movement was a highly-diverse population whose primary common connection was enrollment in an institution of higher education. Not infrequently, even student status was not required for identification with the movement. Any activity or uprising of young adults from roughly 18 to 22 years of age could be, and often was, credited to "the student movement." It was not, then, student status so much as dissent itself that shaped the public consciousness of this group.[9]

The University Christian Movement, like the larger student "movement" of which it was a part, afforded students a place of involvement, a community of support, and a forum for dissent. No doubt it encouraged and nurtured students with gifts of leadership. But the strength of the student movements was also their greatest weakness: student life is transient and as such, frustrates the stability necessary to sustain an effort. The life of student structures is very fragile. The University Christian Movement convened in Cleveland, Ohio, over the Christmas holiday in 1967 for "Process '67," an "experiment…to formulate and test a model of what university education should be."[10] But the design of the conference was upstaged by student interest groups that transformed themselves into caucuses: "the Black Caucus, the Women's Caucus, the Radical Caucus, and the International Caucus."[11] The Black Caucus was especially powerful given the prominence of civil rights in the national agenda. The Black Caucus challenged the UCM in the spring of 1969 by requesting $50,000 to support an economic development

---

7 *Quadrennial Reports.* (1968), 170.

8 Shockley, *Campus Ministry*, 96–98.

9 Robert Rankin, ed., *The Recovery of Spirit in Higher Education* (New York: Seabury Press, 1980), 13.

10 *By Faith*, 37.

11 Ibid.

program. The General Committee of UCM buckled beneath the weight, "afraid that its hang-ups about white racism were forcing it to make a necessary discussion for the wrong reason."[12]

In the winter of 1969 the General Committee of the UCM dissolved the organization. Robert Rankin's assessment seems the most cogent one. Rankin, who was an officer of the Danforth Foundation, which funded "Process '67," suggested that the membership of UCM was held together by its common "political dissidence, anger against inequities in racial relations, the threat of militarism, and oppression at home and abroad. Its glue was moral conscience, but a morality with few roots into spiritual disciplines and into continuing communities of faith."[13] He contends that UCM died because it pulled away from the communities and constituencies that had supported it and its predecessor organizations. The decision to disaffiliate was harmful not only in financial and political terms, but harmful because it severed the organization and its members from the spiritual resources that had sustained its predecessors through other trying times.[14]

The paradox of forming a mega-movement of student campus ministry groups in the midst of general distrust of all large institutions may account for part of the dismantling. The burden of administrating such a large undertaking could only have frustrated the students' ability to act and respond in a rapidly-changing social environment.[15] Perhaps the formation of the University Christian Movement had made the only point it could make: that students could dissociate themselves from the traditional structures of mainline American religion and re-configure themselves in a broadly based ecumenical setting of self-determination.

The University Christian Movement's organizing principle "to work for social change through the reformation of the university"[16] seemed consistent with a denominational shift in perspective, which moved the center of campus ministry's attention away from the denominational tradition and posited the university itself as the new center. What this change proposed was, in effect, a loosening of denominational control. It also served to remove campus ministry farther from the central concerns of the churches, which had been concerns of Christian education, liturgical and pastoral ministry to denominational students and potential

---

[12] Ibid., 86.

[13] Rankin, *The Recovery of Spirit*, 13.

[14] Ibid., 14.

[15] Shockley, *Campus Ministry*, 96–98.

[16] *Minutes of the Presbyterian Church* (1968) part 2, 60.

inquirers, and the recruitment of candidates for ordained service—all concerns that served the supporting institution.

The Churches and the Students: Failed Attempts to Communicate

The Standing Committee Report of the Board of Christian Education of the United Presbyterian Church in 1969 included a special statement entitled "The Church and Campus Unrest" which described the time as one of "ferment" on campuses marked by "idealism and frustration, conflict and creativity, destruction, and the building of a new order."[17] A quadrennial report of the United Methodist Church in 1968 summarizing the period 1964-1968 documented the strife:

> As the news came from many a troubled campus last year, bewildered parents and citizens, more or less touched by it all, often asked whether students were positively possessed. Students evidenced keen intelligence, idealism, self-sacrifice, intensity, courage, arrogance, boorishness, ingratitude, disrespect, and sometimes, it seemed, ruthless rebellion. Higher education was dominated by a central fact: the astonishing emergence of the student as a force for change in school and society."[18]

There is some evidence that the denominational officials were wary of student drift to the political Left. One United Methodist source defended the association of some Methodist Student Movements with the New Left as "consistent with biblical understandings of the church that is ready to spend itself,"[19] a defense that suggests that an opposing view required this rejoinder. Where earlier generations had spoken of the church/academy relationship as somewhat antagonistic and the church's presence a necessity in the midst of the academy's secularism, this same Methodist report casts the church and academy in the role of partners with a common end: "to make common cause with the university in helping tomorrow's leaders learn to distinguish between fads and permanent things,...to broaden the view of the landscape, which includes the immediate and practical aspects of life but a vista also upon man's eternal destiny."[20]

---

[17] *Minutes of the Presbyterian Church* (1969) part 1, 457.
[18] *Quadrennial Reports.* (The Commission on Entertainment, Methodist Publishing House, 1968), 167.
[19] Ibid., 171.
[20] Ibid., 172.

The Campus Minister: Role Confusions and the Danforth Study

Students were not the only members of the campus ministry community to assume a new role as the decade of the 1960s moved toward its end. Campus ministers comprised what was becoming a growing niche of specialization in ministry. Phillip Hammond, described as a "sociologist of occupations,"[21] studied campus ministry as an emerging profession. Hammond posited that as an organization adapts to its environment and maintains its identity, it typically deals with its radical elements by segregating them, while drawing upon their ideas for renewal. His thesis was that "for Protestant churches the campus ministry serves as an organizational device for segmenting radicals....[I]t siphons off potentially disruptive personnel, thus serving the safety-valve function; and especially it contributes to organizational change, thus serving the leavening function."[22]

For his research, Hammond mailed surveys to all Protestant campus ministers, receiving a 79 percent response, which he compared to over 4,000 parish clergy. The comparison revealed marked deviation. Campus ministers were more interested in international affairs and less interested in the denomination. Campus ministers more strongly agreed with the need for more social action than did their parish counterparts.[23]

The Hammond study further maintained that campus ministry functioned to retain leaders in the ordained ministry of the church who might otherwise drop out, but also sustained radicalism within the church that, if campus ministers returned to the parish, could further radicalize the church. It was also suggested that radicalism returned to the church via the students who were influenced by campus ministers.[24] Any fear that such radicalism posed a viable threat to the church was offset by the finding that, by a 2 to 1 margin, campus ministers, if they left campus ministry, would prefer teaching to the parish[25] and by the tendency among students to disaffiliate with the traditional parochial structures.

The work and role of the campus minister, like many other roles in modern American society, became a specialized ministry. When students rebelled against institutionalized paternalism and sought to engage the

---

[21] Danforth, vol. 2 , 3.

[22] Ibid., 4–5.

[23] Ibid., 6. Hammond's survey and conclusions are open to critique. It is difficult to determine, for example, how generational and/or experiential differences might account for deviation between the two groups compared.

[24] Ibid., 9–11.

[25] Ibid., 8.

issues of their time, they turned away from the more traditional ministries of worship and study and asked the church to support them in a new, and for that time, unaccustomed ministry of active political and social reform. The challenge to change that many campus ministries posed to the church positioned those ministries as special and outside the central focus of the institutional church as custodian of tradition and witness in Word and sacrament. Such specialized ministries were accorded less emphasis as essential components of the churches' mission and were treated more as add-ons, even to the extent of being called "experimental."

In a similar vein, the United Presbyterian Board of Christian Education in 1968 described a changed role for the campus minister. According to A. Myrvin DeLapp, Associate General Secretary of the General Division of Higher Education, the former role of campus minister as pastor-counselor gave way to one of mediation. The campus minister, through the engagement of contemporary issues, was on campus to mediate between university and society. It was even proposed that the campus minister be conceived as "minister in higher education," or director of an institute that functions as an action-resource center on campus.[26]

One such proposal in the Episcopal Church indicated that "The Church Society for College Work[27]...after two decades and more of investment in student work, campus pastor work, and experimental campus based ministries, [determined] that its resources and time might be best used...as an institute for studies. It has begun to see its associations less with colleges and universities as such and more with organizations such as the American Academy of Arts and Sciences, the Center for the Study of Democratic Institutions, and the American Assembly."[28]

Kenneth Underwood, director of the Danforth study, in his own report of the findings revealed something of the confusion of the time and the dilemma it posed for the campus minister. The stated goal of the Danforth study was directed toward social policy, defined as "the ordering and reordering of the resources and personnel of whole institutions and movements in the context of the needs and aspirations of nations,

---

[26] *Minutes of the Presbyterian Church* (1968) part 2, 57.

[27] The Church Society for College Work existed alongside the official denominational structure and saw itself as the research and development arm of the church's campus ministry program.

[28] Frank Alsid de Chambeau, "An Exploratory Ministry in Higher Education: Analysis and Recommendations," Unpublished paper, 30.

peoples, and societies."[29] Campus ministry, according to Underwood, was a window through which to view the upheavals of American society that preoccupied the period under study. "Profound and serious divisions in the body politic of the Church are clearly revealed in controversies now taking place over the status and function of the experimental and specialized ministries."[30]

Underwood's vision positioned campus ministries strategically between the two institutions that ministry serves: the church and the university. But he saw the role of campus ministries as stimulus and guide to the church. It was his vision that campus ministries would utilize the resources of the university to renew and reorder the church.[31]

Underwood can be criticized, as he has been by successors, for adopting too sanguine a view of the university. Furthermore, his vision of campus ministry and the institutions it serves is skewed by the assumption that the university has more to offer the church than the church has to offer the university. In this regard, Underwood betrays a bias that certainly was not shared by the leadership of the church—lay or ordained—in its conception of why it was on campus and what its role on campus was to be.

"The purpose of education in the church and university, or better, the best test of its quality, is that it enhances the capacity of laymen to achieve just social policies," wrote Underwood.[32] For his part, the role of the church is "to contribute by its social policies to the building of a just, peaceable, and beautiful commonwealth."[33] What is missing from Underwood's vision is the role of campus ministry as bearer of tradition, nurturer of faith. These roles, derived from the missionary impetus that conceived of campus ministries as the bearer of denominational worship and care to the secular arena of the university, are subsumed—or overwhelmed—by the vision of campus ministry as architect of social policy.

Arguably, Underwood addressed the need to reconcile the church with the culture of which it was a part. His report emphasized the need to recover *vocation* as a foundational principle for life's work. He was critical of the tendency to emphasize technique over vocation and of the tendency of professional schools to such narrow specialization as to

---

[29] Danforth, vol. 1, xx.
[30] Ibid., 3, 9.
[31] Ibid., 17.
[32] Ibid., 92.
[33] Ibid., 94.

make comprehensive social policy impracticable.[34] In that regard he recovered a valuable component of campus ministry's mission.

But in his zeal for a utopian vision of the university as a model for society, where students in the professions interact across disciplines, Underwood threw the balance. That is not to say that his vision is folly; indeed, it is a noble vision. But the emphasis Underwood placed upon the university and upon social policy was not consistently balanced with emphasis upon the institutional church. In that regard Underwood evidenced the bias that campus ministry had a greater allegiance to the university than to the church. His bias is reflected by the campus ministers themselves who, as cited earlier, indicated that if they were to leave campus ministry they would prefer teaching to a career in parish ministry.

When Underwood turned his attention to the clergy's experience of role conflict, he identified as a source of that conflict the inability of the church to integrate its own approaches to life. The segmenting of religious life into compartments of prayer and social action, for example, made for a fragmented spirituality. What is less evident is any sympathy for dysfunction created by competing visions of campus ministry. Underwood's vision of campus ministry was shared by many practitioners of campus ministry and gained support among the ideologues whose denominational reports envisioned campus ministries as research institutes and campus ministers as brokers of social policy, as was the case in a heretofore cited report of the United Presbyterian Board of Christian Education. And Underwood's vision was evidently shared by those Episcopal visionaries and others who advocated a more experimental approach to church work on campus. But the wilderness between such visions and the hard realities was the landscape upon which campus ministry lived. Denominations struggling with social chaos, declining membership, and scarce resources wondered often, and painfully, if such visionaries had lost sight of reality.

At the heart of it, the primary measurement of campus ministry so far as the institutional church has been concerned is self-serving: how many students attend? How many converts to the denomination? How many vocations to ordination? Because the questions persist to the present day, one can presume they were of equal or surpassing concern then, as well. By the end of 1970, in the aftermath of Kent State and Jackson State, with war raging in Vietnam, the answers to these

---

[34] Ibid., 418.

questions were disheartening. Caught between the rock of that institutional demand and the hard place of impracticable, impossible visions was a marginalized campus ministry and those who served it.

Some, like Myron Bloy and Paul Schrading, brought energy and creativity to this demanding time. Both urged campus ministers to use their marginality as a gift, reminding that it is easier to change and to desire change when one is not at the core. Schrading saw campus ministry as a place where new community could be created, where old patterns could be abandoned and new territory charted.[35] But even Bloy acknowledged that to live under such circumstances, the campus minister must be a relatively mature adult sufficiently secure to help students work through their own convictions.[36] That was much to ask, especially in a culture where so much was in flux and among a people who had much reason to doubt. The experience of marginality in this time was a tension that proved, for many, untenable.

Denominational Turmoil

As noted in previous chapters, funding for campus ministry has never been adequate to the vision held by campus ministry national staff. By the late 1960s and early 1970s that inadequacy was strained further. In some cases, funding dissipated. What happened has remained confused, but some possible clarity may be gained by looking beyond campus ministry in particular to examine what was happening in the larger church. Because campus ministry is but one portion of a many-faceted ministry, it may be helpful to consider its relationship not only to the whole but to an ever-expanding constellation of partners in ministry.

In 1967 the Episcopal Church had created the General Convention Special Program as a means for assisting African-Americans, Native Americans, Hispanics, and poor whites.[37] It was widely and hotly criticized, especially at the local level. In 1969 the GCSP granted $30,000 to the Malcolm X Liberation University in Durham, North Carolina, arousing opposition from the bishop and diocesan leaders. The Diocese of North Carolina cut its pledge to the national church by $160,000.[38] Similar grants were made to projects and organizations perceived by

---

[35] Paul Schrading, "A New Campus Ministry," *Theology Today* 26 (January 1970): 472.

[36] Myron Bloy, "Alienated Youth, Their Counter Culture, and the Chaplain," *Lutheran Quarterly* 21 (February–November 1969): 251–62.

[37] Booty, 60.

[38] Sumner, 50.

some to be subversive or dangerous to the community. From the perspective of the special grants reviewing process, such suspicions and charges—some of which betrayed racial hostility—justified the "impartiality" or at least the greater objectivity of an outside review mechanism. From the perspective of the local opponents, the removal of control from the local community was a new kind of paternalism that communicated blatant mistrust and impugned local competency to judge.

Into this atmosphere of contention the Inter-Religious Foundation for Community Organization lobbed a stunning volley: the Black Manifesto. This manifesto, adopted in the spring of 1969 at a meeting held in Detroit, charged that African-Americans had unwillingly lived "as a colonized people inside the United States," a country that victimized them even as it deployed them in the attainment of its industrial status. The manifesto was addressed to white Christian churches and Jewish synagogues and demanded "reparations" in the amount of $500,000,000 from those same churches and synagogues. The drafters of the manifesto calculated that amount as "15 dollars per nigger."[39]

Less than a month after the Black Manifesto was adopted in Detroit its demands were made specific. In a letter from James Foreman to Presiding Bishop John Hines the demands made of the Episcopal Church came to "60 million dollars immediately to fund the program of the Black Economic Development Conference, 60% each year of profits on assets, and an accounting of the total assets of the Episcopal Church in all dioceses."[40] Tempers flared on all sides. The General Convention of the Episcopal Church in 1967 had approved a special session of convention for 1969 at the University of Notre Dame in South Bend, Indiana. It was a session that included not only elected denominational deputies, but large numbers of women, ethnic minorities and young people specifically invited to attend. It was the first time the convention had ever been held on a college campus and the first time that such an assembly allowed not only for the conduct of legislative business, but for conference as well.[41] From August 31-September 5, 1969, the Special General Convention deliberated the demands of the manifesto and debated response.

The Special General Convention neither rejected the demands of the manifesto nor capitulated to them. In the end a grant of $200,000 was made to establish a special fund entrusted to the African-American

---

[39] Booty, 60.
[40] Ibid., 61.
[41] Sumner, 52.

clergy of the Episcopal Church to be contributed to the Black Economic Development Corporation. In the wake of the Notre Dame special convention, some members left the Episcopal Church and revenues declined as funds were willfully withheld from the national church.[42] A budgetary shortfall of more than $1 million by 1970 required the national church office to reduce its staff by one-fourth; a year later the staff was reduced again by half: from 204 persons to 110.[43] Judging from the Journal of the special convention of 1969, cause for dissatisfaction was manifold and not relegated solely to matters of racial strife. The Special General Convention adopted an amended budget of $14,171,000 for 1969, $1 million under the figure authorized for that year by the convention in 1967. The revised budget reflected a shortfall in revenues created when twelve of eighty-nine jurisdictions failed to meet their pledges.[44] Furthermore, The Executive Council reported, "It is clear that [campus] ministries must be developed by experimentation, since few effective ones exist. It is also clear that new forms of mission are needed for a university world which seems not to know its own mission at the present time."[45]

The Episcopal Church was not alone in its agonies. In 1969 the United Presbyterians reported that lack of budget increases in the previous three years had forced staff and program cutbacks; receipts to the General Assembly from congregations declined 4.16 percent in 1968 alone.[46]

While Presbyterians played an active role from the earliest days of the desegregation drama, tensions reached a critical point and elicited widespread attention in May 1971 when the Golden Gate Synod's Ethnic Affairs Committee, having requested and received funds from the Council on Religion and Race for Angela Davis' defense, paid $10,000 to her defense fund. Although the following General Assembly could not rescind the grant, it did vote 347-303 to seriously question the appropriateness of the grant. But, in addition, twenty Black Presbyterians gave another $10,000.

The merger in 1968 that created The United Methodist Church changed drastically the structures of that church. From 1939 most African-American congregations of the Methodist Church were segre-

---

[42] Booty, 61.
[43] Sumner, 52–53.
[44] *Journal of the Special General Convention* (1969), 259.
[45] Ibid., 272.
[46] *Minutes of the Presbyterian Church* (1969) part 1, 906–7.

gated in a "Central Jurisdiction"—a non-geographical jurisdiction based on race alone. In 1968, the Central Jurisdiction was eliminated and its congregations and programs folded into the merged United Methodist Church. Over the next four years all segregating structures were to die. In addition, in 1968 a Commission on Religion and Race was established within the new denomination. Along with the quadrennial emphasis on "A New Church for a New World," the 1968 General Conference created a Fund for Reconciliation. The goal was to raise $20 million over four years for reconstruction in Vietnam, and for minority empowerment and development at home.[47] Electing to meet on their own in 1968, African-American Methodists called the First National Conference of Negro Methodists in Cincinnati and formed a new entity within The United Methodist Church called Black Methodists for Church Renewal.

Campus ministry, one of the most vocal advocates for racial integration and civil rights, found new partners in the denominational enterprise in the form of new staff officers and new programs created by the civil rights crusade. But the resources of the churches were not expanding quickly enough to fund the old agenda and the new. In fact, campus ministry, especially in relation to civil rights, was unwittingly thrust into the unenviable role of John the Baptist, who, having successfully heralded a new day, was required to step aside so as not to block the dawn. In an era of dwindling resources and heightened demand, one had to decrease in order that the other might increase.

Neither can it be said that the resulting change that left campus ministry more financially vulnerable was calculated. For understandable reasons, including the sheer enormousness of post-war expansion, the mainline churches were more reactionary than deliberate in the establishment of ministries on campus. The church tended to react as best it could to a rapidly changing culture. As the culture and its campuses changed, campus ministry itself changed from work with veterans and families to something more approximating an extension of the youth ministry of the church into the student young adult population. The church followed its constituency to campus and to the suburbs. But plans were often made on the run, and the national judicatories never funded those plans completely. The visions of those specifically responsible for and committed to ministry on campus were never fully realized. And throughout the era under study, few if any of

---

[47] *Journal of the Methodist Church,* ed. John L. Schreiber (1972) vol. 2, p. 1800. Denominational officials estimated that the program actually raised almost $29 million and created 800 new ministry projects across the church.

the numerous studies and reflections regarding the church on campus examined the ecclesiological questions about what involvement in campus ministry meant to the larger understanding of what the church is.

In previous periods, when social cohesions were different, campus ministry—like Sunday School—was but one dimension of Christian education. The splintering of the culture into varied special purpose groups changed this. Infants, pre-school and elementary-grade children, adolescents, junior and senior high youths, college students and young adults—along with the aged—all became "special purpose" groups in the eyes of the adult population that ordered the institutions of the society. In their marginal position on the churches' agendas, campus ministries joined all the aforementioned constituencies—generational, racial, and otherwise—seeking a claim on the churches' resources.

The increased division of ministry by generational, topical, and other interests changed the life of the church. New ways of communication were sorely needed, though slowly implemented. In the Pastoral Letter from the House of Bishops to the Episcopal General Convention of 1970, the image of the Tower of Babel was invoked as appropriate to a "crisis in communication where emotion-packed words make it extremely difficult for us to understand one another."[48] Many quoted in a variety of contexts the line from the popular movie of the time, *Cool Hand Luke*: "What we have here is a failure to communicate." The failure was widespread. It became increasingly difficult to bridge the differences. Episcopal bishops urged the General Convention of 1970, increasingly divided into conservative and liberal factions, to seek God's healing and forgiveness, and each other's.[49] The Standing Committee on Education of the Presbyterian General Assembly of 1970 noted a generational warfare that directed hostilities toward the youth of society and asked their General Assembly to "reaffirm its faith in the essential idealism and integrity of [our] young people, working as they are for a more just and healthy society."[50] Episcopalians in 1970 began a General Convention Youth Program as an effort to heal division between the generations and explicitly named university and educational processes in need of attention. Recommended funding was to be $250,000 a year for the triennium.[51]

---

[48] *Journal of the General Convention* (1970), 20.
[49] Ibid., 21.
[50] *Minutes of the Presbyterian Church* (1970) part 1, 362.
[51] *Journal of the General Convention* (1970), 306–7.

Not a little of the churches' contentiousness was related to the sheer number of vocal groups each claiming legitimate, worthy causes and ministries within a climate of diminishing financial resources at the national level. The custodial model of stewardship that saw monies collected by a national bureaucracy for distribution was being tested. The Presbyterian General Assembly of 1970 reported expenditures of almost $7.6 million from its reserves. Although the churches of the denomination increased giving overall by nearly one percent, funds directed to the General Assembly declined nearly three percent. The Board of Christian Education, which derived significant income from publications printed and distributed by the denominational press, reported giving down by $245,000 and reduced its staff by twenty-seven persons. A half-million dollars was cut from the Board's giving to denominational colleges; $150,000 was still given, however, from reserves to campus ministry.[52] But in 1972, for the first time in nearly thirty years, no money was dispensed from the reserves of the Board of Christian Education to campus ministry.[53]

The Episcopal Church's experiment with a different method of stewardship—the General Convention Special Program—was still a testy issue when the General Convention gathered in 1970. Despite a number of challenges, the GCSP was continued and expanded, with a proviso that no monies be given to any group or individual engaged in or advocating violence as a means to carry out a program.[54] A budget of $23,686,376 for the triennium was passed, but was divided into two categories of receipt: Half of the total was the committed income of apportionments, the other half was a "faith challenge" made of designated gifts.[55] College work, then funded under the category of "Specialized Ministries"—which included persons with special needs, the armed forces, youth ministry, and industrial missions—was budgeted $60,000 of the committed income, down from almost half a million dollars in 1963, with an additional $10,000 if the designated gifts materialized.[56]

The United Methodists reported in 1972 that although total church giving for all causes increased 7.12 percent, total benevolence giving had declined 5.04 percent. Their report observed that "…there obviously has been a trend during this quadrennium to use a greater proportion of all

---

[52] *Minutes of the Presbyterian Church* (1970) part 2, 52, 88.
[53] *Minutes of the Presbyterian Church* (1972) vol. 1, 1095–96.
[54] *Journal of the General Convention* (1970), 301ff.
[55] Ibid., 595.
[56] Ibid., 598.

available funds at the local church and annual conference levels, and to use such funds for non-benevolent causes." [57]

CULTURE, CAMPUS, AND CHURCH:
RETREAT TO PRIVATISM

The financial strains and pains emanating from the reports of this period reflect both the inflationary economics of the time and what a number of reports freely acknowledge as distrust and disenchantment with social and political institutions, including the church. The Vice-President of the United States was forced to resign amid charges of corruption in the early 1970s, confirming suspicions that would continue to grow in the coming decades and contribute to cynicism about government.[58] This disaffection, as it built over the latter portion of the 1960s, gradually became the basis for a retreat into *privatism*. The patterns of fragmentation we have noted in earlier chapters as response to social complexities set the course for a privatism that has been ably examined by Robert Bellah and others.[59]

Such privatism has both individual and collective faces. In 1971 the Journal of the Presbyterian General Assembly reported "trends toward decentralization and regionalization."[60] Disenchantment with denominational hierarchy increased during the tumultuous time of the late 1960s when denominational leaders possessed sufficient bureaucratic strength to direct church affairs contrary to the desires of the grassroots membership, pursuing programs and interests not favored by the majority. A study of members in fifteen major denominations undertaken in 1972 observed a "schizoid image of the church, split between the intimate local congregation on the one side and the remote, impersonal denomination on the other" and "a tendency to concentrate resources on the community level and downgrade the denomination."[61] Parochialism became more and more evident as the 1960s gave way to the 1970s.

---

[57] *Journal of the Methodist Church*, ed. John L. Schreiber (1972) vol. 2, p. 2026. Given the apparent success of the Fund for Reconciliation, this statement does not seem quite fair.

[58] Flowers, 122.

[59] Robert N. Bellah, et al. *Habits of the Heart* (Berkeley: University of California Press, 1985; repr., New York: Harper & Row, Perennial Library, 1986).

[60] *Journal of the Presbyterian Church* (1971) part 1, 737.

[61] Wuthnow, *Restructuring*, 98.

Campus ministries, as Richard Ottaway observed in 1971, were increasingly called to function as connecting links between alienated groups in growing systems.[62] The dilemma of campus ministry was that it, too, was caught up in the tempers of the times. Hardly exempt from the prevailing experience, campus ministry was also critical of the institutions it served. And campus ministry was, because of its associations with the youth culture, subject to the generational suspicions that smouldered between that youthful constituency (of which the chaplain might also have been a member) and those elders who deliberated church policy and dispensed church resources. Alvin Hoksberger and others noted that in such times of tension greater—not less—accountability is necessary between church and campus ministry. [63] But such communication did not come easily.

Campus ministers found it increasingly difficult to account to either the church or the university in such a milieu. Bishops of The Episcopal Church reported from the worldwide Anglican conference at Lambeth Palace in England in 1968 that members of the denomination were "free to attend the Eucharist in other Churches holding the apostolic faith as contained in the Scriptures and summarized in the Apostles' and Nicene Creeds." In 1967 the Confession of the United Presbyterian Church U.S.A. denied that belief in any particular confession could be held as a standard of membership or a criterion of belief.[64] Still, campus ministers could satisfy neither parents nor judicatory officials that student religious pilgrimage was allowable, perhaps even desirable, within the held policies of the denominations. But neither could mainline campus ministers adequately communicate to universities that rigid sectarianism and proselytism were no longer consistent with the practices of their denominations.

Despite attempts to broaden the vision of campus ministry within denominations the attitude that campus ministries were to provide for distinctive denominational groups and that they were to recruit on behalf of the denominations persisted at the grassroots and in the local judicatories of the denominations and within the universities. John Snow wrote in 1971 of members of the church outside the university community that "...they, like many of the academic community itself..., are also

---

[62] Richard N. Ottaway, "How the Chaplain Can Influence the Structures of Society Via the University," *Anglican Theological Review* 53 (January 1971): 40–41.

[63] Alvin L. Hoksberger, "Where the Church Meets the Campus," *The Princeton Seminary Bulletin* 64 (March 1971): 44.

[64] Wuthnow, *Restructuring*, 92.

suspicious that the chaplain is putting them on. How quick the institutional Church is to dispense with these chaplaincies when money gets tight is an indication of its latent distrust of their value."[65]

Campus ministers, then, were faced with the impossible task of reconciling an ever-expanding array of diverse groups and interests on campus and within the church. And they were faced with the enormously difficult business of reconciling two institutions that were estranged, sometimes at enmity but more often in apathy. Between 1969 and 1970 church attendance among the college educated fell by 6 percentage points—a notably large proportional drop for a single year. In the previous decade—from 1958-1968—church attendance among the same group had fallen by 11 percentage points. Yet church attendance among those without college educations dropped only 5 points from 1958-68 and in the year 1969-70 remained constant.[66]

Among the varied constituencies sharing life in the American culture there emerged a more identifiable division between the college-educated and those who had not known the college experience or its benefits directly. Wuthnow has indicated the role this division played in the constitution of church structures and policies and in the conflicts that pitted these groups in combat during the late 1960s and early 1970s.[67] But he also posited that in this same period the role of education itself changed by virtue of its enormous influence in the economy. Education contributed goods and services to the culture through its research activities. But education became also at this time "a major means of stratifying the society into different subcultures, of promoting technology, and of

---

[65] John Snow, *Christian Identity on Campus*, ed. Myron B. Bloy, Jr. (New York: Seabury Press, 1971), 102.

[66] Wuthnow, *Restructuring*, 161–62.

[67] Based on information found in General Assembly records, lists of those who served on the Presbyterian Board of Christian Education in 1960 and 1970 were obtained. In the membership for 1960: 4 of the lay people held Ph.D.s; of the 20 clergy serving local churches, only 1 of the churches had under 600 members, while 15 had over 1000 members (including 7 churches of over 2000 members). In 1970, the Board boasted nine lay persons with earned doctorates. Of the fifteen clergy serving local churches (there were three or four more professors on the Board in 1970 than there were in 1960), there was still only one from a church of under 600 members, while 10 were serving churches of over 1000 members. Only one pastor in the two years surveyed was designated as an associate.

One can plausibly argue, based on this evidence, that younger, less wealthy clergy and laity, as well as small churches were underrepresented in this era. We suspect that a similar assessment could be made of the other two denominations under study here.

maintaining the country's competitive position in a world economy."[68]
As college-educated membership in the churches declined, and those
who valued education less highly remained in the churches, the work of
the campus minister grew more difficult.

The Department of Campus Ministry of the Division of Higher
Education in the United Methodist Church produced a book in 1972 entitled *Campus Ministry: An Affirmation of Transcendence in the Midst of
Turmoil*. It maintained that "campus ministry of the 1970s strongly
emphasizes a ministry of mission in the world....Theological reflection
leads campus ministries, today, to reject an isolated ministry based on a
personal and pastoral piety and turn instead to an activism and
involvement in the social and political spheres of our existence...."
Among the points of active engagement, the authors listed ecology,
urbanization, the racial crisis, the military industrial complex, and the
Vietnam war. The book made bold to claim: "The present student generation is attempting to implement the values their parents and heritage
held as ideals."[69] From this perspective, the book is exemplary of the
painful gap between the generations, and between the varied ministries
of the church. This major report, intended to defend campus ministry
and encourage support for it, established a case for campus ministry that
stood largely in opposition to the prevailing culture of the church it
addressed. For just as the church membership was seeking a more
personal, pastoral piety and decrying social and political activism, this
report claimed the opposites as the bases for campus ministry. Insult was
only added to injury in the naive and erroneous assumption that these
values were widely held by the parents of this generation of students.
The report acknowledges the difficulty of interpreting campus ministry
in an atmosphere of unrest and disruptions, aggravated by selective
media coverage that overplayed the worst aspects of campus violence.
But the report seems oblivious to the ominous gulf between its perceptions of its audience and the reality.

A restructuring of the United Presbyterian Church U. S. A. in 1973
dissolved the Board of Christian Education. Though there was grief over
the death of the Board, which had been the primary conduit for information from and extending resources to higher education ministries, there
was optimism and hope for greater life for the whole church. The practical reality of the restructuring was that financial reserves previously held

---

[68] Wuthnow, *Restructuring*, 163.

[69] *Quadrennial Reports*. (The Commission on Entertainment, The Methodist
Publishing House: 1972), 35.

by the Board of Christian Education (including publishing profits) and similar boards, would be surrendered to the United Presbyterian Foundation, interest from which would be available to the General Assembly General Mission Budget.[70] Those monies had sustained Presbyterian campus ministries for nearly three decades.

By 1973 the wave that was the "baby boom" had crested and was poised to recede. As Richard Nixon assumed his second term of office, the war was finally ending, but soldiers returned to a bitter homecoming. Allegations of political chicanery linked to high-ranking Republicans in the Cabinet and even the President himself cast a long, dark shadow. The new generation of students faced rising unemployment and relentless inflation. After years of extroverted activism, it was a turning of time to a more introspective privatism.

The universities sorted through the pieces and looked through the economic recession to a receding pool of traditional (18-24) college-aged applicants. The churches were consumed with the internal struggles wrought of the changes that could no longer be checked. Each turned to their own affairs. Drawing unto themselves, institutions and individuals took up their own healing.

---

[70] *Minutes of the Presbyterian Church* (1973) part 1, 474.

5

RESTRUCTURING AND INTROSPECTION: THE CHURCH BESIDE ITSELF, 1973–1980

INTRODUCTION

American churches, government, business, and other institutions have grown up together, sharing boon and bane, and enriching one another through the cross-fertilization of ideas and influences. The post-Civil War industrialization of the nation encouraged a growth and an appreciation for expansiveness that spread throughout American institutions. It was in this period that bureaucracies were developed to oversee and manage enlarging systems of governance and management.[1] Churches, like business and other institutions, were enchanted by the notion that bigger is better and that expansion is the measure of vitality. The cycles of development have at times altered fortunes and posed challenges, but as the nation expanded so did the institutions within it, the churches being no exception.

The post-World War II era brought national recovery from the Great Depression and inaugurated a period of unparalleled economic and social growth. The resources of enthusiasm and money and the cultural

---

[1] Ben Primer, *Protestantism and American Business Methods* (Ann Arbor, MI: UMI Research Press, 1979).

values of the time encouraged an explosive expansion in every area of American life. The exuberance of this growth in the economy, in the churches, in the government and elsewhere mandated, but also made possible, a division of labor. As institutions grew and labors divided, the energies conserved and released allowed for more growth—until the growth slowed, stopped, or worse, reversed into decline.

In the 1950s, as the post-World War II boom on campus accelerated the churches' role in that setting and numerous campus ministries were established, college work was commonly affiliated with the educational components of denominational ministry, including Christian education (and by association, Sunday Schools), youth ministry, support for denominational colleges and universities, and a growing number of divisions fed by the "baby boom." By the late 1950s and early 1960s, the churches' corporate organization which had begun in the early 1900s had succeeded in fashioning denominational hierarchies of governance with a new layer of institutional leadership. The sheer size of the churches' national structures demanded a managerial bureaucracy at the national level and the diversity of church program required more attention and closer administration than periodic conventions could effectively manage.

But American mainline denominations, American businesses, and American government itself began to decline by the mid-1960s. Many factors have been cited for this decline. One thesis that bears repeating here is a shift in America's global relationships. This interpretation sees this perceived reversal not as an absolute decline, but rather as the difficult transition to stabilization. The United States has for many years enjoyed a disproportionate share of the world's resources. The United States must adjust to its "natural entitlement" of about 18 percent.[2] By extension, American mainline denominations enjoyed a hegemony that has been challenged by religious pluralism, ethnic diversity, and heightened individualism.

A similar disproportionality applies as well to the university. Residential campuses experienced a marked challenge from commuter schools. The homogeneous campus populated by single-sex, racially uniform, denominationally affiliated students gave way in this period to a heterogeneity that crossed every boundary. By 1970 the press was reporting a financial depression in higher education. Inflation, diminished endowment return, and new appropriations going to community

---

[2] *The New Yorker* 65 (8 May 1989): 31.

colleges and the health sciences contributed to the funding crunch. Federal funding priorities for defense, welfare, unemployment, crime and health care all edged higher education lower in the national budget.[3]

Campus ministry, and certainly particular configurations of campus ministry, had also assumed an overestimated prominence. The Presbyterian hope of a denominational ministry on every campus met defeat because it reflected a disproportional model. Free-standing denominational campus ministries with expansive physical plants and ordained professional staff may also represent a disproportional goal.

Lastly, in the period of the late 1960s and early 1970s American citizens began to challenge the common assumption that big is always better. A Harris poll in 1972 showed a strong anti-establishment bias throughout the country.[4] The prominence of overwhelming institutions—including government—led to grave suspicion. George Orwell's *1984*, with its images of repressive governmental control, seemed perilously close not only in years, but in the networks of surveillance made possible by a Federal Bureau of Investigation, a Central Intelligence Agency, and an expanding network of computerized data. Liberation from such authority, regardless of its source or its beneficence, became a priority for many. In its place, new patterns of organization were demanded, with open accounting and local governance.

SOCIETY:
IS THERE A BALM?

Shortly after Nixon's inauguration to a second term in 1973, negotiations ended America's involvement in Vietnam and soon the veterans were returning home. The social and political cleavage created by the war became, at best, an ambiguity, depriving the homecoming veterans of positive recognition and, in some cases, engendering outright hostilities. The exposures of the Watergate scandal that revealed corruption throughout the highest levels of the federal government further demoralized the nation and contributed significantly to what Roof and McKinney identified as the diminution of "national ideals and messianic concep-

---

[3] Henry, 134–35, 142–51. Despite appearances, the 1960s was not a period of affluence for higher education. After inflation, constant dollars expended computed to $1542 per student in 1958 to just $1621 in 1971.

[4] Ibid., 137.

tions of America as an instrument of divine purpose."[5] When Nixon resigned from office and Gerald Ford assumed the presidency, the nation wanted nothing more than to be healed, but seemed bereft of the resources to effect a cure.

Patience may have seemed a luxury in these times. The inauguration of Jimmy Carter in January, 1977 indicated the desire of the nation to get past the ravages of political scandal that so marred the previous Republican administration. Carter brought an appreciation for the grassroots and a quiet determination to the office that, while momentarily palliating, gradually grated on the sense of urgency that attended American life.

CAMPUS:
BROKEN BONDS, LOST CIVILITY

In the early 1970s Lansing Lamont, a reporter who returned from five years abroad to examine the American university campuses, characterized the mood he found on campus as "Lost Civility," an accurate and somewhat prescient characterization that became a subject of increasing concern on campus and in the culture itself.[6] What Lamont observed was a breakdown of trust on campus that gave rise to selfishness. Campus crime increased, not only in the numbers and types of crimes against students, but more alarmingly, the numbers and types of crimes perpetrated *by* students. The same loss of any clear sense of the common good that marked the general culture, in this evidence, extended to the life of students as well.

The transition to college was different in the 1970s than for previous generations. Throughout the 1950s and into the 1960s students made the transition from home to campus with the commingling of dread and excitement that attends any new adventure. New relationships and new challenges along with the dynamics of social and academic competition attended the transition. By the mid-1960s the competitive edge sharpened, but still there were the touchstones of family and the familiar institutions, including denominational campus ministries, to assist the transition.

---

[5] Wade Clark Roof and William McKinney, *American Mainline Religion: Its Changing Shape and Future* (New Brunswick: Rutgers University Press, 1987), 28.

[6] Horowitz, 255.

The difficulty of doing ministry or serving these students in any way, however, was further complicated by changes in the educational community. By the early to mid-1970s the residential campus, and the four-year baccalaureate program, were but one facet of a multi-dimensional system of higher education. Commuter education on residential campuses and on new commuter campuses designed for a particular constituency added a transience heretofore unknown. Students did not come to campus to live, but only to work. They treated the campus, in large measure, rather perfunctorily. Campus was but one place and education but one dimension of lives that were filled with other concerns, including family and employment obligations. Increased emphasis upon higher education as professional credential spurred many people to return to school. Some who married young returned to earn their deferred degree. Others who had degrees came back as special students to continue their education, either to learn newer technologies or techniques, or to enhance their earning potential. Spouses once dependent upon a partner's income, after divorce came to campus to secure credentials for self-support. And among the undergraduate community, returning Vietnam War veterans shared classes with students who labored five, six, or more years to complete the baccalaureate degree, not because they were slow or poor students, but because the financial burden of higher education required employment to support its cost.

Another complicating factor was that in the 1970s patterns of divorce and remarriage in the United States created a growing number of students who, by the time they left home for college, had already sustained the breakup of their family. The economic recession of the early 1970s only heightened the competition for jobs, while runaway inflation drove the cost of education and everything else upward. Students of the 1970s were often under increasing financial and social pressure, but with fewer resources to call to their aid. Their autonomy, sometimes enforced by family dynamics that from childhood had cut them off from significant relationships, was made a virtue. The reward of solitary study and long hours in the library was better grades, better grades gave an edge in a sharply competitive market, and the competitive edge was the key to future security.

Students learned to keep their own counsel, to remain aloof. They continued to date and be sociable, but perhaps family divorce made them wary of commitment. Also, the advancing women's movement and the gay liberation movement made sexuality and relationships more complex. Women and men were learning new ways of relating to one another, often in coeducational settings where even residential privacy offered no respite from the pressing questions of male-female interaction. A kind of introspective withdrawal seemed to characterize many students of the period. This characteristic was consistent with the times, which were marked as noted earlier, by the fragmentation of the culture.

The crises of change and erosion of ethical and moral foundations were perhaps ironically symbolized by an observation that comes not from the social historians, but from an architectural historian. Paul Venable Turner published a series of articles in 1974 on the subject of alternatives to new construction, a matter prompted by sharp reductions in campus growth. Turner observes:

> The most radical type of transformation (radical, at least, in light of the history of the American college) involved the campus chapel, that indispensable core of the old-time sectarian college, but now virtually abandoned at many institutions. A separate article on this problem reported that the planner Richard P. Dober estimated there were nearly four hundred college chapels in America that were unused and ripe for recycling. Dober held a conference on the subject at Oberlin College in Ohio (whose Cass Gilbert-designed chapel was one of the four hundred), which focused on the conversion of these relics to performing-arts centers or audio-visual-communications facilities. Significantly, the planners did not recommend demolishing these outmoded buildings, as they probably would have done ten or twenty years earlier. The new economic realities, and preservation consciousness, now conspired to save the physical structures, even if their original use was abandoned.[7]

The anachronism of campus chapels was, however, not a sign of religion's demise. It could not be said that the campus of the 1970s was irreligious. On the contrary, there were many religions. That any one of them should be considered central to the life of the university was unthinkable; their mere proliferation made chapels, as symbols of dominant tradition, expendable. "The challenge," as Roof and McKinney wrote, "is no longer to accommodate new and different religious groups, but rather to adjust to a broader pluralism of religious and secular ideologies. Civility is no longer the issue, but the character of the *civitas* itself."[8]

A growing pluralism, especially in higher education, made room for greater diversity. Horowitz suggests that the "culture of the outsider

---

[7] Turner, 304.
[8] Roof & McKinney, 38.

emerged triumphant in the 1970s."[9] Those outsiders included that widely divergent assembly of people who did not conform to the white male (and to a less extent white female), relatively affluent, 18-22 year old group that was the dominant culture on American campuses until the 1970s. Those outsiders brought with them a different set of standards and expectations.

With the dominance of the outsiders there came to campus a new set of concerns, many of them related to securing and maintaining comfortable economic independence. To that end, students were more than ever concerned to secure credentials that would improve their job prospects and their future earning power. The colleges and universities within which they studied were also accused of self-seeking opportunism as they reordered curricula and, as some argued, pandered to what was called the "me" generation.

By the 1970s American colleges and universities had seen the crest of the baby boom and, with it, the passage of their gravy train. They, too, had followed America's fortunes with expanded campus facilities, faculties, and a host of new resources in a newly created category of administration that included greatly enhanced student services. Colleges and universities were, like the church and numerous other social institutions, big business. But their market share was changing. The institutions were changing. They were in flux, as the dominant leadership gradually gave way to the outsiders. Throughout all American institutions women, people of color and of a variety of ethnic and sexual persuasions were taking their places, slowly but surely. But these constituencies were not yet sufficiently mature to clarify or articulate a new set of values.

CAMPUS MINISTRY

Students and Campus Religious Climate

An article from the *Vassar Quarterly* in 1974, written by a 1971 alumna, provides a sketch of the religious climate on campus. Julie Thayer wrote of "increased attendance at religious services and increased enrollment in religion department courses" but rightly demurred from calling the phenomenon a revival. "Revival is a misnomer; it implies that old religious forms and beliefs 'live again.' At Vassar today the emphasis is not on old traditions which are revived, but on students awakening to

---

[9] Horowitz, 263.

an appreciation of the religious dimension of their lives and sharing their discoveries in a caring religious community."[10] Thayer, who had herself been a student assistant (lay) chaplain at Vassar, recalled the late 1960s and 1970 as a time when chapel was packed and "litanies of anguish" over the war in Vietnam unified the students, "swallowing up our differences in the overriding similarity of the urgent issues confronting each one of us."[11]

Thayer chronicled waning interest in denominational ministries in the late 1960s and 1970s and the ecumenical chapel-centered board that evolved. But by 1974, she reflected, religion had a broad profile and included many different activities. Enrollment in religion courses at Vassar in 1974 increased to the point that the department enjoyed the highest number of students per faculty member and religion majors numbered 44, as compared to 16 only three years previous.[12] Denominational groups were popular again, and attendance at services of denominational worship had replaced the campus-wide gatherings. "The theme of caring community appeared over and over again in my exploration of religious experience.... Worshipping together can break down barriers to closeness for students who feel isolated."[13] But she did not perceive this change in religious activity indicative of "retreat from action and political commitment."[14]

Thayer observed that students seemed less trusting of "tidy, logical plans to solve problems which may be rooted deep below the rational surface of the human mind and the institutions it creates."[15] But these students were no less concerned with matters of personal integrity than the previous generation of students. Indeed, they evinced a "vocational consciousness" that sought the consistent balance of work, family, friendship, and leisure in a life "filling their own needs and serving the needs of other people by sharing capabilities and insights."[16] She described a Sunday chapel worship service. It "centered around the theme of standing alone in independence and self-respect, a companion service to one on loneliness held a week before," grounded in readings

---

[10] Julie Thayer, "The Caring Community: Religious Awakening at Vassar," *Vassar Quarterly* 70 (Winter 1974): 25.

[11] Ibid.

[12] Ibid., 28.

[13] Ibid.

[14] Ibid.

[15] Ibid.

[16] Ibid.

and a sermon on "the steadfastness of Job and the stubborn strength of Martin Luther."[17] Yet for all the vibrancy Thayer found on the Vassar campus, and the many echoes of it that abounded elsewhere, religion's vitality accounted for only a portion of student energies.

Among those ideologies that competed for time and attention on campus, few were as pronounced as self-absorption. Barbara Jurgensen, comparing students in 1974 to their counterparts in 1969 observed that students in 1974 were less utopian and faddish. They felt the pressure of possible unemployment even as they yearned for well-paying jobs. They were not at all interested in campus activism. Campus ministry no longer followed student action; if there was to be any action, campus ministry had to stimulate it. That is not to say that students were uncaring. Rather, students in 1974 viewed problems as global, requiring a more reforming than revolutionary response. But when students were agitated enough to speak out, their concerns were most often local. They could be exercised about campus alcohol policies or gender-integrated housing. And if and when they were in church, they were less interested in innovative liturgy than they were in traditional patterns.[18]

Denominational Climate: Political Division and Restructuring

Reflecting upon the missionary character of campus ministry, Shockley described ministry on campus as "the church beyond itself."[19] By 1973, some campus ministers claimed their role as prophetic and consequently saw themselves as the church *ahead* of itself. In this regard they shared much in common with their parochial colleagues. Jeffrey Hadden's *The Gathering Storm in the Churches* drew upon the findings of the Danforth study to ascertain that the cleavage between the pulpit and the pew threatened to widen.[20] The 1960s and the 1970s saw clergy and laity divide along the political spectrum. Mainline Protestant clergy of that period tended to fall to the left, or liberal, end of the spectrum, while the laity tended to dominate the right, or conservative, end.

Within the churches, other lines of demarcation were in the early 1970s beginning to show more prominently. Congregations tended to take on distinct religio-political postures or identities. No longer bound

---

[17] Ibid., 26.

[18] Barbara Jurgensen, "Campus Scene: A 1974 Overview," *The Christian Century* 91 (18 December 1974): 1200–1.

[19] Shockley, *Campus Ministry*.

[20] Jeffrey K. Hadden, *The Gathering Storm in the Churches* (Garden City, NY: Doubleday and Company, 1970).

geographically, parishioners were free to commute to the church of their choice. In many instances members of a given denomination could find within reasonable proximity to their homes several churches of their denomination whose political and/or socio-economic distinctions were their distinguishing characteristic. Proliferation of churches in the 1950s and 1960s meant that by the 1970s members or prospective members could not only choose a denominational preference but, within that preference, could affiliate with a congregation compatible with their own political posture. Within the denominations themselves, however, such distinctions presented a different picture.

While congregations could adopt a distinct posture and gather unto themselves compatible adherents, denominations—by virtue of their size—were required to harbor a greater diversity of opinion. As the mid-1970s approached, parties and partisans within denominations became more visible and more vocal. Lines tended to emerge over specific issues. In the Episcopal Church, revision of the Book of Common Prayer, the ordination of women to the priesthood (and later, the episcopate), and the place of gay and lesbian members within the church were all issues that emerged in the early 1970s and continued to factionalize the denomination. For United Methodists and Presbyterians, as for the Episcopalians, issues of human sexuality, and homosexuality in particular, became points of contention.

Mainline denominational churches, on the whole, were edged from their centered, quasi-established position in the 1970s as Catholicism saw some increases in membership, especially in those regions where immigrants from Hispanic and Latino countries tended to congregate. But the greater incursions into mainline hegemony were launched by the conservative evangelical churches. Often independent, sometimes possessing massive, state-of-the-art television networks and charismatic leadership, these groups espoused a more fundamentalist reading of the Bible and promoted a life ordered by that discipline. Given the disorder and complexity of modern American society they found many adherents.

Within such an environment and among students of this generation, evangelical campus ministries seemed to enjoy an advantage. Campus Crusade for Christ, Navigators, and InterVarsity Christian Fellowship, as well as a host of newer and more extreme groups espousing fundamentalist or literalist Biblicism, often attracted more students than their mainline denominational counterparts. Students found in these groups, as the general public found in their parochial counterparts, much that was appealing: these groups offered easy, even instantaneous, fellowship to the lonely and frightened. Most importantly, they offered the promise of security in systems of defined discipline and comparative certainty. But their attraction, while notable, was never more than relative. Except for very rare cases, they could never claim a majority of students on a given campus, or even a majority of all the Christian students on a given campus. Indeed, many students who initially affiliated with these groups early in their college years later found their disciplines restrictive and repressive. While they were frequently helpful in assisting student transition to the diversity and complexity of campus life, once the need for such assistance was over, students abandoned them.

The economic travails of the mainline denominations continued into the 1970s as budgets reflected continued reductions. Various "re-organizations" of denominational bureaucracies made it increasingly difficult to determine how monies were being spent. Indeed, it seems at times as though the greatest creative energies of the churches were spent in crafting Byzantine financial reporting systems. While monies for ministry in higher education had for many years been shuffled from department to department—appearing under diverse categories like Christian education, youth work, or mission—in this period they occasionally disappeared altogether.

In 1974 the Presbyterian Church U.S.A. presented a budget reduced twenty percent from the 1973 level. A line item for United Ministries in Higher Education (UMHE) in the amount of $534,000 seems the sole national support for campus ministry.[21] To further confuse matters, the UMHE report for 1974 was not presented by an educational unit but by the Assembly Committee on Ecumenism and Church Union.[22]

It is difficult to know whether this confusion was intentional legerdemain or sheer neglect. The confusions and/or outright lack of intention throughout the mainline denominations' short history of campus ministry may, in this instance, simply have played themselves out. It is equally possible that bureaucratic expediency, seeking to shore up collapsing finances, contrived to consolidate previously apportioned monies by rearranging the resources to their benefit, and at the expense of agencies ill-equipped to mount a political alternative.

By 1975 the Presbyterian General Assembly embarked on a reorganization "that the General Assembly's and the synods' programs and budgets be developed together so that they form a whole mission which

---

[21] *Minutes of the Presbyterian Church* (1974) part 1, 430.
[22] Ibid., 120.

united the church."[23] The budget for 1975 was divided into three goals: Preparing for Mission, Doing Mission, and Enabling Others to Do Mission. Within these three categories seventeen sub-categories were detailed. Campus ministry and denominational colleges came under the "Doing Mission" heading and were one of several programs listed under the sub-category of "Serving the Needs of Persons."[24]

United Methodists, Presbyterians, and Episcopalians once again held national meetings in 1976 as their quadrennial, annual, and triennial schedules coincided. The Presbyterian General Assembly made modest refinements to their organizational system. An allocation of $504,084 ($30,000 less than the 1974 allocation, which, in these inflationary years, represented an even smaller allocation) was made to United Ministries in Higher Education, this time under the heading of "Enabling Other Judicatories: Allocation to Aid-to-Field," again under the sub-category of "Serving the Needs of Persons."[25] Among the UMHE emphases for that year was programming for congregations to interact with community colleges.[26] That UMHE was working with community colleges was not unique, but the attention directed toward congregations as a base for campus ministry represented a new direction.

The United Methodist Board of Higher Education and Ministry, and its newly established National Commission on United Methodist Higher Education, were urged "to review thoroughly the role of the Church in higher education and the condition and status of institutions, campus ministry programs, and other agencies related to higher education" and to submit their review to the General Conference of 1980.[27] Resolutions for "Churchwide Support for Institutions of Higher Education" and "Churchwide Support for Campus Ministries" were adopted without significant opposition.

The Episcopal Church in 1976 debated women's ordination, homosexuality and the clergy, and a proposed revision of the Book of Common Prayer. Heated opposition by small but vocal minorities who protested any or all of these liberalizing actions and media coverage that accentuated this dissension all but overshadowed a rather important initiative of this General Convention to raise money for mission and ministry projects that would be different from the General Convention

---

[23] *Minutes of the Presbyterian Church* (1975) part 1, 366.
[24] Ibid., 374.
[25] *Minutes of the Presbyterian Church* (1976) part 1, 284–85.
[26] Ibid., 538.
[27] *Journal of the United Methodist Church*, ed. John L. Schreiber (1976), 1416.

Special Program, the ill-fated design that had engendered much grass-roots resistance. The new program was called "Venture in Mission."[28] The campaign, from the financial development perspective, offered no real distinction from any large fund-raising program. It looked very much like what many Americans frequently encountered from college and university alumni/ae associations, civic, philanthropic, and cultural agencies. But compared to the GCSP, Venture in Mission was a radical departure. The program was purely elective; no diocese would be required to participate. Before any monies were raised in a diocese's campaign, the diocese would gather proposals from its membership. Meanwhile, at the national level a committee received and reviewed proposals for national and international projects. After projects were selected, goals for funding were established. The only condition set was that for every dollar a diocese designated for a local project, an equal dollar would be committed to the national and international projects selected for denominational outreach. All the programs would be identified and goals set before fundraising began. Then, and only then, were monies solicited. In most cases professional development consultants managed the campaigns, greatly enhancing efficiency and productivity. The original goal of $100 million was proven quite a modest proposal when, at the end of 1985, it was revealed that the eighty-five participating dioceses had raised more than $170 million.[29]

The importance of the campaign went far beyond the impressive revenues. Venture in Mission signalled a new direction for the Episcopal Church that was replicated in other ways in other mainline denominations. In one sense, Venture in Mission failed, for it did not succeed in turning the denomination's attention from internal strife and self-consuming arguments; those continued and, in some cases, grew even more acrimonious. Venture in Mission did succeed in releasing unrealized potentials, success which is all the more impressive for being won within a time of great internal pain for the denomination. The campaign proved beyond a shadow of a doubt that a denomination could not only survive turmoil and change, but could actually thrive within it. The real learning of Venture in Mission was that support and enthusiasm were forthcoming from the grassroots, if they were respected.

Campus ministry sometimes benefitted from the design. In one diocese, a gift from a student ministry initiative represented the first dona-

---

28 General Convention, 1976, 168.
29 Ibid.

tion to that local campaign. In the same diocese, students on a different campus were the beneficiaries of a new center constructed largely as a Venture in Mission project. Elsewhere in the country, Venture in Mission monies helped rehabilitate an Episcopal campus center and provided seed money for the establishment of a new campus ministry on an urban commuter campus. The Venture in Mission design honored the church's membership and greatly increased local commitment to ministry.

But this was not, generally, a good period for campus ministry expenditures at the national level. In 1977, for example, the United Presbyterian General Assembly approved expenditure of only $299,438 to United Ministries in Higher Education, compared to their 1976 allocation of $504,084.[30] The drop was precipitous. In 1979 the United Presbyterians reported campus ministry under the heading of Ministries of Health, Education, and Social Justice and lodged it under the subheading of Mission in Education and Health.[31] It was reported of UMHE that the Program Agency of the Presbyterian Church U.S.A. "provides staff services for several of its key programs," but there is no clear indication of national funding.[32] It was as though campus ministry disappeared. No longer significant in denominational consciousness, campus ministry and those who were practicing it, even where vital, were often invisible at the national level.

The Episcopalians met in Denver in 1979. Their triennial convention wrestled with two major agenda items: the second and final vote on the Book of Common Prayer, and a raft of resolutions concerning the ordination of gay and lesbian persons. Ministry in higher education had not been on the agenda of the Episcopal General Convention for years.

But some Episcopal campus ministers did not rely on the national church for direction. Wofford Smith, then Episcopal chaplain to the University of Maryland in College Park, rehearsed in 1979 the history of the Episcopal Society for Ministry in Higher Education (ESMHE). ESMHE was founded in 1968 to create a new network after the elimination of national staff from the provinces. It attempted, with little success, to serve also as the denominational lobby for campus ministry interests. As a voluntary professional organization, the political function of the organization sometimes strained the relationship with the national staff officer for ministry in higher education. In the first ten years of its existence, however, ESMHE's membership grew from 100 to over 500

---

[30] *Minutes of the Presbyterian Church* (1977) part 1, 334.
[31] *Minutes of the Presbyterian Church* (1979) part 1, 186.
[32] Ibid., 351.

members, including campus ministers, bishops, parish clergy, and lay academics, including some students. Smith predicted that as ESMHE matured it would become a more credible agent for administering campus ministry within the denomination. He pointed to the steady growth and improvement of a voluntary provincial network that gradually replaced the defunct provincial staff positions, in many cases to better effect for their involvement of more grassroots initiative.

Campus Ministry Strategies and Evaluations

Within this changed culture, there was a role for mainline Protestant campus ministry. Robert McAfee Brown observed the university world of 1974, a world of competing and often covert value assumptions: "Whatever else campus ministers do, they have an obligation to raise questions about the value of assumptions of the community they serve, particularly when others are failing to do so."[33] Campus ministry's marginality and "ec-centricity" (its standing outside the center), reasoned Brown, allowed campus ministers to facilitate connections between different persons in the university community.

Brown's observations, taken from a review of campus ministry grants made by the Danforth Foundation, are critical of the foundation's stated goal of bringing some common purpose to the educational community.[34] The university, according to Brown, simply did not share that goal. The university was too diverse and complex a community. Brown concluded: "If campus ministry has a place in the strategy for influencing higher education, it has something to do with the minister's ability to bring together people who ordinarily ignore each other and to function as a broker for exchanges that would otherwise not occur."[35]

Some campus ministries were able to fulfill this bridging function. That they were distanced from the traditional, mainline churches may not have hurt them in the eyes of students and others who had grown suspicious of the traditional institutions. In that regard, campus ministries shared much in common with those who were adrift and had suffered estrangement from institutions and individuals they had once trusted. In the early 1970s campus ministries, especially those that possessed free-standing centers, were havens not only for students but for lonely and isolated church members. They could attract, as the mainline

---

[33] Robert McAfee Brown, "Selections from a Review of Danforth Campus Ministry Grants," *CSCW Report* 32 (January 1974): 3.

[34] Ibid., 6.

[35] Ibid., 16.

congregations could not, those who were disaffected by the institutional church. They offered sanctuary to those who had suffered disappointment in religion or who had been distanced by reason of age or politics from the local parish. And they offered a low threshold of entry for those who were curious but suspicious of larger or established communities that might make claims upon their lives they were not ready to commit.

But denominational campus ministries in the 1970s were not always gatherings of malcontents. Because they retained denominational ties and bore denominational identities—if sometimes obscurely and obliquely—they were still connected to the larger church. For that reason, they salvaged for the churches some who, though embattled, were not content to separate themselves entirely from their tradition. And because these campus ministries remained within the denominational fold, even if on the *avant-garde* or lunatic fringe of it, they provided a point of continuity with denominational tradition. Students looking for something of what they had experienced positively in their parish high school youth group, regional youth gathering, or denominational camp setting found a place. Those who had grown up, as many had, with no experience of church membership also found a place. And those who, for reason of their politics, their race, their feminism, or their sexuality, had suffered pain from their denomination made tentative approach and often found a welcome embrace.

There was also, however, a pronounced downside to the location of campus ministry. Denominational campus ministries, with rare exception, were cut off from one another. While ministries continued to function on many campuses, lines of collegial contact were down. Unlike the National Lutheran Campus Ministry staff, which mandated annual meetings of all Lutheran clergy deployed in campus work, other mainline denominations relied upon voluntary and casual association. The ties structured in the Association of Presbyterian University Pastors weakened after that denomination joined UMHE.[36] Enthusiasm for united campus ministry initiatives waned and in the 1970s both the United Methodist Church and the Episcopal Church withdrew from UMHE. Neither the Methodist nor the Episcopal churches had ever established a mandatory national denominational network of campus ministers as the Lutherans or Presbyterians had. Within denominations, groups like the Episcopal Church Society for College Work and the

---

[36] See Charles William Doak, *History of the Association of Presbyterian University Pastors, 1930–1965* (unpublished D. Min. dissertation, San Francisco Theological Seminary, 1985).

Episcopal Society for Ministry in Higher Education provided elective voluntary associations among colleagues in campus work. Reshaping campus ministry, without an adequate mechanism and regular occasions for communication and conversation, seemed impossible.

United Methodists laid plans to rebuild some of their national staff and resources. In 1977 the national Commission on United Methodist Higher Education issued its report on higher education ministries. In his forward to the first report, Paul Hardin wrote:

> The United Methodist Church is called upon by the Gospel to address the Word of God to the whole of higher education. Thus, the United Methodist Church is present in institutions of higher education to call people to the Lordship of Christ; to encourage teaching and scholarship that is both intellectually rigorous and humane; to hold institutions accountable for humane values; to help institutions fulfill their mission to people; to gather a community of the faithful; and to help people within the university anticipate and work for a better society. For all these reasons, the National Commission on United Methodist Higher Education has declared that the United Methodist Church should continue and strengthen, with faithfulness and imagination, the witness of its ministry in higher education.[37]

Declaring higher education "probably the most formative agent in society today," the report holds that higher education demands the fullness of ministry described in the Danforth study: sacerdotal ministration, prophetic inquiry, pastoral care, and administrative governance. The report also acknowledges that the shape and exercise of these roles is contextual, each institution requiring its own recipe for balance.[38] Campus ministry will, however, evince concern for persons, for the freedom of inquiry, for values, and for global perspective.[39] Because of the expanse of campus ministry, new directions in this work will require campus ministers and local pastors to place more emphasis on the ministry of others, openly inviting lay participation in ministry and equipping that ministry through education aimed at addressing ministry in a learning society, ministry in a pluralistic society, ministry to community colleges, and ministry involving laity and local congregations. New directions in campus ministry will also include new patterns of

---

[37] *Ministry on Campus*. A United Methodist Mission Statement and Survey Report. (Nashville: National Commission on United Methodist Higher Education, 1977), 11.

[38] Ibid., 19.

[39] Ibid., 20.

staffing and new financial support.[40] Interestingly, the report suggests that communication and accountability will play a signal role in securing future resources. It indicates that "...as churches both locally and in conferences become more aware of the faithfulness and accountability of campus ministry and of the new directions of that ministry, new patterns of support should be provided...."[41]

What the report does not make clear is where responsibility for such accountability is lodged: will it be the task of the campus minister or ministry to initiate this communication, or will the churches be forthcoming in their relationships to the campuses? It may be supposed that the intention suggests a two-way street with mutual accountability, but lacking clear directives the mechanisms for such communication could become problematic, especially in times when individuals and institutions were prone to introversion.

Perhaps the more insightful information from the report is the results of a nationwide survey of United Methodist campus ministers that, among other things, assessed relational perceptions. Summarizing the findings, the report says:

> campus ministers believe their constituents would have them emphasize pastoral goals such as witness and religious nurturing of students and would de-emphasize social criticism, ministry to socially ostracized groups, and attention to issues of racism and sexism. Whether these beliefs are accurate is unknown. What is clear, however, is that the ministers believe a gap exists between their views and those of their constituents.[42]

Because each minister was allowed to determine who his/her constituency was, the finding is all the more intriguing. Whether the campus minister defined the constituency as the student and faculty population served on campus, the local congregation or board that supported the campus ministry, or the denominational bodies that endorsed the ministry, the bottom line is quite clear: campus ministers perceived themselves to be, by their own admission, out of touch. Regardless of the accuracy of their perceptions, the Methodist campus ministers polled were either intentionally or unintentionally at odds with the primary communities of relationship.

---

[40] The point on finances is significant because United Methodist monies available for campus ministries at the national level had declined to the lowest point in the period under investigation in our study.

[41] Ibid., 23.

[42] Ibid., 41.

Authors of the survey suggested in their analysis that the bulk of campus ministry funds were spent on professional staff—not a surprising finding.[43] The survey does not provide a detailed analysis of campus ministry income by source, but reports from a survey of annual conference treasurers revealed that campus ministry support at the conference level grew from $4.4 million in 1972 to nearly $5.5 million in 1975. Support for campus ministry accounted for 22.2 percent of all conference higher education expenses in 1972, but dropped slightly in 1973 and stayed below this level through 1975.[44] Confirming a point made earlier in this study, this decline in percentage support for general campus ministry was directly related to competition with the racial justice priorities of the church. According to the report, "…annual conference contributions to black institutions increased by 155.9% between 1972 and 1975. Annual conference support for all other higher education activities grew by only 24.4% during that period."[45]

Robert Rankin, himself a member of the team that drafted the United Methodist report in 1977, wrote in a separate article the same year of what he perceived to be a revolution and paradigm shift in campus ministry. Rankin was the Danforth Foundation administrator who had overseen the Underwood project. He praised the work of the Lilly Endowment and the Danforth Foundation, who were both consistent and even insistent in their support of ministry on campus, but acknowledged that limitations were ahead.[46] The foundations were withdrawing much of their financial support, support that had provided not only collegial and ecumenical gatherings for campus ministers and other professionals concerned for this facet of the churches' ministry but, functioning as independent funding sources, had provided significant funding for leadership and creativity in this field of ministry. Denominational funds, whether national, regional or local, were barely able to maintain campus ministry and were always attached to the doctrines and dictates, not to mention the moods, of the denomination. Private foundation funding made possible research and conversation that simply could not be had elsewhere.

Rankin also observed that the Protestant evangelical and the Catholic charismatic movements would pose a serious challenge to the mainline

---

[43] Ibid., 55.
[44] Ibid.
[45] Ibid., 56.
[46] Robert Rankin, "Revolution in the Campus Ministry: The Evangelical Challenge," *The NICM Journal* (Winter 1977): 166.

denominations. Noting that mainline denominations, excepting the Lutherans, Baptists, and the United Methodists, had reduced financial support for campus ministries, he predicted that these ministries were "vulnerable to attack from evangelicals at the right and predatory academics at the left," the latter being those academics so steeped in logical positivism that they would undercut by any method the work of the church on campus.[47]

Rankin thought that the evangelicals filled a vacuum in campus ministry created by the demise of the University Christian Movement. He reasoned that rather than lament the evangelical resurgence, mainline denominational campus ministries might actually learn from them. He cited the Campus Crusade for Christ practice of assigning staff the responsibility of raising their own salaries from constituents who share their own passion for this mission and provide not only financial, but moral and spiritual support, for their staff. Echoing the findings of the United Methodist report cited above, he urged that a healthy future campus ministry depended not only upon restoration of financial support, but "the formation of mutual confidence between ministers and their constituents."[48]

Creative attempts to expand and enhance mainline campus ministry are under-documented. Only a few examples survive in the literature. One reported experiment was the unique experience of a small, six-year-old church in a college town that adopted the Clinical Pastoral Education (CPE) model to the training of its lay membership for campus and other ministry.[49] The CPE model was severely modified. There was less structure for theological reflection, for supervisor-student interaction, and it lacked the intense peer-group experiences that encouraged the personal growth that is one of the chief benefits of the CPE model. Because the participating laity ministered in a variety of settings, experience was not always readily transferable from one setting to another. The conclusion of the experiment was that while the CPE model failed in the parish setting, the discipline of case study based on practical ministry did expand the congregation's caring ministries. The model reveals that at least someone was willing to venture creatively into uncharted waters.

This being said, adventure was not a high priority in 1979. Dissatisfaction with national leadership, or the perceived vacuum

---

[47] Ibid., 158, 165.

[48] Ibid., 166–67.

[49] John M. Mann, "Use of the CPE Model in Developing Congregational Campus Ministry," *The Journal of Pastoral Care* 32 (September 1978): 191–99.

therein, fed a burgeoning nostalgia. People lamented the loss of "the way things used to be." Campus ministers, especially those who had been around for any length of time in the profession, were particularly prone to reminiscence. As is often the case of nostalgia, it was not that the past had really been so much better; the pain of the moment only made it seem so.

It was legitimately a time to look back, to reflect, in order to look forward with a clearer vision. In 1979 Leo Sandon, Jr., re-examined the Danforth Study on its tenth anniversary. He concluded that the study had had little measurable impact on the church, the university, or social policy, but it had been influential for campus ministers. Its key social statement was the primary importance of the university; its key theological statement was H. Richard Niebuhr's radical monotheism; and its key ethical statement was Niebuhr's responsible self.[50] Almost immediately, said Sandon, the study was received as dated. The Danforth study was met in 1970 with a "prevailing rhetoric that [was] radical, while the study came across as establishment reformism."[51] The following decade, he maintained, represented a retreat from the prophetic and governance modes that Underwood emphasized and had moved toward localism. Ecumenical commitments waned and denominations truncated all specialized ministries. Sandon felt that, for the 1980s, campus ministry might well emphasize the functions of prophetic inquiry and interdisciplinary approaches to ministry articulated in the Danforth report. Commenting on the pictures sent from Apollo 8 in 1968, Sandon wrote:

> As an international community of memory and hope, the church has the perspective and the spiritual resources to contribute to meaning and a sense of fraternity, which are the great needs of our time. In the local congregation persons can experience supportive, nurturing community and know that the local group is the microcosm of the catholic macrocosm.[52]

Overall, Sandon concluded, the Danforth study's "essential vision is painfully appropriate to the decade ahead."[53]

---

[50] Leo Sandon, Jr., "Prophetic Inquiry and the Danforth Study," *The Christian Century* 96 (February 1979): 128.
[51] Ibid., 129.
[52] Ibid., 140.
[53] Ibid.

Later in the same year, *The Christian Century* published "a sympo-sium on current concerns in campus ministry."[54] Rabbi Daniel Leifer of the University of Chicago wrote that after the 1967 and 1973 Arab-Israeli wars and the ethnic and racial revivals, "Like everyone else on this planet, the Jews have swung closer to the particularism and away from the universalism of their heritage."[55] Robert L. Johnson of the University of North Carolina at Chapel Hill, wrote of the campus despair echoed in the songs of Jackson Browne and James Taylor: "The power of death, the immensity of space, the certainty of entropy, the 'long-distance loneli-ness,' the fragility of community, our political paralysis...."[56] Davida Crabtree, Director of the Greater Hartford Area Campus Ministry, which encompassed four institutions, maintained that economic issues predom-inated. She saw her task as working for greater partnership between the church and the university, to help the church see that campus ministry is two-way and not just a mission of the church to the university. The dan-gers of parish-based campus ministry, from her perspective, consisted of the campus minister's temptation and/or tendency to manage the status quo instead of leading, deferring to the congregation's needs over the needs of students or the university, and the temptation of the church to think that parish-based campus ministries can replace full-time campus ministers—a fallacy, Crabtree believed.[57] Joseph C. Williamson, a pastor in Boston, provided a different point of view, suggesting that a parish base provides a critical distance from the power structures of the university and allows the church to guard its integrity.[58] While no unified sense of purpose is discernable in the symposium, it is clear that practitioners were thinking and strategizing for the future.

Ecumenical Ventures

In 1974 the Lilly Endowment granted $1.5 million to establish the National Institute for Campus Ministries (NICM). The three-year grant enabled the foundation of an organization to serve Protestant, Jewish and Catholic campus ministries. It was intended that after the first three years, NICM would receive funding from its sponsoring judicatories. The NICM initiative grew out of the National Center for Campus Ministry

---

[54] "A Ministry to Students: A Symposium on Current Concerns in Campus Ministry," *The Christian Century* 96 (17 October 1979): 1002.
[55] Ibid.
[56] Ibid., 1003.
[57] Ibid., 1004–1005.
[58] Ibid., 1006.

which, by the early 1970s, was pronounced moribund. Myron Bloy, of the Episcopal Church, was one of the incorporators and saw NICM as a means for equipping campus ministers with a theological rationale for their work. He suggested that campus ministers did not know their role; he implied that neither did the churches—else the support of an independent foundation and the creation of an institute might not have been necessary.[59]

Within this shifting environment there were attempts to exercise greater creativity in campus ministry. While the ecumenical models of the UMHE type, from which the United Methodists withdrew and some other denominations decreased financial support, were less prominent, more voluntary cooperation at the local level could be seen. This tendency was likely most pronounced in the Episcopal Church and grew out of accords with Catholics and Lutherans in this period. Local covenants between Episcopal and Catholic dioceses and/or Lutheran synods encouraged the campus ministry community. For example, a covenant between the Catholic and Episcopal campus ministries at The College of William & Mary in Virginia allowed full participation in all aspects of ministry excepting the Eucharist. In time, local guidelines even made provision for eucharistic sharing. But each ministry retained its paid ordained leadership, effectively doubling its capabilities. Out of this effort many shared programs, including a student drama company, grew and prospered. A Lutheran and Episcopal venture of similar scope and design was organized at the University of Minnesota at Minneapolis-St. Paul about the same time. Such partnerships, often involving students and lay leadership in prominent roles, nevertheless relied heavily upon the personalities of the campus ministers and their initiative and commitment to ecumenical relationships.

Programmatic initiatives also opened avenues between previously estranged partners. Cordial relationships were sometimes made with InterVarsity Christian Fellowship (IVCF), whose skill at motivating student leadership to organize dormitory-based Bible study and prayer

---

[59] "A Boon to Campus Ministry," editorial in *Christian Century* 91 (18 September 1974): 836. It is interesting that Bloy assumed that campus ministers did not know their role because they were unable to communicate their role and their function to the churches they served. It was an odd twist that revealed a reversal of relationship: if campus ministry was to serve the church, why was the burden of mission placed upon the servant? Was it not the responsibility of the church to articulate, or at least assist in the articulation of, its mission on campus? Bloy's assertion is indicative of the distance that stood between the church and its mission to higher education.

complemented the sacramental and/or social ministry offerings of main-line campus ministries. Because IVCF eschewed denominational identity, yet encouraged church membership and participation, there was no conflict of loyalties other than those posed by constraints upon student time.

Cooperation with Catholics in the 1970s brought to the Episcopal and other mainline churches the creative energies of the Cursillo movement, a program of spiritual catechism originally developed in Europe to recover lapsed church members and provide an intensive reorientation to the church through a structured weekend retreat. Adaptations of the Cursillo model brought the structured retreat design to high school youths and, in time, to college-age young adults. The design proved ideal for the highly mobile, spiritually introspective populations of all ages who struggled at the edges of the churches. Because the weekend retreat represented a limited commitment of time and the design established a pattern for sustaining long-term relationship beyond the weekend, such experiences sometimes netted impressive results. The experience was so salutary for individuals that some, previously marginalized, gained new self-confidence, identified sound gifts within themselves, found a foundation for their ministries in renewed commitment to Christian community, and achieved leadership within their campus or parish settings.

MOVING BEYOND DIS-APPOINTMENT

As the decade of the 1970s neared its end, campus ministry had come to terms with its dis-appointment—that is, that the denominations were unclear as to what they wanted from campus ministry and, therefore, could not determine what resources campus ministry needed to get the job done. Even in The United Methodist Church, where both appreciation and funding continued to support it, campus ministry was joined by many other concerns. In no sense was campus ministry any denomination's favored child. In this time a generation of campus ministers, some whose careers spanned nearly the scope of this study, approached retirement. Another generation, many of them members of the baby-boom, were taking up these ministries.

Because of its marginal character, campus ministry attracted a tremendous diversity of ordained leadership. In the Episcopal Church, for example, though women were ordained there were few parochial positions that would employ them. A number of them found their entry into ordained service through campus ministry. Increased support for Black campuses, made possible by the reforms of the civil-rights era, secured more chaplaincies in those schools. Gay and lesbian clergy found a place in ministries that welcomed creativity and afforded some distance from parochial scrutiny. The community of campus ministry, though sometimes bereft of financial resources, also enjoyed the freedom of its isolation. In spite of—or perhaps even because of—its imposed weakness, it found a new strength in new relationships and alliances, and—in many places—in its smallness.

In many ways campus ministry was uniquely poised to greet the coming decade. Maintaining respectful distance from, but a continuing affiliation with, the supporting denominational structures, campus ministry was less a ministry *of* the churches. It was a ministry in its own right and, increasingly, on its own terms. Neither beyond or behind, campus ministry was—in nearly every conceivable sense of the expression—the church *beside* itself.

—⚐ 6 ⚐—

SEARCHING FOR NEW APPOINTMENT FOR THE CHURCH ON CAMPUS: 1980–1990

INTRODUCTION

Mainline campus ministry met 1980 with a distinct advantage. In the fifteen years from 1965 to 1980, campus ministries had from one perspective "taken it on the chin." As the baby boom cohort aged and thus changed the demographics, as social priorities claimed a greater share of diminishing denominational resources, campus ministry was pushed farther from the centers of denominational concern at the national level. Campus ministry was also pushed farther from the centers of denominational governance. In their marginality, campus ministries were challenged earlier than most specialized ministries to take responsibility for themselves. They were, with few exceptions, not identified with the college or university administration. They were relatively remote from denominational, even local, judicatory authority. They were in some cases—as in the case of the Episcopal ministries—even beyond canons, whose preoccupation with parochial structures neglected any ministry that did not conform to that model. They were, in their marginality, specially situated for the 1980s.

In other respects, too, campus ministry gained advantage. Wuthnow reported that in 1970 only 21 percent of the adult population over the age of 25 had completed at least some college education; by 1980 that figure had grown to 32 percent. While denominations exhibited grave—near hysterical—concern over shrinkage in church membership, campuses saw an increase in enrollments, which rose from 8.6 million in 1970 to 12.1 million in 1980. As other institutions shored up wobbly finances and wondered whence the next penny would come, higher education expenditures increased from $23.4 billion in 1970 to $50.7 billion in 1980. Higher education even enjoyed a favored position in the American economy since two-thirds of all American exports were in high-technology industry, and that field was growing.[1] Roof and McKinney rehearsed similar statistics and concluded that the consequences of these demographic changes to organized religion were manifold:

> It must accommodate a more informed and less parochial constituency, adjust to new cultural orientations and values brought on by expanding scientific and technological constituencies, bridge gaps between better educated and less on a wide range of social, political, and moral issues, conform divisions between those arguing for symbolic interpretation of Scriptures and those insisting on a more literal approach. Perhaps no aspect of change in the social basis of American religion has produced greater strains in the past couple of decades than the shifts in education and class.[2]

Campus ministry, by 1980, was positioned as one of the few ministries—perhaps the only ministry—of the church that enjoyed sufficient distance from structures of authority that were held in suspicion *and* sufficient proximity to a growing proportion of the population, at precisely the point where that population was bridging the personal transitions from one level of education and class to another. That such opportunity was present seems evident from our present perspective; how the institutions of academy and church, and, more pointedly, campus ministry, responded to such opportunity in their own time was, however, uneven.

Some campus ministries realized the advantage and acted upon it with unusual creativity and much hard work; individual examples could be noted in all denominations. These campus ministries took initiative and developed and encouraged new styles of organization and leadership. Surrounded as they were by a new generation of descendants of old Tom Paine, who maintained "My mind is my church," a generation

---

[1] Wuthnow, *Restructuring*, 167.
[2] Roof & McKinney, 65–66.

characterized well by Robert Bellah's "Sheila"—whose religion was so personal she identified it as "Sheilaism"[3]—some campus ministers despaired, but others adopted the style of the apostle Paul at Athens, respecting any foreign altar as evidence of a religious sensibility open to conversation.

CAMPUS:
THE PURSUIT OF SELF-INTEREST

Since all students did not conform to a single design, it is difficult to determine what, if anything, they held in common. Perhaps their most common characteristic was a self-interest that had little experience of or appreciation for popularized familial and communal values that reflected more nostalgia than reality.

United Methodist bishops, using a phrase echoed by leaders in other denominations and non-denominational evangelical churches, called for a return to the "sanctity of the home."[4] Home for the student of 1980 was not as the bishops may have recalled it. Between 1967 and 1977 the divorce rate in America doubled.[5] In 1969, 55 percent of the mothers of first-year collegians were full-time homemakers; by 1979 only 29 percent were.[6] The students' sense that the world was falling apart, and that survival was to be found within, came from a long and early experience of loss and childhood retreat into self. Even in the most traditionally configured households, patterns of living had changed considerably by the 1980s. Changes in the African-American household wrought by social policy were manifold. Some households were adversely affected by economic conditions that split families, creating more single-parent households. In other instances, a rising African-American middle and upper class frequently competed with the prevailing culture on its own terms, and paid comparable costs in divorce, overwork, and ambition. Students from African-American and from ethnic communities new to America were under increased pressure to achieve, either to carry the family into a new generation of prosperity and security or to safeguard and advance a status already, but only tentatively achieved. In all house-

---

3 Bellah, 221.

4 *Journal of the United Methodist Church* (1980), vol 1, ed. John L. Schreiber, 188–89.

5 Arthur Levine, *When Dreams and Heroes Died* (San Francisco: Carnegie Foundation for the Advancement of Teaching, 1980), 14.

6 Ibid.

holds, regardless of status or race, increased mobility and patterns of family relationships tended to minimize time spent together as family and often eroded the quality of what time there was in the family setting.

For some students, painful experience in the loss of a mother or father, and even siblings, to divorce made them careful of intimacy and shy of affiliations that required the risk of friendship. Some knew the destructive patterns of an alcoholic parent, or an abusive one. Some struggled with sexuality and the uncertainty that attends such revelation in society. Some wrestled with womanhood or manhood, insecure in what gender signified in them and would require of them. Some negotiated the difference of race or ethnicity that was traced in their features and in the skin, this difference setting them apart from their contemporaries on campus, their presence on campus setting them apart from their contemporaries at home.

For some the lack of experience with intimacy drove them deeper within. Guarded in themselves, these students, when they chose to engage with campus ministry, did so tentatively. They sought the places that made no immediate claim and that in respectful distance conveyed a welcome. Others sought just the opposite: communities of discipline and sizeable number, where behavior was easily defined and codified, and the crowds sufficient to guarantee anonymity in conformity. For these, the evangelical organizations held greater attraction.

The generation of students on campus in the 1980s have been characterized as selfish, "me"-centered. The label was likely wrong; it was certainly unfairly applied if limited only to them. Like their parents, these students sought recovery from a chaos they did not fully comprehend and thus frightened them all the more. They were part of an entire society that was turned inward and more conservative. Horowitz interviewed students on campus in this period and asked them to clarify the pressures with which they lived. As one student responded,

> It's fear of not having what you have right now....What I consider to be successful...is maintaining the comfort level that you grew up with, basically....Now there is a lot of pressure because we're starting out at this level and now we have to say this is where we want to be....We're running six figures for married people with two children.[7]

The situation of an earlier generation had been completely reversed. Those who had known the deprivations of the Great Depression and the

---

7 Horowitz, 266.

struggle of World War II easily envisioned a better world and one of more affluence than had preceded their own time. Their children and grandchildren, who knew the deprivations of affluence and the cost of influence, feared a worse world and one of less power than had preceded their time. The former generations, rich in relationships and poor in goods, had parlayed family ties and party loyalties into affluence and prestige. The latter generations, rich in goods and bereft of intimacy, sought to parlay money and influence into security and relationship. Lacking that, they would succumb to fatalism and a concomitant hedonism. As Arthur Levine assessed them, there was "a growing belief among college students that, if they are doomed to ride on the Titanic, they ought at least to make the trip as pleasant—make that as lavish—as possible and go first class, for they assume there is nothing better."[8]

The students of 1980 were the first generation for whom *in loco parentis* was a dead issue.[9] They were, therefore, the first generation of students to enjoy the autonomy of true young *adulthood*. But they were ill-equipped to embrace adult autonomy. In 1969 a survey of first-year college students indicated that 82 percent of them thought that developing a meaningful philosophy of life was essential or very important; in 1979 only 53 percent of their counterparts held the same opinion.[10] Unlike their parents and grandparents, this generation grew up in an era of governmental and institutional disintegration; their civics lessons were gleaned from television, from televised hearings on Watergate and similar disclosures of malfeasance in authorities. Neither did they grow up with religious education. For the most part, they were only nominal church-goers and their churches were not particularly inclined to teach them.

These factors alone, however, do not account for the totality of a changed life on campus. Just as there were changes in students and in the churches, so too were there changes in the colleges and universities that contributed to the dominance of self-interest in the 1980s. David Riesman wrote of the relationship between the rise of consumerism in American society and its effect upon the academic community.[11] Schools expanded

---

8 Levine, 105.

9 Ibid., 129. It should be noted that, while students may want freedoms that are incompatible with ideas of in loco parentis, students, parents, and administrators expect the university to provide services (such as counseling) that can be construed as parental functions.

10 Ibid., 112.

11 David Riesman, *On Higher Education* (San Francisco: Jossey-Bass, 1980).

in the 1970s, despite the demographic projections of lower young adult enrollments, creating a more competitive market in the education business. Colleges and universities grew more conscious of public relations and marketing, and students became a more powerful determinant, dictating by preference and choice the shape of the academy in much the same way consumers shape products in the market. As schools sought to attract students to campus, features that students deemed attractive and desirable were more frequently accommodated, and features deemed onerous or unpopular were eliminated.[12]

Together, the heightened consumer orientation of schools, the shift in power from faculty and administration to student and public opinion, the increased responsibility accorded student young adults and their lack of preparedness to exercise it, and above all, the conspicuous absence of religion at the heart of it all contributed to what Robert Rankin identified as a loss of "spirit" in higher education.

CAMPUS MINISTRY

A New Appreciation for Tradition

Those campus ministers and ministries that were most effective in the 1980s may trace a goodly measure of that effectiveness to rootedness and confidence in a particular tradition. While a breadth of ecumenism was necessary to open conversation, grounding in a particular tradition was necessary to prevent loss of a center. In the 1980s it was not the lowest common denominator, but the highest integrity that served best. Paradoxically, while Americans eschewed denominations in greater numbers in the 1980s, they were no less respectful of distinctiveness. How to be distinctive without being dogmatic (in the derogatory usage of that word) was an issue of exceeding importance.[13]

Tradition, a virtual synonym for "stagnation" and "irrelevance" in the late 1960s, was appreciated anew. The "fear of forsaking...heritage"[14] was one of the most pervasive forces in the mainline denominational churches in the 1980s. This fear was often conservative for the best of

---

[12] Riesman, 7.

[13] Peter Berger, *The Sacred Canopy* (Garden City: Anchor Books, 1969). Berger explored a market model of ecumenism. In the market, pure competition is too costly in money and image, but the market will not bear just one religious product. Different packaging needed to identify—and justify —separate entities.

[14] *Journal of the United Methodist Church*, vol. 1 (1980), 180.

reasons; it was "conservative" in the genuine meaning of that word. It was that respectful fear that was the necessary attendant to a time of change, a time given over to dealing with the real crisis, or turning point, of this generation—the changing shape of authority. Affecting that change required attentiveness to conserving the fundamental principles of one's religious heritage. Whether it was the fundamentals of Christianity in the broadest sense or the foundational principles of a given denomination, attention to this conservation was an important part of the transition from what had been known to what was yet to be.

The Continuing Turn Inward

Part of the renewed desire to conserve stemmed from the multivalent quest for a personal faith. Churched and unchurched citizens alike drifted away from social concerns to attend to personal ones. For the churched the drift sometimes led to a passivity that was characterized by its detractors as apathy. There is scant evidence to support that designation. People did continue to feel, sometimes quite deeply, about many important issues; that they did not always feel for others as deeply as they felt for themselves represented not a lack of feeling, but rather a re-directing of feeling. Having been exhorted to get in touch with their feelings, they did just that. And having been encouraged to look after themselves, to literally take care, they sought those communities and ministries that supported them.

Some did, indeed, adopt a modern quietism, retreating into self even as they remained within the accustomed pew. These stayed in place, but tuned out. They rarely initiated conflict, but their mere presence was considered a stumbling block to activism since that quiet presence anchored communities eager to sail. Others opted to leave familiar pews and sought out new ones in the growing number of full-service consumer-oriented churches that met their wants in services and activities promising a high degree of anonymity—a place to be alone with others—and a low expectation of commitment.

Others espoused small-group life under discipline as a spiritual journey to changed behaving and believing. Alcoholics Anonymous, the first modern para-church to pioneer the use of a structured discipline based upon religious principles to reverse addictive behavior, gradually spawned constellation groups to assist those enmeshed in the systems of addiction. In the 1980s similar groups proliferated for treatment of drug addiction; compulsive sexual addictions, including sexual abuse; physical abuse; and eating disorders—with similar ancillary groups for friends and family members whose lives are affected by the principle in treatment. These small-group programs helped many people find a point of affiliation around common interest or issue, even as they assisted the community and culture in identifying long-denied abuse and educating to destigmatize and promote positive disciplines for ordered recovery.

Not everyone who turned inwards stayed there. Sometimes the journey inwards was to gain strength for life in the world. On some campuses, new methods of Bible study achieved remarkable results with students. Students in a drama group chose plays with a biblical or justice theme and, as part of their preparation, read and studied relevant portions of the Bible together. At Yale, students were organized into Bible study and prayer groups by gender affinity. Male students gathered to consider what it meant to live as men (and women as women), and undertook Bible study and reflection as a central component in their conversations. Programs like Habitat for Humanity and a host of work/study options, domestic and foreign, provided opportunity for integrated Bible study and social action.

Continuing Assessment

With the assistance of a Danforth Foundation grant, Rankin edited *The Recovery of Spirit in Higher Education* in 1980.[15] Rankin's book examined four faith groups—Jewish, Catholic, Protestant evangelical and Protestant liberal—and proposed "to explore three elements of faith and ministry...regarded as indispensable: spirituality, action, and community."[16] In his contribution, Parker Palmer opined that what was singularly absent from the time was any sense of wholeness, that culturally speaking there was no need for more surgeons, but a crying need for

---

[15]   In the preface, Gene L. Schwilck noted that the Danforth Foundation in its early years supported endowments and grants to encourage public and private universities to establish departments of religion, and had supported nearly seven hundred persons in study and research fellowships and internships in campus ministry. Additional grants had supported campus ministry projects in peace studies, ministries with minorities, women in campus ministry, values education, and discussions among evangelical, charismatic, and ecumenical campus ministries. Rankin's book represented one of the last campus ministry projects underwritten by Danforth, a foundation established to "serve the needs of young men and women, particularly their educational needs, with special emphasis upon the cultural and spiritual aspects of education." Gene L. Schwilck, preface, *Recovery of Spirit*, ix.; "The Program of the Danforth Seminary Interns," (St. Louis: Danforth Foundation, 1957), 3.

[16]   Robert Rankin, "Beginnings," *Recovery of Spirit*, 18.

persons who could sew.[17] Palmer saw the campus minister as one who could create "a clearing in which members of the university can see past the thickets of disciplinary fragmentation, the biases of class and culture which hedge in the campus, into the needs of the world community, the yearnings of the human heart, the divine requirement for love and justice."[18] It is not enough to see beyond "the surface of cultural illusions"; the campus minister must also see "beyond the brokenness as well."[19]

Ronald Sider, in his essay, posited that "…the only solid foundation for campus ministry in the 1980s is a thoroughly biblical—and therefore thoroughly radical—faith."[20] Sider noted that a biblical foundation demands confession across the spectrum of Christianity—that both evangelical and liberal Christians have their failures to confess. Evangelicals must accept culpability for neglecting biblical imperatives to do justice and seek to amend it; liberals must do likewise for their neglect of evangelism and lack of fidelity to the central biblical doctrines of the faith.[21]

Community was the theme of Myron Bloy's essay. "The basic business of human culture is to devise stratagems, like the family or like the tribe, to help us mitigate" the fight between the human desires to be in and to flee community.[22] By the 1980s this was the toughest of all businesses for the campus minister. Not only did the very structures of campus life—which were highly individualistic, competitive, mobile,

---

[17] Parker J. Palmer, "Contemplation and Action in Higher Education," *Recovery of Spirit*, 107.

[18] Ibid., 103.

[19] Ibid., 105, 111.

[20] Ronald Sider, "Resurrection and Liberation," *Recovery of Spirit*, 157.

[21] Ibid. Sider rightly points to the catholicity demanded of campus ministry. Beyond the limited notions of ecumenism—limited in the sense that ecumenism might better have been defined as inter-Christian relations—remained an advancing array of non-Christian faith communities to be considered, and a swelling variety of perspectives within each denomination to be taken into account. Campus ministries that persistently neglected these realities, or purposely denied them, would not likely continue. Those which met the decade well and survived it engendered respect for diversity, including respect for evangelical/liberal differences. Dialogue with Catholics and Jews constituted but one part of the conversation; collegial cooperation with InterVarsity Christian Fellowship and similar evangelical campus initiatives were important in honoring pluralism and encouraging scriptural study. Solid, biblical preaching assisted the formation of a biblical faith by taking maximum advantage of the worship gatherings that constituted for many students their primary contact with the church, either in the local community or on campus.

[22] Myron B. Bloy, Jr., "The Ministries of Faith Communities," *Recovery of Spirit*, 202.

and overcommitted—militate against the formation of community, but neither faculty nor students seemed to have any experience by which to ascertain or access the components of community. The disciplines of research which prevailed over the skills of teaching made many faculty introspective and asocial. Preoccupation with study and achievement, heavily influenced by television and computers, retarded the social skills of students. Bloy observed that when one does run across a community of faith in academia, it usually is spiritually disciplined, morally engaged, theologically reflective, and collegially led.[23]

Joseph C. Williamson contributed a piece on "A Mainline Parish-based Protestant Ministry with Students," a report of a federated parish whose ecclesiology was based not on conversion or sacraments as means of grace, but the covenant community itself.[24] The leadership, clergy and lay, wanted students to affiliate with them, but within certain boundaries set by the congregation. Anyone wishing to join ought to care about the city and its people and be able to live in the tension between religion and politics. The congregation's leaders thought of the church as a "nonsectarian sect."[25] The uniquely interdenominational nature of the congregation set it apart from the denominational norm, a distinction that was both asset and liability. The congregation did have sufficient sense of itself that it could set conditions for affiliation that served both to introduce the congregation to any inquirer and to define the congregation's mission. But the conditional nature of congregational affiliation made student or faculty participation a self-selected option; thus the

---

[23] Ibid., 212–13. Campus ministries that were able to envision and encourage new models of community made significant strides. Emphasis upon diversity, patience with reticence, and sensitivity to time constraints encouraged lively small-group interaction and sometimes built up campus communities of impressive size. Students indicated that these qualities, which distinguished campus ministry from fraternity and sorority life, and from what they recalled as homogeneous congregational structures that demanded conformity, attracted them and nurtured them in these campus ministries.

An informal poll of approximately 60 students active in campus ministry from 1976 to 1990 solicited reflections on their experience. The responses of nearly 40 students yielded information used here and elsewhere in this study.

[24] Joseph C. Williamson, "A Mainline Parish-based Protestant Ministry with Students," *Recovery of Spirit*, 288–89.

[25] Ibid., 292. Denominational parish-based campus ministries can be hampered by similar expectations that preclude invitation to, or tolerance of, the tentative seeker. Reconciling this tension was often a key component in reaching the campus population and continues to be an important consideration, especially when it is suggested that more campus ministries be based in near-campus congregations.

congregation served largely as a congregation of the converted, a community based upon shared commitment to specified programs and principles.

Concluding reflections by Rankin observed that his three dimensions—spirituality, action, community—were interwoven but the communities of faith were not. "I found that, while I longed for catholicity in our relationships, the realities, the needs, and the hopes for campus ministry now and in the immediate future, and recovery of Spirit through them, lie in the mystery and power of the differences among the four faith groups."[26] He proposed that "...the new denominationalism might reinvigorate campus ministry."[27]

But Rankin also expressed his concern that campus ministers had cut themselves off from the churches, and that the Danforth Foundation— via its support for professional campus ministry associations and conferences—may have been an unwitting accomplice to this estrangement. Two years later, in 1982, in a different publication, Rankin reflected upon Danforth's involvement in campus ministry projects and their decision to withdraw from those projects.[28] The work of Danforth did, in his estimation, help enlist the interest and aid of the Lilly Endowment, whose support insured that some important work in this area of religious concern would continue. Lilly funded the establishment of the National Institute for Campus Ministries—not for the purpose of pursuing the formation of social policy, which had guided the Danforth initiative under Underwood's direction, but "for the professional development of campus ministers and others in the academy concerned about the spiritual health of higher education."[29]

Rankin's concern was legitimate. The distance and distrust that separated campus ministry from the church and from the university was the most prevalent and pressing problem of the period. The NICM, though excellent at encouraging interfaith and interdisciplinary conversation, did little to foster rapprochement among these essential, yet estranged, partners in the campus ministry enterprise. That work fell largely to the campus ministers themselves. It was—and continues to be—hard work, requiring time, energy, and patience. It calls the diplomatic function of ministry to the fore. The apostle Paul's notion that

---

[26] Robert Rankin, "Reflections," *Recovery of Spirit*, 307.

[27] Ibid., 309.

[28] Robert Rankin, "Comments on Campus Ministry as the Church's Phoenix," *The NICM Journal* 7 (Summer 1982).

[29] Ibid., 76.

Christian ministry includes functioning as ambassadors (2 Corinthians 5:20; Ephesians 6:20) is borne out in the experience of those who seek to establish renewed ministries on campus through the healing of old relationships and the making of new ones.

Andrew Foster explored the ministries of his Episcopal colleagues in the early 1980s.[30] In reports of his impressions he noted some pronounced distinctions that set the campus ministers of this period apart from their immediate predecessors. Among the more striking observations was his impression that campus ministers of the 1980s had recovered a sense of the "priestly" component of their ministry. In the wake of the Danforth report, which had placed primary emphasis upon governance, priestly ministry connoted only something external. The priestly dimension of campus ministry, as Foster interpreted the Danforth report, was simply the category under which religious worship services and related functions were filed. It was not a dimension that seemed in the Danforth study to inform the role or the self-identity of the campus minister. Foster's observation may well have originated from specific and fundamental differences between Anglicans and their Reformation siblings. But beyond those distinctions, the phenomenon he encountered did signify that something had changed in the ministers themselves, and that "something" was worth pondering.

"The last thing I expected to find in my travels and conversations with Episcopal chaplains," wrote Foster, "was a resurgence of and strong emphasis upon the particularly priestly functions in campus ministry. What did surprise me, however, was that at the heart of all my conversations there was a deep affirmation expressed about this aspect of our work and identity, even at a time when I expected the chaplains to be most perplexed and demoralized."[31] This reaffirmation of the priestly was not a revival of a liturgical role or the affectation of prelacy. These campus ministers did not perceive themselves to be the dispensers of correct theology or spiritual answers or the examples of model Christian behavior; nor did they believe others perceived them as such. It was a shift of some subtlety, "a movement away from an exemplary role and towards an emblematic role in society."[32]

In their priestly role, these campus ministers considered themselves a bridge,

---

[30] Andrew Foster, "Campus Ministry: Discoveries on the Road," *Ministry Development Journal* (Fall 1984): 4–8.

[31] Ibid., 7.

[32] Ibid., 8.

...a living connection between the Church and the university, between Christian belief and cultural unbelief, between people who have encountered God and those who are still searching. Even when not pursuing an overtly religious agenda, much of the priestly role is played out by staying in touch with networks which exist on campus, connecting people with one another, and people with issues of vital importance.[33]

What Foster found, it seems, was an evolutionary adaptation in the campus minister. These ministers, perhaps in ways different from their predecessors, came to campus ministry with a different experience of both the church and the university, one that was particularly well-suited to the time and the reality. For them, the marginality of campus ministry was not exile, but opportunity. To borrow an image that John Fortunato developed in his own study of gay and lesbian spirituality, these campus ministers knew the strength of "embracing the exile."[34] Many of them knew from the outset the difficulty of their ministry and had accepted it willingly as challenge and opportunity. Also, many of them shared the ambivalence of society toward both the university and the church, a love-hate relationship that gave them deep affection for and critical distance from each. Consequently, in their willingness to confess this tension they established their affinity with many in both institutions, and others found within them a sympathetic meeting place.

Where a previous generation had organized vigorous, vocal protest of institutions, these campus ministers took a different tack. Instead of marshalling extremes into confrontation with each other, they were more inclined to work both ends against the middle. They encouraged student, faculty, and administrators to undertake their own ministries. Aided by liturgical and theological changes within the churches, and unhindered by custom in ministries that changed rapidly with transient populations, they provided education and opportunity to a growing body of laity. In this regard they were, much as Shockley indicated, "the church beyond itself."

New Wine in New Skins: A New Student Movement

The early 1980s marked a turning point for mainline campus ministries in the revival of student leadership. Campus ministries that did well throughout the troubled time between 1965 and 1980 were those

---

33 Ibid., 7.
34 John Fortunato, *Embracing the Exile: Healing Journeys of Gay Christians* (San Francisco: Harper, 1987).

that gave the students themselves authority and guidance. Authority alone rarely suffices to sustain any campus organization; the transiency of student generations and the seasonal nature of the academic year make it difficult for student organizations to survive. Their lives are too fragmented in too many different and legitimate ways to allow for stability. But neither is guidance alone sufficient, for it can too easily translate into authoritarianism and control. If anything marks the 1980s it was a new collegiality between campus ministers and their primary constituency: the students.

At the local level this collegiality was evident in the proliferation of "peer ministries," the practice of identifying natural student leaders within the community, equipping them, and authorizing them to conduct much of the important work of ministry with their peers on campus. In some instances, student peer ministers were stipended; in others they were volunteers. Some were designated as peer ministers, others functioned in the role but as leaders of their campus ministry organization—members of student "vestries" or boards.

Students also took a prominent role in regional campus ministry. In one province of the Episcopal Church, for example, an annual campus ministry conference organized and planned by the campus ministers was given over entirely to a student team drawn from participating campuses. The campus ministers made themselves available as "consultants" to the planning team and offered initial guidance and training in conference planning and design, but remanded full responsibility to the students themselves. Shared leadership improved the quality of the conferences: themes pertinent to student interest were addressed by speakers and learning designs selected by the students, which in turn increased student participation. Division of labor lightened the load while including more people. Wider participation enhanced diversity. Governance issues actually became less of a problem. When considering the options for the social components of the conference, even students who were of legal age to consume beer and wine elected for non-alcoholic refreshments out of respect for their peers who were active in Alcoholics Anonymous and similar programs.

Denominational student gatherings in many mainline churches had ended in 1969 or shortly thereafter, as the student movement collapsed. In the early 1980s, however, Presbyterians, United Methodists, and Episcopalians restored national student gatherings. Usually held over the year-end, Christmas/New Year academic break, these conferences drew 300-500 students from each denomination to events that included addresses by and conversation with noted lay and religious figures; small, peer-led group sessions on widely ranging topics and concerns, such as human sexuality, alcohol and substance abuse, fundamentalism, and intimacy; Bible study and worship; and recreational sports. The revitalized meetings were different in several respects from their predecessors. Though students had a major role in planning the conferences, emphasis was not placed on the creation of a student hierarchy or bureaucracy.

The Episcopal gathering in 1983, the first in nearly 30 years for that denomination,[35] probably represented the extreme in this regard. A student planning team with representation from the nine provinces of the Episcopal Church worked with national staff and representative campus ministers to design a gathering that included no mechanism for the election of officers and no formal business sessions for the deliberation of policy. Instead, the entire conference was given to education and community. The result was a gathering that emphasized connection and communion, while respecting difference.

Rapprochement with the University

Within the universities in the 1970s and 1980s administration of student life and services achieved the status of a specialized profession. Demand for student services brought personnel trained in student organization and recreation, mental health and preventive medicine. Deans of Students and their advisory staff, previously drawn from the academic faculty, were more often hired from an increasing pool of specialists in academic administration. These administrators seemed more amenable to collegial relations with other professionals. Many of them recognized and valued the contributions that campus ministries made on campus. On one campus, for example, a modest accounting of the campus ministries revealed that the religious community held over $5 million in real estate assets, and devoted nearly $1.5 million annually to staff and program expenses—all a voluntary contribution to campus life.[36] Administrators and campus ministers worked together on the hard issues present on the modern campus. Increased diversity in the dormitories and classrooms meant the increased possibility of prejudiced or bigoted behavior as students encountered the different. The virulence of racism and sexism were particularly troublesome. Race-related and sexuality-related harassment sometimes issued in acts of vandalism or

---

[35] Except for one called "Morningstar" in 1974.

[36] Statistics are drawn from a survey in 1989 of campus ministries at the University of Chicago.

physical violence. As Marie Susan Hoffman observed in 1984, students of that era had much difficulty integrating any "faith life with their academic and social development."[37] Campus ministers were often helpful in mediating and providing education in the midst of such trouble. And campus administrators relied upon personal and professional associations with campus ministers in the adjudication of such problems.[38]

The Denominations: Which Vocation? What Resources?

As one after another the mainline churches faced the turning of the decade of the 1980s, each contrived to stimulate renewed vigor and numerical increases in membership and income through appeals to evangelism. Despite their protestations to the contrary, denominational officials were hard put to convince the more cynical members of the churches' lay and ordained leadership that their mission appeals were not just "church growth" schemes by lean and hungry wolves clad in fleecy clouds of theological rhetoric.

But what does evangelism look like on a campus? What would be its purpose? Wayne C. Olson, director of Metropolitan Indianapolis Campus Ministry, pointed to what would likely be an important component in the success of any evangelization enterprise when he suggested that campus ministry at a public college had become an exercise in remedial religion. By necessity, he maintained, campus ministry endeavored to supplement and even correct the teaching of well-meaning local congregations and pastors, as well as parents. Sometimes, he continued, students need help unlearning previous truth affirmations.[39]

It was true, to be sure, that campus ministry did frequently play such a corrective role in the lives of students previously acquainted with the church. Moreover, by the late 1980s the number of students with previous experience of Christian education—or any other religious education, for that matter—was a distinct minority on campus. More and more, the campus population was largely ignorant of religious tradition. Within this culture, evangelization of any kind would entail far more than encouragement and campaigns.

---

[37] Marie Susanne Hoffman, "Christian Vision in Academe," in "Symposium: Campus Ministry," *Theology Today* 41 (July 1984): 190.

[38] Courtney Leatherman, "Students and Administrators Turn to Religious Leaders for Help With Such Problems as Racism, Homophobia," *The Chronicle of Higher Education* (28 March 1990): A35–36.

[39] Wayne C. Olson, "Campus Ministry as Remedial Religion," *The Christian Century* 105 (13 April 1988): 381.

Joseph Kitagawa, former Dean of the University of Chicago Divinity School, was asked what he perceived to be the single greatest challenge to the mainline Christian churches in the last decade of the twentieth century. His reply was a simple one. Kitagawa maintained that Christianity, and mainline Christianity in particular, had become a "family affair." That is to say that the Christian story was familiar only within the confines of a particular family of people, and their sharing of the story heavily dependent upon an increasingly specialized vocabulary. Christians are quite good at and comfortable with the story, so long as the conversation is within that confined family. But there are fewer of such people in American society. There are more and more nominal Christians with little education in the specialized vocabulary and less experience of the liturgical routines of the church that function to convey this teaching. Moreover, half of those who say they are Christians do not know who delivered the Sermon on the Mount.[40] Documents like the United Methodist mission statement on grace are not likely to be comprehensible, then, even to the majority of the churched. Moreover, there are growing numbers of non-Christians in the culture, adherents of Islam, Buddhism, Judaism, and a host of other religious systems. To these, Kitagawa suggested, the telling of the story would present Christians with a new challenge. Christians will have to develop a whole new way of speaking about their religion and a new way of telling their story.[41]

Campus ministry would be a logical place to formulate apologetics, but if they were being produced, they went largely unreported. Robert Conn, in a paper written in 1984 for the National Committee on Campus Ministry of the United Methodist Board of Higher Education and Ministry, stated: "Sadly, at present, no coherent and accessible theology of higher education has captured the imagination of the church, nor has any vision of ministry in that setting. That doesn't mean campus ministries now reel in disorientation. It does mean that most denominations have paid scant attention to an important historical particularity."[42]

It was, perhaps, premature to expect a coherent vision for campus ministry so soon after the disarray of the 1960s and 1970s. But there was

---

[40] George H. Gallup, Jr., Robert Bezill ed., "Looking Ahead to the Year 2000," *Religion in America* (Princeton, NJ: Princeton Religion Research Center, 1990), 7.

[41] These viewpoints were related in private conversation between Joseph Kitagawa and Sam Portaro in 1989.

[42] Robert H. Conn, "Campus Ministry: A Mandate for Wholeness," *Plumbline* 12 (March 1984): 24.

a vision to be seen from a different vantage—at the local level, in scattered regions, and in periodic national assemblies of students. The role of the denomination was not to formulate or promulgate a theology or vision for campus ministry but rather that "the church must discover how to do some of its traditional religious tasks and do them in higher education. Those tasks are the development of community, a sense of vocation, and a drive for mission."[43] The tasks of ministry were being done in higher education and, in some instances, they were being done quite well. That they had not yet been fully *discovered* was an accurate observation. What the denominations at the national level lacked, especially in the Episcopal and Presbyterian cases, was not only a renewed vision for campus ministry, but also how and with what resources to re-equip—to re-appoint—campus ministry in order for that ministry to fulfill its vocation.

The General Assembly of the Presbyterian Church U.S.A.[44] accepted a Life and Mission Statement in 1985 that maintained:

> We are called to equip the body of Christ. The work of equipping involves the whole community. First of all, it includes the equipment of all members for their ministry of service in the work of the world to which their baptism has ordained them. Basic Christian education nourishes our vocation of servanthood. Leadership education equips those called and ordained to particular offices of ministry...because they furnish the leadership critical for the church community's life and work.[45]

Yet nowhere in the practical affairs of the church was there any indication that campus ministry might play a significant role in this work of equipping, and at a point in the lives of many young adults when vocation is uppermost in their consciousness.

This blindness may stem, in part, from the failure of the church to address the integration of vocation, a failure painfully evident in the confusion between vocation and career exhibited by parents and students alike, a confusion aided and abetted by the culture. Horowitz reported:

> One of the saddest voices I heard was that of a youth girding himself up for the law school that he did not want. I was disturbed not only by his resignation but also his failure to make a true choice. Much of grim professional-

---

[43] Ibid., 25.

[44] This denomination was formed by the merger of the UPCUSA and the Presbyterian Church U.S. in 1983.

[45] *Minutes of the Presbyterian Church* (1985), part 1, 50.

ism is mindless professionalism. And it can be enthusiastic as well as resigned. What characterizes both is calculation rather than experience.[46]

The prevailing contemporary experience of vocation is apparent in parental attitudes that separate work from religious activity and are passed on to children in vocational guidance that occasionally lapses into what could only be considered abuse—the violent refusal or diminishment of a child's genuine talents buried beneath parental expectations of conformity and productivity. The universities themselves are of little assistance, for as Ernest Boyer noted, universities have lost *their* sense of vocation: "Scrambling for students and driven by marketplace demands, many undergraduate colleges have lost their sense of mission. They are confused about their mission and how to impart shared values on which the vitality of both higher education and society depends."[47]

Reversing this trend is not easy, but campus ministries made some important progress. It is important for the church to have a solid sense of its own vocation, to be secure in its own mission, on campus and elsewhere. Shockley in 1985 suggested that the renaissance of denominational student conferences may have been, at least in part, an indication that students found denominational identity attractive and helpful to the shaping of their own identity.[48] Central to a denomination's identity is a clear understanding of what its specific gifts are and how they relate to the larger vocation of the Christian church. Institutional integrity has grown in importance in the wake of institutional crises of authority and credibility. The distinction between what a denomination says of itself and what it reveals of itself is essential to its evangelical mission.

The irony, and possible benefit, of the diversity hailed by mainline Protestant churches in the mid-1980s is that such diversity actually requires greater denominational integrity. In a more diverse society, especially on campus, religion found a new place. Though deprived of its historic dominance, it found a new power. No longer rejected for its arrogant assumption of superiority, or its authoritarian demands of conformity, religion—and American liberal Protestantism in particular—experienced a new attractiveness as a religion of choice.

---

[46] Horowitz, 272.

[47] Ernest L. Boyer, *College: The Undergraduate Experience in America* (New York: Harper and Row, 1987), 3.

[48] Donald G. Schockley, "Campus Ministry: A Contrarian Investment Strategy," *The Christian Century* 102 (23 October 1985): 952.

In a setting of increased diversity new demands pertain. As Boyer observed,

> All parts of campus life...must relate to one another and contribute to a
> sense of wholeness. We emphasize this commitment to community not out
> of a sentimental attachment to tradition, but because our democratic way of
> life and perhaps our survival as a people rest on whether we can move
> beyond self-interest and begin to understand better the realities of our de-
> pendence on each other.[49]

Campus ministries in the 1980s played an important role in those places where they were able to add to the diversity of the individual's and the community's experience of the specific lessons to be learned of and within a specific religious tradition and context. The specific gift of liberal Protestantism, as obvious as it may seem, is its liberality. That is not to say that this gift is superior to the other gifts of other churches or faiths. It is to suggest, however, that the integrity of liberal Protestantism resides in its attempt to hold in communion a diversity of opinion.

In this regard mainline, liberal Protestantism is well-suited to the modern campus. Roof and McKinney discovered in their research that people found the demythologized beliefs of the liberal churches more congruent with life.[50] They also reported in 1987 that almost 40 percent of the nation's adult population is aged 18-34;[51] but that population is underrepresented in the mainline Protestant churches. United Methodism's claim to twenty-eight percent is likely the highest representation of that age group in any of the churches in this study. Young adults are far better represented in the conservative churches and, compared with moderate and liberal Protestants, the conservative churches are more successful at holding onto their members.[52] No one to our knowledge has yet examined whether conservative churches hold youth by conscious design or because of maturational and social factors that make a conservative model more attractive to youth seeking order and discipline in the transition to adulthood. But Roof and McKinney also found that the young adult cohort is vastly overrepresented among those who switch from a church to nonaffiliation. As many as 80 percent of those who disaffiliated were under 45 years old.[53] And those who switch

---

49 Boyer, 8.
50 Roof & McKinney, 163.
51 Ibid., 154.
52 Ibid.
53 Ibid., 172.

to no religious preference have measurably more education and higher occupational prestige than those who remain affiliated.[54]

These statistics only heightened the urgency of Boyer's concern. "Is it too much to expect that, even in this hard-edged, competitive age, a college graduate will live with integrity, civility—even compassion? Is it appropriate to hope that the lessons learned in a liberal education will reveal themselves in the humaneness of the graduate's relationship with others?"[55] If his questions were rhetorical, they seemed pointedly directed toward one constituency that had historically concerned itself with the same concerns: the church.

United Methodist Renewal at the National Level

In 1980 the General Conference Special Program on the Church and Campus report was presented. This program offered a theology for campus ministry maintaining that the search for truth needs a grounded relationship in God; that secular culture needs to hear the good news; that faith can be renewed through vital study, as Wesley once called the church to knowledge and vital piety; and that the whole church needs to share in college and university ministry. Practical components of the program included the training of campus ministry advocates at the annual conference level; development of campus ministries as part of the Ethnic Minority Local Church emphasis; support for the resuscitation and reformation of a United Methodist student movement; and the revival of *Orientation*, a publication identified with the Wesleyan heritage and tradition directed at students and young adults.[56]

Training annual conference advocates for campus ministry placed priority on the regional and local dimensions of ministry, where interest was strongest and initiative forthcoming. Partnership between campus ministry and ethnic minority local church emphasis focused on local work and modeled a collegial relationship with others as opposed to an adversarial or competitive model. Advocating support for student initiative through a United Methodist student movement directed resources to the primary lay constituency of campus ministry, promising support for grassroots organization and activity. And the revival of a publication

---

[54] Ibid., 176.

[55] Boyer, 279.

[56] Ibid., 1837–38. It must also be noted that local church women's groups, prior to the merger in 1968, often assigned a member the task of advocating for campus ministry, as well as helping to make connections between the home church and the campus ministry.

directed to the grassroots represented attention to the growing need for good communication, and avenues of communication, essential to the health of pluralistic communities.

The United Methodist Church continued its inclination to support higher education for racial and ethnic minorities in the United States, and launched a major new effort in Africa. At the General Conference of 1988, two major programs won approval: a $100 million endowment to be established for scholarships for United Methodist students attending United Methodist-related institutions, and the establishment of a United Methodist-related all-Africa University in Zimbabwe.[57]

But campus ministry at the national level was also strengthened with budget and personnel. National staff positions in this decade increased from one to three. Program expenditures increased several hundred percent. Some endowment monies made national student gatherings a financial possibility.[58]

Presbyterians: Campus Ministry Regains a Home

The United Presbyterian Church U.S.A. reported in 1980 that all program units of the denomination had been reduced to five in order to increase flexibility, focus, unity and administration.[59] United Ministries in Higher Education (UMHE) and Higher Education and Ministries in Public Education were combined to form a new entity called United Ministries in Education (UME), which was allocated financial and personnel support under one of the five Presbyterian program units. The unit also supported the denomination's colleges and leadership development, all out of a budget of $1.4 million.

In 1981 the Presbyterian General Assembly received a report on "The Church's Mission in Higher Education."[60] The report is rather unremarkable in most aspects. It reiterated the familiar proposition that the church's presence on campus is necessary as a stabilizing influence in a culture of competing value systems and to call university research to "the ethical and responsible use of new knowledge."[61] Nor was there anything unusual in the counsel that "the church...is committed to call the university to serve society and to be inclusive, just, and humane in its

---

57 *Journal of the United Methodist Church* (1988), F–88.
58 This information was not readily available in published denominational records but was generously provided by Don Shockley and Lisa Hanson.
59 *Minutes of the Presbyterian Church* (1980), 245–46.
60 *Minutes of the Presbyterian Church* (1981), 378–84.
61 Ibid., 380.

own life" or the notion that the church might actually learn from and within the university, "reexamining its own past,...its present life, and exploring projections concerning the future."[62]

The report proved important, however, as a means to re-secure an office for campus ministry at the national level. Campus ministry had been adrift since 1973, when the Board of Christian Education was eliminated. The denomination was contemplating a new restructuring and campus ministry sought a berth. The report called for an adequately funded and staffed national office of higher education to oversee church-related colleges, especially those church-related schools serving racial minority constituents. It called for grant programs to fund students, faculty, and chaplains to study at institutions unlike their own and for more materials to interpret the work of the church in higher education to local churches. The report urged that college presidents, chaplains, and higher education ministries be put on denominational mailing lists and included in the same mailings that were sent to parochial clergy in order that communication might be two-way.[63]

In 1982 the Program Agency Report reveals an Office of Ministries in Higher Education.[64] The restoration of this office placed an advocate in the national structure who could initiate funding requests and safeguard allocations, especially in lean times when budgets were challenged. The same report surmised that it would take at least four years to implement the goal of securing a higher priority for higher education in the church's program agenda.[65]

The Episcopal Church: Challenging Diminishments

Campus ministry in the Episcopal Church had benefited from the Venture in Mission Program. The General Convention in 1982 received encouraging news that over the past six years the Venture in Mission Campaign had received over $150 million and was still increasing. A new program of "Jubilee Ministries" was created to provide additional outreach to the hungry and aged. The "Next Step in Mission" program

---

[62] Ibid.

[63] Ibid., 381–82.

[64] *Minutes of the Presbyterian Church* (1982) vol. 1, 362.

[65] Ibid., 393. In 1986, however, only strong lobbying by college presidents, campus ministers, chaplains, and sympathetic allies, secured a Committee on Higher Education within the denominational structure—as opposed to the suggested proposal, which relegated higher education ministries to a minor slot in a larger unit. Letter from Douglas King, March 1, 1992.

called each congregation to a new ideological campaign that would not be measurable in quantitative terms, as Venture in Mission was. The "Next Step" called congregations to examine themselves with renewal and mission in mind, and to commit their resources accordingly.[66] In a departure from more recent practices, the General Program budget report for 1983 was presented in a detailed format. The good news was a refreshing openness in a more forthright accounting. The bad news was that of a total national budget of $20,883,000 for 1983, only $43,000 was budgeted for program in Ministries in Higher Education. [67]

From the students' perspective, the church lacked both dollars and presence on campus. In their Pastoral Letter to the General Convention of 1988, the Episcopal House of Bishops addressed the "Young People of the Episcopal Church in the United States and Around the World." Forty young people attended the convention and helped shape its concerns. One of those concerns presented by the youthful visitors was the tendency of clergy and bishops to absent themselves from gatherings of youthful members of the church. Bishops cannot be shepherds, the youths reminded them, if their sheep never hear the shepherds' voices.[68] It was, however, at this General Convention that funding was approved for National Student Gatherings to be held at least once in each triennium. Two of these gatherings had already been staged and funded, presumably from a piecemeal gleaning of program budget categories; now they would have funding of their own. Still, Ministries in Higher Education was budgeted at only $65,000 for the coming year, the denomination's major higher education funding being allocated to its campuses serving the racial minorities.

New Connections and Directions for the 90s?

Two events in 1990 indicate that a new story is taking shape, if only tentatively. The first was the Presiding Bishop's Consultation on Ministry in Higher Education, a gathering in Washington, D.C., in February of Episcopal campus ministers, parochial clergy, bishops, faculty, administrators, and students. Designed and implemented by a few interested campus ministers, with the cooperation of one bishop, the event was criticized by some as a "top-down" event, planned by too few people

---

[66] *Journal of the General Convention* (1982), A–2.

[67] Ibid., AA–185. By comparison, $1 million was designated for Black Colleges; Women's Ministry received $35,500 and the Board for Theological Education, $38,000.

[68] *Journal of the General Convention* (1988), 7.

and organized in an hierarchical fashion. It began as an independent initiative, but the Presiding Bishop subscribed and lent his name to the gathering even though he attended only a modest portion of the meeting. Presentations were made by a variety of speakers and were of high quality, but many present expressed a desire for more small-group time and conversation. Students were included largely as an afterthought, and those who attended articulated dissatisfaction with that status. But the event was beneficial in that it provided the first forum ever to include the fullness of the campus ministry community. Though the ratios of representation were disproportionate and the gathering of nearly 300 people too small to allow for an adequate cross-section of so diverse a constituency, the energies experienced from even a taste of such cross-disciplinary conversation indicated to some that this type of meeting should continue and that the national church structure could positively serve campus ministry by providing resources to that end.

The second event was a year-end gathering of nearly 2100 students and campus ministers in Louisville, Kentucky. Meeting from December 28, 1990, to January 1, 1991, the Louisville event brought together students from eleven denominations. Student gatherings of a similar type, but on a smaller scale—like the Episcopal Gathering of 1983—had progressed to the point that it was deemed timely to attempt a reunion of the whole, the first since the demise of the University Christian Movement in 1969. This time denominational meetings were interspersed with plenary assemblies. In this way, separate polities were honored and shared activities encouraged. The joy of the gathering seemed less one of shared commonality than of shared community. Difference itself was celebrated as a gift.

There is little question that campus ministry in 1990 and beyond is and ought to be different from what it has been in the past. Campus ministers understand what others of their churches have yet to learn: that a new kind of leadership is required and that old patterns of dependency and paternalistic structure are being challenged. As Clyde Robinson wrote in 1990, the churches need to move beyond the foundational model of campus ministry, to ministry that involves the local congregations in priestly-pastoral work with students; that links the resources of higher education with the church's priorities on behalf of justice, peace, and the integrity of creation; and that recognizes and supports not just ministry *to* , but the ministry *of* students, faculty, and administrators.[69] The responsibility of campus ministry is the challenge to stand independently and to work collegially within a community of varied ministries. Our research suggests what every campus minister and every person familiar with campus ministry knows: that there is no one way, no single method for doing campus ministry. Each is uniquely shaped by the institutions its serves and by the resources God has given it.

There is, then, no "model" that emerges from what we have seen and studied. But that is not to say that there are no learnings. What we have learned, and invite others to explore, are intimations of new relationship. These are not new ways of doing campus ministry so much as they represent new ways of thinking about campus ministry among ourselves and of representing campus ministry to a larger community of ministry. New perceptions among ourselves of our ministry may lead to greater clarity of our own specific ministries wherever we are. The ability to refine and communicate those specific ministries as gifts in themselves leads us to a new place in our relationship with others in the church who share our common concern for the ministry of Christ and the Gospel. That new place does not wait upon others to define our ministry, but invites us to take initiative for our own ministries, and to fashion these ministries as offerings in themselves. When we know who we are and what we are about, we are the better able to share with others the gift that we have to contribute. Such a changed posture brings us to our denominations, and to our local communities, not with hat in hand as beggars seeking yet another handout, but with real gifts in hand, ready to contribute what we have to a shared enterprise. The partnerships that can emerge promise to be exciting and fulfilling.

It is important for us to remember that it was campus ministers and their students who were among the first to call for a redistribution of the churches' resources to the growing number of diverse people and important social concerns that challenged the structures of our denominations. As the diversity of the church grew and the demands of ministry with it, campus ministries were among those whose budgets were reallocated to equally important mission. Campus ministers have liked to think and speak of themselves as pathfinders, as the *avant-garde* of the church. In this regard, they have certainly fulfilled that role, learning to live without

---

[69] Clyde O. Robinson, Jr., "Grandeur, Misery, and Challenge: Ministry in Higher Education in the Nineties," *A Point of View* 2 (21 November 1990) issued by The Presbyterian Church USA Committee on Higher Education, 8.

hierarchical guidance and centralized financial support nearly three decades before other colleagues in ministry were challenged to do so.

But campus ministry does need re-appointment. Ministries need to be re-equipped with the resources necessary to fulfill their vocation. The next section is one attempt to define both that vocation and its necessary equipment.

$-\maltese\ 7\ \maltese-$

CAMPUS MINISTRY:
A PRIESTHOOD OF ALL BELIEVERS

THE DANFORTH REPORT:
A BEGINNING

Kenneth Underwood, in the Danforth campus ministry study, published in 1969, examined what he called the "experimental" and "specialized" ministry on campus. One of the primary interests of the Danforth study was the person of the minister. Underwood identified four categories or modes of campus ministry: priestly, pastoral, governance, and prophetic. His categories provided dimension and shape for campus ministry that established this work as a full, though specialized, ministry in its own right, something more than an appendage to or an extension of the church's ministry. The fullness of campus ministry, the Danforth study maintained, embraced all four characteristics identified in the report.

Underwood's work was undertaken in a time of crisis, as indicated in previous chapters. It was a time that challenged the identity and role of all professional ministers. Distrust of traditional, institutional authority and enhanced appreciation of the laity for their own ministries were but two of several factors that called the identity of the professional clergy into question. Moreover, campus pastors lived with changing dynamics in church and university that questioned their efficacy, suspected their motives, and compounded their anxieties.

One of the difficulties of the Danforth study is that it was dated almost as soon as it was published. Between the time the study commenced in 1963 and its publication in 1969 society, church, and campus all changed radically. The whole culture was torn by Vietnam, by conflicting reactions to the civil rights movement and other fledgling liberation movements, by the violence at the Democratic National Convention in 1968, and by the assassinations of Robert Kennedy and Martin Luther King, Jr. All of these general tensions were expressed in churches in a multitude of ways. These factors—coupled with declining revenues for new ministries and the implosion of the Student Christian Movement in 1969—conspired to challenge the relevance of any reformist strategy that looked to the university with such sanguine eyes as Underwood's study did.

Still, the study represented a considerable achievement. Most denominational campus ministry mission statements reflect the ecclesiastical biases of the authoring institutions and frequently neglect to deal with the university on the terms of the university. The strength of the Danforth study was its willingness to do just that and, thereby, to challenge the strategies—articulated or not—that the churches were practicing. But the study was published at a time when the university had neither time nor inclination to listen and when denominational monies were being funnelled elsewhere. The Danforth Foundation itself, in spite of the report's call for increased funding for campus ministry, was subject to changing perspectives and priorities. For the most part, only those persons who were self-interested in campus ministry—denominational executives and the campus ministers themselves—waded through the 964 pages of the report. Thus, it never reached the wide, interdisciplinary audience for which Underwood had hoped.

The study has, nevertheless, been a benchmark in campus ministry since its publication, especially Underwood's four categories of ministry. But those categories reflected Underwood's biases. For example, Donald Shockley correctly noted the tendency of the report to lean heavily upon the prophetic dimension of ministry, even in its characterizations of the other three categories.[1] Similarly, even though Underwood sought to address the totality of ministry on campus, the bias of the Danforth

---

[1] Shockley, *Campus Ministry*, 98–99.

study, and its influence, was largely limited to the clergy. The role of the campus minister, while still important, comprises but a portion of ministry on campus. Further, Underwood urged abandonment of an imperialistic and patronizing perspective that defines campus ministry as the church's ministry *to* the university; the university has its own ministry, on campus and elsewhere. From the Judeo-Christian vantage, all human activity is divinely ordered, God making use of a variety of ministrations to effect God's will and design. The work of the university, no less than the work of the church, is essential to that design. If campus ministry is to be a reconciling, mediating ministry between two essential institutions, it shall need to cultivate ministry that holds and conveys genuine respect for both institutions, and for all those who minister within them. Within the university—and the church—campus ministry no less than any other must concern itself with *total ministry*, accounting for the ministry of all people, and their human institutions.

Building upon the work of Underwood, and those who contributed to the Danforth report, the defining categories of priestly, pastoral, governance, and prophetic are helpful only as a beginning point.

PRIESTLY MINISTRY:
NURTURING RELATIONSHIP

Traditionally, the priestly functions of ministry are liturgy and worship, sacraments and study.[2] Preaching, celebration of the sacraments, and catechetical instruction are among the tasks associated with the priestly office even in post-Reformation traditions. Beyond these functional tasks, the essential role of the priest is the nurture of relationship with God. Through the sacraments, we are introduced to God and signify and maintain our relationship with God, with our neighbors and with ourselves. Thus the priestly function is one of formation. This function is shared with the entire community of ministry. The priestly ministry of God's people is manifested in *vocation*. The notion that one is "called" to a particular work has long been the anchor of the faithful life. The sense that one's daily activity—the exercise of one's gifts and energies—is grounded in some greater reality is the means by which

---

[2] *The Standard College Dictionary* defines "priest" as "one especially consecrated to the service of a divinity, and serving as mediator between the divinity and... worshipers in sacrifice, worship, prayer, teaching, etc." *Funk & Wagnalls* (New York: Harcourt, Brace & World, Inc., 1963), 1070.

religious people have discerned that elusive "meaning" in human life and experience that seems to pose a struggle for all generations. "The famous collection of songs written by medieval students preparing for the priesthood, *Carmina Burana*,...gives voice...to an age-old suspicion that the universe is ruled by Fortune, not by Providence, that life has no higher purpose at all, and that the better part of moral wisdom is to enjoy life while you can."[3] Sharon Parks has suggested that the "capacity and demand for meaning" lies at the heart of faith itself, that faith is "the activity of seeking and composing meaning in the most comprehensive dimensions of our experience."[4]

The meaning of one's life is derived from relationship. The relatedness of oneself as individual to the whole of life is invitation to an ongoing conversation with all that constitutes the "other." That one's life is response to a call is the basis of vocation; that one's life is response to a call originating in God is the basis of the Christian concept of vocation. The voice of God, Christian tradition and experience affirm, is manifold. The call may come in silence, in unspoken need that beckons one's personal initiative. The call may come in mystic vision, in the recesses of meditation wherein one's mission or task takes on vivid clarity. The call may come from the mouth of another person, in the recognition and affirmation of specific abilities or in the challenge to attempt a new venture. The call may come from an institution, from a community within which one's talents are recognized or commissioned. The vocational conversation extends through the whole of life, not only life's length but its width and depth.

GOD CALLS:
LIFE AS ANSWER

Vocation pertains not only to one's livelihood, but to every aspect of one's life. Thus, vocation is essential to meaning. For meaning consists both in the determination of what my life means to me and what my life means to all others. Vocation extends not only to one's work, but to one's love. Indeed, the Judeo-Christian tradition posits creation itself upon God's "calling forth." For the authors of Genesis the proclaimed word of

---

[3] Christopher Lasch, "The Illusion of Disillusionment," speech reprinted in *Harper's Magazine*, (July 1991): 20–21.

[4] Sharon Parks, *The Critical Years: Young Adults and the Search for Meaning, Faith, and Commitment* (San Francisco: Harper & Row, 1986), xv.

God "said" all things into being. "And God said" was the formula by which the dialogue was begun; that all things *are*, is response to God's saying, God's calling.

For the Christian, too, the prologue to the Gospel of John establishes the conversational foundation of creation. For that author, the Word of God was manifest in the particular person of Jesus and that Word evoked response. It is possible to see Jesus himself as vocation incarnate, and the relationship with Jesus as the fundament of Christian vocation. Meaning in the Christian life is derived not only from what is perceived of God in the person of Jesus but extends to all of creation as Jesus suggests that the believer is to seek the conversation not only with him, but with all his brothers and sisters—all other human beings—and implies that even in their silence or absence, the rocks of earth itself give voice to the call (Luke 19:40).

Vocation finds its measure in the balance of fitness and readiness. That balance is aptly captured in the Greek, and biblical, notion of *kairos*. *Kairos* is a quality of time. Usually rendered in biblical scriptures as the expression "in the fullness of time," *kairos* gives expression to that equipoise of fitness and readiness that characterizes meaning. The conversation of vocation, the struggle to make meaning of one's life, seeks that quality which is *kairos*, that balance between fitness and readiness. One can be fit for a particular kind of work, but not yet ready to undertake it for lack of training or skill. One can be fit for a particular task, but not yet ready to undertake it for lack of physical prowess or emotional maturity. One can be fit for an intimate commitment, like marriage, but not yet ready to undertake it; or fit to conceive and bear children, but not yet ready to provide for their care and nurture.

The tension between fitness and readiness is well chronicled. Again, reaching into religious resources, that tension is known within the biblical image of "testing." The fitness and/or readiness of Abraham and Sarah to undertake the covenant's demands are examined in the book of Genesis. Moses protests his own fitness and readiness when called by God in the book of Exodus, and then is saddled with responsibility for convincing the Israelites through his leadership that they are both fit and ready to leave Egypt and take up their own vocational conversation as a people. The prophet Jeremiah denies his fitness to undertake his mission, and claims youth as impediment to his readiness—both of which are challenged and put to rest when the youthful prophet proves the right person at the right time for the task at hand. Jesus signifies a readiness to serve in his submission to baptism at the hands of his cousin John, but seems to have opened to question his own fitness in the ordeal of the wilderness immediately thereafter. The zealous Saul, who seemed (from a Christian point of view) neither fit nor ready for any godly service, was convinced otherwise by the abrupt visitation of blinding insight on the road to Damascus that rendered him an entirely new person in the apostle Paul—and much of his early work among the Christians consisted in having to convince them that he was both fit and ready to serve them.

The process of discerning vocation is lifelong. Young adulthood is itself a moment of *kairos*. "Young adulthood is marked by the capacity to take self-aware responsibility for choosing the path of one's own fidelity....One becomes a young adult in faith when one begins to take self-conscious responsibility for one's own knowing, becoming, and moral action—even at the level of ultimate meaning-making."[5] Though different theories of human development ascribe different characteristics to adulthood, many agree that age alone is not determinate. That being the case, the biblical record suggests that Abraham and Sarah, Moses and Jeremiah, Jesus and Paul were all acting in a manner analogous to "young adults" at that point in their lives when each began to take self-conscious responsibility, even—and one could assert *especially*—as they took responsibility for what Parks called "ultimate meaning-making."

THE PRIESTLY MINISTRY OF INSTITUTIONS

The work and role of the church in the life of the young adult has long centered on the matter of vocation. Higher education began in America—at Harvard College, The College of William and Mary, The College of New Jersey (now Princeton) and King's College (now Columbia)—under the aegis of the church and for the purpose of equipping suitable candidates for ordained ministerial service. Though the scope of higher education broadened considerably to include a wider range of academic disciplines, the initial commitment to vocation never wavered. Well into the twentieth century, even on campuses founded by the states, the notion that higher education prepared students for a life of service to the commonweal prevailed in the statements of mission or purpose that defined the institution's *raison d'être*.

For both the church and the university vocational formation is fundamental. Indeed, indulging in intentional tautology, the vocation of the church and the vocation of the university are profoundly vocational. For

---

5 Ibid., 77.

the church, vocational formation lies at the heart of the baptismal covenant, the sacramental worship, the preaching and the teaching—all of which are aimed at communicating the relationship of God to the creature and all of creation, and nurturing the creature and creation in the establishment of mutual relationship with God. The Christian church proclaims the fitness and the readiness of all to live in responsible relation to God, to neighbor and self. All Christian believers are called to share in this ministry of formation; indeed, it is this ministry which constitutes responsible relationship with God—that we love one another, care for one another, relate to one another, as God has loved, cared for, and related to us.

For the university, no less than the church, vocational formation is fundamental. One need look no farther than the familiar ritual incantation of the commencement exercise that welcomes the newly graduated into "the company of educated women and men." Which is not to say that graduates are welcomed into knowledge, but intelligence. Education, at its root, means "to bring up, to develop"[6]—a process of formation. Educated women and men are presumed to be formed. They have been formed in intelligence, which is to say that they have been formed in "the faculty of perceiving and comprehending meaning,...the ability to adapt to new situations, and to learn from experience."[7] Knowledge may be attained through education and experience, but knowledge is not the end product of education. The end product of education is, according to its own ritual acclamation, educated women and men.

INSTITUTIONAL IMPEDIMENTS TO PRIESTLY MINISTRY

Both church and university, then, make their meaning in the nurture of persons and in the formation of those persons as individuals responsible for making meaning in themselves and in the company of others. For that reason, the religious enterprise and the educational enterprise have frequently been united. Certainly, in the American experience of higher education, the role of the church in founding colleges and universities suggests a wedding that saw church and university as partners in common mission. Why, then, do church and university know their present estrangement?

---

[6] *The Standard College Dictionary*, 420.

[7] Ibid., 702.

The full answer to this question is beyond the scope of this study, but likely begins in the departures each institution has made from its initial mission. The drift away from common cause has its roots in the nineteenth century, or even earlier. But our research suggests, if only superficially, that particular enticements after World War II further aggravated the estrangement and complicated the path to reconciliation.

The university was encouraged by war's decimation of its enrollments and government's desire for its expertise to turn its attention and energy to research in a new way. Research was always a part of the learning and teaching experience, but technological research became a commodity and became, for the university, a source of income as the nation's need for technology expanded. After the war, increased demand for research and larger enrollments enabled by the GI Bill gradually shifted the academy's focus from education to knowledge. Education was revalued by the society: it was no longer esteemed as formation in intelligence, preparation for a life of meaning, but was valued more highly as the accumulation of knowledge and the refinement of skill. Education became less important as a preparation for living and more important as a tool for earning. Pluralism on campus introduced the tension between neutral governance on the one hand, and restrictive, even exclusive, governance on the other. Those who espoused neutrality—often demanded as a condition of governmental monies—either restricted all religion from campus or indiscriminately granted all religions free expression. Some private schools, often founded by religious bodies, imposed restrictive governance and freely exercised sectarianism, but forfeited governmental grants as a consequence. Debates over the proper balance of research and teaching and of moral governance increase and modern controversies over curriculum are deeply related to these questions and confusions of mission.

The church, too, was affected by the forces of war and culture. Spurred by post-war growth, churches proliferated and bureaucratization expanded accordingly to tend the administration of them. Emulating American business, the church followed constituencies and directed resources into suburbs with sometimes deleterious consequences in rural and urban settings. As the culture moved away from institutional religious commitment and adapted to greater diversity of religious choice, denominational loyalties eroded. Additionally, the fragmentation of the society—including society within the churches—made new demands upon the institution, which, structured to administer loyal and relatively homogeneous groups, was challenged to administer greater diversity. The role of choice in the life of Americans further complicated the churches' mission. Like the university, the church was and is stimulated by the competitive market environment of the prevailing culture. Some churches tended to configure themselves intentionally to meet market desire. Others renounced the market approach, but avoided action that would challenge existing memberships to change—which was but another capitulation to market dynamics. Mainline denominational campaigns of evangelism cannot fully evade suspicion that their real motivation is simply institutional, and hence financial, growth. And just as the university debates the role and substance of its curricular canon, the church is likewise divided in the debate over the role and substance of its scriptural canon, some advocating fundamental adherence to literalism, and others to liberalism in interpretation.

The tension between institutional maintenance and institutional mission represents a new common bond between university and church. "Discerning our native gifts is difficult for many reasons. We live in a culture that tells us there is no such thing as a gift, that we must earn or make everything we get."[8] Difficult as this reality is for the individual, it is all the more difficult for organizations. Vocation has also an institutional dimension. Sometimes articulated as institutional purpose or organizational mission, the vocation of the collective—like that of the individual—depends upon inherent gifts and their exercise in service to others. The insistence that there is no gift, that everything must be made or earned, has created for both American universities and churches a genuine crisis of vocation. Church and university now confront the grim reality that each is failing at its original mission. To what other conclusion can we come when we appraise a society that counts unprecedented numbers of the well-educated among its citizenry, and a society whose level of religious membership and commitment has not appreciably diminished in over sixty years, but whose members confess a growing poverty of meaning in their personal and communal lives? It is doubtful that life's meaning has changed. But our ability to make meaning despite abundant educational and religious resources suggests that we have strayed off course. If the voice of God is heard in the voice of society, then the voice that cries out for meaning, or even asks tentatively after it, suggests to faithful and discerning believers in both church and academy that these institutions are called to re-examine their gifts for nurturing

---

8 Parker Palmer, "Practicing the Public Life in the Congregation," *Calling of the Laity*, ed. Verna Dozier (New York: Alban Institute, 1988), 66.

those relationships with God, neighbor, and self from which meaning are derived.

Neither church nor academy will retreat to its previous mission. The struggle will continue, even as it does in the life of every person, and many resources will be necessary to the process. Campus ministry may expect to play a role in each of these institutions as each struggles with its own vocation. The primary role of campus ministry, however, will not likely be immediately recognizable at the institutional level in either the church or the university. Neither campus ministry nor any other single constituency in church, university, or society possesses sufficient authority or power to assure institutional response.

The work of Robert Bellah (*Habits of the Heart*; *The Good Society*) posits that since the late 1960s institutional authority has been displaced in the American culture by a greater sense of autonomy and individual authority. Lacking a clear, denominationally stated mission and institutional cohesion, the role and influence of campus ministry will continue to be most pronounced at the local and individual level. To the extent that individual campus ministries recover their own historical commitment to vocation, they may exert influence at every level, thus inducing reform. We found throughout our study of denominational statements a consistent recapitulation of campus ministry's role in the process of vocational formation. Though it waxed and waned, sometimes to the point of virtual disappearance, that thread remained consistently, and persistently, present. That it has emerged out of our own more localized experience as an impressive and important ministry on campus indicates that it is not only an essential component of mission, but may serve as an integrating theme that unites the tremendous variety of campus ministries in a single enterprise.[9]

The most probing religious question posed by campus ministry anywhere it goes is simply the vocational: "Why are you here?" Examining this question, and coming back to it again and again, can be unsettling in the very best sense. But posing that question and struggling to discern the answer to it gives shape and meaning to life. The process of vocational formation which reflects upon that question with consistent discipline is familiar to those who know the traditional disciplines of

---

[9] Among our contemporaries we acknowledge that Donald Shockley (*Campus Ministry: The Church Beyond Itself*) and Clyde O. Robinson, Jr. ("Grandeur, Ministry, and Challenge: Ministry in Higher Education in the Nineties," *A Point of View* No. 2 (21 November 1990): 1–8) have also identified vocation as a central concern of campus ministry.

religious formation. The catechisms of the Christian tradition frequently framed the question for the religious inquirer or novice believer. Those who pursued the call to ordained vocation or the vows of monasticism undertook an intentional reflection upon the same question. Even in our own time, the consideration of candidates for ordained service in the church continues to seek the balance of fitness and readiness in a disciplined process requiring study, experiential learning, prayer and meditation, and seemingly constant conversation with the varied communities of the church represented in committees.

VOCATIONAL FORMATION FOR THE MINISTRIES OF THE LAITY

But the greater portion of the church's ministers—the laity—are less familiar with a disciplined integration of life that leads to meaning, and the available data indicates that this will continue to be true. Since 1966 Alexander Astin and his associates at the University of California in Los Angeles have surveyed entering first-year college students. Their profiles reveal that in 1967 nearly 83 percent of those students surveyed considered it essential or even very important to develop a meaningful philosophy of life. By 1973 that figure dropped to 69 percent[10] and continued to fall until, in 1991, it reached a low of 43.2 percent[11]. Conversely, the profiles revealed that in 1967 43.5 percent of those students surveyed deemed it essential or very important to be very well-off financially.[12] That figure rose in 1991 to a high of 73.7 percent.[13] Graduated into society, the values continue to shape us. As one observer noted: "...the workplace is this nation's great, unrecognized church; each workplace, each profession has its own culture, its own set of values. They are largely unexamined, but they are relentlessly inculcated, relentlessly enforced. For many, this religion is more persuasive, more powerful than anything they observe on Sunday. It can become a false god we place

---

[10] Astin, Alexander W., et. al *The American Freshman: Twenty Year Trends, 1966–1985* (Los Angeles: Higher Education Research Institute, UCLA, 1987), 97.

[11] Ibid., quoted in "The Year's College Freshman: Attitudes and Characteristics," *Chronicle of Higher Education* (30 January 1991): A31.

[12] Ibid., 97.

[13] Ibid., quoted in "The Year's College Freshman: Attitudes and Characteristics," *Chronicle of Higher Education* (30 January 1991): A31.

before the real one."[14] Clearly, values have changed and the search for meaning itself has been displaced by a quest for material security.

Gregory F. Augustine Pierce, past president of the National Center for the Laity, recounted his own youthful spiritual pilgrimage: "I kept looking for it in the wrong places: in church, in spiritual books, in prayer, in fasting, in retreat centers, in days of recollection—in 'silence, solitude and surrender.'"[15] Pierce found, ultimately, that his true spirituality—the only spirituality that spoke the truth to him—was "the spirituality of work."[16] Out of that realization, he edited one of a growing number of works on vocational formation of the laity.[17] Frank Macchiarola, president of the Academy of Political Science, a professor of business at Columbia University, and former chancellor of the New York City School system, wrote in his essay for the collection that "...the modern world encourages and supports the development of lives without reflection. People suffer a great deal because of their failure to reflect upon what has the most meaning in their lives."[18]

Davida Foy Crabtree, a parish pastor, described an innovative approach to ministry. She and a number of laity in her congregation decided to concentrate their efforts on visiting with and listening to members of the church on the job, in their daily lives. They suspended Bible studies and traditional programs on spiritual devotion and gave themselves over to a process of learning. She reported the discovery of an important principle:

> By beginning with their lives, we were validating the authority of the laity and empowering them to reflect on the faith. When we had begun with Bible study and theology, we had started on ground where the clergy had authority....When we begin with their lives, however, we begin where they

---

[14] Chris Satullo, "The Lord Catches Us in Our Craftiness," *Of Human Hands: A Reader in the Spirituality of Work*, ed. Gregory F. Augustine Pierce (Minneapolis, MN: Augsburg Fortress Press; Chicago: ACTA Publications, 1991), 94.

[15] Gregory F. Augustine Pierce, "A Spirituality That Makes Sense," *Of Human Hands*, 15.

[16] Ibid.

[17] *Of Human Hands: A Reader in the Spirituality of Work*, ed. Gregory F. Augustine Pierce (Minneapolis, MN: Augsburg Fortress Press; Chicago: ACTA Publications, 1991).

[18] Frank Macchiarola, "Finding the Courage to Take Risks," *Of Human Hands*, 37.

have authority. We provide an opportunity for them to talk about their work and to reflect on the impact of that work on the rest of their lives.[19]

Crabtree's discovery echoed the finding of the Gallup organization that Americans "want their churches to help them learn to put their faith into practice; to shed light on the important moral issues of the day; to help them learn how to serve others better and to be better parents. Americans understand that for their faith to be meaningful, it must be real and have a real impact on their day-to-day lives."[20] Thus, the observation credited to an unnamed college president: "...the church needs to think of itself as having a ministry *of* education, rather than the present ministry *to* education."[21]

A CALL TO NEW DIRECTION

The insistence that faith's meaning is derived from ordinary experience is hardly new, nor is it confined to the modern American experience. One need look no farther than the theological doctrine of the Incarnation to find that relationship with God is based in human experience. Relationship with God, at least for Christians, is not disembodied or ideological. It is quite tangible and personal, based upon the indisputable apostolic succession that traces all Christian relationship to personal encounter with the historical person of Jesus. Quite apart from the hierarchical claims that surround the notion of apostolic succession, each Christian claims a history, a genealogy, in a lineage of unbroken continuity to the company of friends—the women, men, elders, youths, and children—who lived with and related to Jesus and whose stories comprise the record of that relationship in scripture. For Christians, then, turning attention to the intersection of religion and daily experience is both *discovery* and *recovery*. It is discovery in that it takes one beyond the accretions that have obscured that ordinary revelation; it is recovery in that it is the taking up not of something new and different, but of something quite traditional and familiar.

Yet there is vague discomfort, and sometimes even outright disagreement, with a Christian ministry that intentionally turns away

---

[19] Davida Foy Crabtree, "They Bring Their Work to Church," *Of Human Hands*, 114–15.

[20] Gallup, "Looking Ahead to the Year 2000," *Religion in America* (Princeton), 12.

[21] Eric O. Springsted, *Who Will Make Us Wise?: How the Churches Are Failing Higher Education* (Cambridge, MA: Cowley Publications, 1988), 123.

from the routine. Crabtree's decision to depart from the standard fare of Bible study and personal devotion and to relegate attendance at worship to lesser status surely raised questions and perhaps resistance and resentment. But in so doing, Crabtree was still on hallowed ground. She reversed the institutional trend that sees the institution as an end in itself and returned to a way that sees the institution and its life as means to an end. In going to people in the workplace, in sharing with them the daily stuff of their lives, Crabtree and those who shared her ministry were following a path taken by many before. For these missionaries, the church, its history, its scriptures, its instruction, tradition, and worship were all resources in the rearguard, which is where support is logically located. With their support behind them, these modern-day missionaries ventured into the field. Again, they did nothing that Jesus before them had not done.

WHY CAMPUS MINISTRY?

Our experience on campus is consonant with Crabtree's parochial venture. Engagement with others—and an abiding spirituality—are derived from the daily encounter in the workplace. But the frequent rejoinder to this experience is the question regularly heard: if this is the basis of campus ministry, then why does the church not have ministries in all workplaces? It is a good question. However, while campus ministry bears some resemblance to industrial missions and other workplace ministries, campus ministry is still distinct from those initiatives.

Campus ministry is different from other workplace ministries because, at least for the student population, campus is not only where they work but where they live. Furthermore, higher education for the American student is a point of transition. Regardless the student's age or reason for being on campus, higher education is a turning point. For the young adult, newly graduated from high school and living away from home for the first time, college entails many new experiences that form not only work life, but emotional, affectional, and political life, as well. It is a time for making commitments, to be sure. But it is also a time of conscious sorting and sifting. Even the older student usually returns to campus as a point of transition: to take up a deferred ambition; to test a latent talent; to adjust to widowhood or singleness; to undertake a familiar discipline at a new level of competence.

Ministry to faculty, administrators, and staff within the university does bear some affinity to other workplace ministries. For that reason we are inclined to see these constituencies as secondary to the student population in the priorities of campus ministry. If campus ministry might be likened to hospital ministry—an apt analogy—the hospital chaplains' first priority is patient care, but that patient care entails daily ministry to and among an extended network of other ministers. A hospital chaplain cannot disregard the needs or the gifts of nurses, doctors, administrators, or staff. But neither can the hospital chaplain devote primary care to those constituencies without neglecting service to the patient. Campus ministry is, then, an institutional ministry.

Beyond the institution, however, whether it be campus or hospital, all constituencies are linked to other primary ministries. Faculty, administrators, and staff—if they are committed religious people—have an established relationship with a pastor and congregation elsewhere. Except for rare exceptions, the chaplain is for them something other than their primary pastor. In many instances, the campus chaplain—like the hospital chaplain—functions as colleague within the university or hospital. But the same is equally true of the relationship between student and campus minister. For students do frequently come to campus from previous experiences of parish life, and it is anticipated that they will go on to a commitment to parish life after graduation. But for the brief time they are on campus, they may find within the campus minister a collegial mentor. It may well be that this relationship more nearly approximates the role all ordained ministries are to seek, though modern mobility and the fragmentation of society raise very difficult obstacles to such relationship—at least within existing models of church structure.

A CALL TO CONVERSATION

"The way theology and ethics are done in mainline churches is too greatly conditioned by the styles of university and seminary discourse."[22] To approach theology and ethics from the academic model is increasingly foreign to the experience of most Americans. The resulting drift away from learning and toward knowledge is inherently destructive. This is the concern of those in the academy who fear that university and seminary discourse is more concerned with imparting particular

---

[22] Tex Sample, *U.S. Lifestyles and Mainline Churches: A Key to Reaching People in the 90's.* (Louisville: Westminster/John Knox, 1990), 5.

knowledge than with nurturing and mentoring patterns of learning and living. That these methods have been replicated in the parish, and anywhere else in society, only reinforces the need to address this matter wherever it arises and to identify it as the gnosticism that it is. Challenging and/or replacing these habits with new ones is the vocational task of all ministry. The urgings of God, audible and visible in the people we serve, suggest that discourse must give way to conversation.

The distinction between discourse and conversation is a subtle one. The root of the word "discourse" means literally, "running apart."[23] It is an apt description of the fragmentation and specialization noted in the historical review of our recent past. "Conversation," on the other hand, is "to live with; turning together."[24] The conversational model undertaken by Crabtree and others represents a corrective to a discourse that, at least for the time being, seems to keep us apart. The conversational model is compatible with the task of mentoring.

A MENTORING COMMUNITY

For the young adult, the mentoring era finds its most powerful form in a mentoring community. The emergence of the more critical and more autonomous self in no way means a shedding of the need for a network of belonging—quite the opposite is the case. Young adulthood is nurtured into being most powerfully by the availability of a community that poses an alternative to an earlier assumed knowing, vividly embodies the potential of the merging self, and offers the promise of a new network of belonging.[25]

The need for such a mentoring environment in the transition to adulthood is essential. How this environment can be sustained, especially for the significant number of Americans who do not experience higher education and, perhaps more importantly, for those whose maturation to adulthood continues well beyond the brief span of a campus experience, is one of the more pressing demands upon the churches today. But the campus is a place through which a considerable number of Americans pass each year, a place where this mentoring community can be estab-

---

[23] "<F *discourse* <L *discursus* < *dis* - apart + *cursus* a running, pp. of *currere* to run" *Funk & Wagnalls*, 380.

[24] "<OF *converser* to live with <L *conversari*, freq. of *convertere* <*com* -together + *vertere* to turn." Ibid., 296.

[25] Parks, 89.

lished, nurtured, and sustained. As such, campus ministry represents an important locus for the churches' learning.

The experience of mentoring in modern campus ministry supports the contention that young adults are receptive to

> any network of belonging that promises a place of nurture for the potential self, even if (and sometimes especially if) its forms are demanding. A place that offers confirmation of one's potential competence and specialness, while also confirming a solid belonging that exempts the fragile self from having yet to stand alone in any real sense, meets the yearnings for agency and communion in their young adult forms.[26]

It is helpful to respect these "yearnings" as legitimate vocation.

A MINISTERING COMMUNITY

For much of its post-war history, mainline campus ministry has been conceived by the churches as an arena for countering the tendency of youthful membership to leave the institution or for cultivating "future" membership or leadership. Both are valid institutional concerns, but each represents a mission impulse that seeks to serve the needs of the institution and only secondarily is concerned with the actual needs of the young adult. Total ministry of the church implies respect not only for the diversity of race, gender, and status of ordination (baptismal, episcopal, presbyterial, and diaconal), but also implies respect for diversity of age.

Youth and young adults are ministers of the church by right of baptism. If Christians believe that God calls each person to fullness of life, then such fullness includes the experience of life's passage into maturity. Thus, progression through the several stages of human development represents legitimate response to vocation. Respect for that vocation translates into respect for the youth or young adult on terms appropriate to maturational status. That being the case, youth and young adults are not the future ministers of the church; they are ministers to the church and of the church in the present.

Students are fulfilling a vocational imperative on campus. One of the important ramifications of the question posed earlier—why are you here?—when posed to the student is that it can be useful tool in discerning whether study is, indeed, the true vocation for that person at that time. Is the student on campus to fulfill a parental expectation? Is the

---

[26] Ibid., 90.

student studying against the hope of future financial security? Is the student enrolled in the discipline she most desires, or is she pursuing the most marketable option? Are there other experiences that might prove more beneficial to this person than the experience of campus? These questions, posed by college advisors, insightful faculty, and campus ministers, are essential to student vocational discernment.

But as the determination is made that the student is truly called to that vocation, the student meets the vocation of higher education: "to inform and nurture the young adult imagination."[27] This vocational mission is consonant with the vocation of the student: informing and nurturing one's imagination is the student vocation. By extension then, the vocation of campus ministry includes the informing and nurturing of the student imagination. Campus ministry's vocation and primary concern is not young adult church attendance. Campus ministry's vocation is developing faith in young adults, and, increasingly, in students of every age.[28] In this regard, campus ministry is a colleague in the vocation of the university: "...we want to educate a given kind of person, we hope for a *people* who will take responsibility for their own meanings, and thus continue to read and write and think throughout their lives."[29]

A COMMUNITY OF IMAGINATION

Those campus ministries which seem to have served the student constituency most *responsibly* are those that have also served students most *responsively*. Informing and nurturing the young adult imagination begins in some appreciation for where they are. Denominationalism no longer defines the social divisions of belief for most Americans. Yet the distinctive marks of particular communities are principal features in a pluralistic culture. The seeming impassibility of this tension was creatively bridged on one campus by reversing the ecumenical agenda.

Denominational ecumenism tends to presume familiarity with and devotion to one's denominational tradition as a prerequisite to ecumenical outreach and activity. It is assumed that a thorough familiarity with one's own tradition is necessary grounding to such sharing. But students

---

[27] Ibid., 132.

[28] Robert T. Gribbon, *Developing Faith in Young Adults: Effective Ministry with 18–35 Year Olds* (New York: The Alban Institute, Inc., 1990), 2.

[29] Wayne C. Booth, *The Vocation of a Teacher: Rhetorical Occasions 1967–1988* (Chicago: The University of Chicago Press, 1988), 272.

only nominally informed of their own tradition, if nurtured within any tradition, are rarely equipped with so thorough an understanding. Moreover, they belong to a culture little concerned for traditional denominational distinctions.[30] Noting that students from Catholic and Episcopal campus ministries were rather freely associating with their friends across denominational lines and indiscriminately sharing sacramental life, two campus ministers sat down with some of those students and asked if they might be interested in formalizing the relationship. The chaplains appealed to imagination.

Out of those conversations, in which the campus ministers instructed imagination by sharing official ecumenical policies, grew a covenant agreement establishing a relationship capable of nurturing imagination. From that relationship, succeeding generations of students were introduced to an imaginative possibility, instructed and nurtured as the relationship progressed in the daily living of student activities. Being in relationship with another body of Christians raised constant questions of distinction as students were challenged to imagine new and different ways of being Christian. Being in relationship also challenged students to acquaint themselves more fully with their own chosen tradition, to the end that the ecumenical venture served to affirm many commitments that had previously been only slight.

In this instance the campus ministry community was the mentoring community. Such communities, however, are not always communities of fixed membership. Indeed, within the campus community, few student communities exist longer than nine or ten months and sometimes they do not last even that long. The transience of student life makes for short, episodic experience and communities that change constantly. The church finds this dynamic foreign and frustrating, but increasingly familiar. At a meeting of clergy in a judicatory heavily populated with military bases, a parish pastor stood up and invited all pastors of congregations with large military constituencies to share the same table at lunch that they might share their concerns. His parish, he noted, had a membership turnover of over ten percent per year. A campus minister suggested that college and university chaplains be invited to share the same table since they lose twenty-five percent of their congregations or more each year.

---

[30] Wade Clark Roof and William McKinney, *American Mainline Religion: Its Changing Shape and Future* (New Brunswick: Rutgers University Press, 1987).

PARISH AND CAMPUS:
THE CHALLENGE OF DIFFERENCE

One must determine if ministry is called to challenge or to change these realities, or if ministry is called to work within them. There is nothing to suggest that increased mobility and transience precludes the establishing of a mentoring community. Indeed, transience can enhance a mentoring community. "The young adult (and his or her culture) most thrives when there is access to a network of belonging anchored in the strength of worthy and grounding meanings that provide a sense of distance both from the conventions of the young adult's past and from the larger society with which the young adult must still negotiate terms of entry."[31]

The balance of these qualities is one reason why campus ministry is so difficult to undertake within the parochial setting, and why campus ministry does not conform to the standards used to evaluate parish ministry. Parish ministry and campus ministry constitute different kinds of community. One can argue the superiority of either, or propose that one should defer to the other, but honest acknowledgement of the difference is required and continuing conversation toward reconciliation is desirable. There are certainly qualities of each ministry that can be of service in the other.

For example, Parks identified the young adult mentoring community as "a network of belonging anchored in the strength of worthy and grounding meanings." The primary expression of the Christian faith community in the American culture is still the parish and the denomination. Campus ministries need that foundation if they are to provide "the strength of worthy and grounding meanings." Campus ministries that in the past distanced themselves too far from those strengths lost their foundation, not only financially but in every other way, too.

But the parish and denominational community, for its part, must acknowledge and respect that young adult mentoring communities need "a sense of distance both from the young adult's past and from the larger society with which the young adult must still negotiate terms of entry." In some instances, those are one and the same. Indeed, it is the expectation (realistic or otherwise) of most parents that their young adult offspring will, after achieving that critical distance from the conventional past, be enticed to make peace with it and fully enter it as an adult. However, campus ministry in the role of young adult mentoring com-

---

[31] Parks, 90–91.

munity may well assist the student beyond the conventions of the past and into a future of a distinctly different character.

This dynamic is particularly difficult for the parish-based campus ministry. Parish-based campus ministry at present is hampered by its proximity to the conventions of the young adult's past, especially if the young adult has grown up within the same religious tradition. Parish-based campus ministries, and all parish-based young adult ministries, may more frequently serve as point of entry for the student or young adult inquirer from another faith, rather than as a community of affiliation for young adults already familiar with the denomination. For the newcomer the parish may, indeed, offer sufficient distance from the past conventions to serve that young adult's growth. But the campus minister in the parish setting is always saddled with an extra burden of mediation since, for young adults, the need to get distance from past conventions may come into conflict with the needs of the parish.

Providing distance from the larger society is no less critical, and no less troublesome. The campus ministry community that provides this distance successfully undoubtedly opens itself to conflict, but especially so if based within a parish setting, and for many of the same reasons cited above. One senior pastor, despite his appreciation and respect for the campus ministry that shared the facilities of his parish, expressed his dismay to the chaplain that so many of the students affiliated with the campus ministry did not match the mainstream profile—or whatever idealized portrait of collegian he harbored. On another campus the senior pastor affectionately (or perhaps not so affectionately) referred to his chaplain/colleague down the hall as "the flake magnet."

THE GIFT OF DIFFERENCE

This distinctive characteristic of the young adult mentoring community is requisite to making that place "that offers confirmation of one's potential competence and specialness, while also confirming a solid belonging."[32] We wrote former students of our acquaintance, some now a decade or more beyond their undergraduate experience, and asked them to reflect upon their experience of campus ministry. With no specific polling instrument, but only their narrative replies, we found a consistency.

---

[32] Ibid., 90.

"I remember finding some friends in Canterbury, as well as finding a number of rather odd people there too....You could be yourself, whatever that might be at the time, and know you were still going to be a part of Canterbury," wrote one.[33] Another wrote that he had "found what I was lacking in other arenas: acceptance, shared examination of life, shared acknowledgement of God's power, and peace in communion....While I felt like a misfit at school, I felt that my differences were recognized as gifts...."[34] One woman wrote of her experience in a Wesley Foundation, in the late 1960s, "I felt a sense of affirmation and personal worth. I felt a sense of eager anticipation because there was always someone new to meet and something good was always about to happen. And the people didn't match....That group anchored me, gave me a sense of belonging."[35] Another wrote that even though he did not take an active role in the local campus ministry, a friend of his had, and what he had observed of campus ministry had a lasting effect, one that ultimately reconciled him to his own church: "I was intrigued that Jeff, who was openly gay, felt welcomed by the church. My law school activities and 'spiritual baggage' prevented me from exploring campus ministries then but I filed away the idea...."[36] The assorted recollections continued, each person returning to a familiar theme: "Acceptance of people from all walks of life,"[37] "challenged me to love some very diverse neighbors,"[38] "a community of faith in which I was unconditionally accepted,"[39] and "the sharing of disparate ways of believing."[40]

These responses also confirm the thesis that young adult education is "an initiation into conversation."[41] But for campus ministry to facilitate this education, it must adhere to the same principles that guide the university. One must acknowledge that many players are required in this conversational process, that no one individual or community can fully equip the young adult. And there must be consonance between what is preached and what is practiced, integrity that connects the principles held up as ideals with the practices of daily life.

---

[33] Roger Schellenberg to Sam Portaro, LS, 1991.
[34] Cal Fuller to Sam Portaro, LS, 16 July 1991, 1–2.
[35] Susan Green to Sam Portaro, LS, 19 July 1991, 4–5.
[36] Brad King to Sam Portaro, LS, 7 July 1991, 3.
[37] Jennifer DiNapoli to Sam Portaro, LS, 25 May 1991, 2.
[38] Tim Swanson, LS, 1991.
[39] Tara Kee, LS, 1991, 1.
[40] John Rebstock, LS, 9 June 1991, 2.
[41] Parks, 140.

Nowhere is this more evident than the young adult upheaval that wracked the nation and all its institutions in the 1960s and 1970s. The genesis of this turmoil, and its outcome in nearly an entire generation of disaffected citizens, was the failure of American institutions to honor these principles. The insistence of a predominantly white, male, Protestant, American hegemony that its vantage was the true one, that its opinions were the right ones, and that those opinions applied universally, were the threads of the racism, nationalism, and sexism that unravelled what had been conceived to be a seamless social fabric. The notion that white, Western men could do it all was challenged by African-, Asian-, Hispanic-, and Latino-American citizens, and by women. The notion that Protestant Christianity was the only true religion was challenged by increased numbers of Catholics, Moslems, Buddhists, and a host of new religions. The notion that American democracy was the only true polity was challenged by Vietnamese resistance to its imposition and by successive waves of ugly corruption at the heart of American government.

The implicit denial that this or any other nation might benefit from the collective energies and imaginations of all those who did not conform to the narrow profile of the predominant leadership represents at the national level the very antithesis of a conversational mentoring community. Furthermore, as heretofore suggested, it was the dissonance between avowed principles—civil and religious—and actual practices that young adults of that generation angrily denounced. Because of that blatant disregard for the integrity of principle and action, a generation of young adults—of all ages—came to a maturity that both denied the efficacy of the dominant institutions and, having created that void of leadership, reinforced innate principles of autonomy that seemed the only alternative in the short run, thus setting the stage for the intense self-centeredness of the late 1970s and 1980s.

Attention to the principles of collegiality and integrity, then, are essential components in campus ministry and provide a clue to the qualities necessary to establish and sustain such a ministry. They are also valuable clues in the seeking of campus ministry leadership. It may be well to ask prospective candidates for campus ministry leadership how their own vocations conform to these principles. Are they committed to and respectful of ministry that is open to all members of the community—including those beyond the denomination? Can they work collegially with a wide variety of other ministers in the conduct of this responsibility? If the contemplated ministry is parish based, it may also be well to pose these questions to the whole congregation, and certainly to its leadership. Can they support and nurture a ministry that does not demand rigid adherence or a single doctrine? Are they willing and able to include the fullness of the academy and the total community as partners in this ministry? And it may be wise to ask of all, no matter their answer to these questions, to account for the relationship between the principles they hold and the conduct of their life and ministry.

That no person or community can achieve perfection on the foregoing points is to be expected. Willingness to engage conflict, however, is a desirable quality in any ministry. This is not to suggest that rabble-rousing is the paradigm for campus ministry—lest that confirm a misapprehension long entertained by denominational churches. It is to say, however, that no ministry can escape conflict, nor would any thoughtful ministry wish to. Conflict is particularly important to the young adult and is an important part of the campus ministry experience. Some students will naturally encounter this conflict when their own experience comes up against new experience. Others will not naturally encounter conflict, especially if they tend to be shy, introverted, or asocial. All of us have developed habits that either blind us to or protect us from (or both) that which challenges us with its difference. Thus campus ministers, like all mentors to young adults, engage conflict with the young adult. Sometimes ministry mediates between the student's experience and existing conflict; at other times ministry must introduce conflict by opening limited human experience to unanticipated or unconsidered possibilities. The vocation to imagination, then, includes the vocation to conflict. It is a call to imagine oneself living beyond oneself, in the company of difference. Campus ministry is, in some ways, uniquely equipped to assist in this particular facet of the young adult mentoring process, especially on large campuses.

THE CHALLENGE OF CONVERSATION:
A MATTER OF SCALE

In a conversation she had with a student from a large university when she was teaching at a small college, Parks described her work with a first-year class at the smaller school, which included work with students on many hard questions fraught with potential for conflict and despair for such young adults.[42] The student from the larger university, a

---

[42] Ibid., 145.

senior, was shocked that first-year students were not devastated by the questions. But the senior student was accustomed to the large university, where much teaching was done in vast amphitheaters and student contact with instructors often limited. It was a campus of high-rise dormitories and little opportunity for intimate friendship beyond a roommate. Parks, on the other hand, was working within a small college where conversation was encouraged and where intimacy, and the smaller scale, increased the tolerance for engagement with conflict. These factors actually made possible a greater tolerance of conflict and enabled a more profound engagement with difficult questions.

The modest scale of campus ministry affords a similar setting for young adults. In fact, another of the consistencies in the mail received from former students reflected that this sense of proportion was a key ingredient in their own development. Even in relatively large campus ministries, involving over a hundred or more students, the essential work of the ministry seems to take place in the small-group setting, where interpersonal relationship is one of the most important learning resources. The vocation to ministry, then, may be a vocation to smallness, to intimacy—especially in times and situations where intimacy is in short supply. Christian ministry, as practiced by Jesus and presumably transmitted accordingly, is intensely personal and thus intentionally modest in its embrace. That is not to say that large ministry is always wrong, but rather to suggest that preoccupation with size can blind us to the virtues of ministry that provides important, even essential, experiences of intimate community where conflict can be experienced and mediated. "Small churches provide places where people can share in an intimate community....The members want to know about each other, to care about each other, to share one's pains and celebrations."[43] Nor is this feature of ministry unique to campus; the present American experience tends in many places to resemble that of the impersonality of the large university campus, suggesting that all modern Christian ministries might evaluate efficacy on merits other than the total head-count.

---

[43] Carl S. Dudley, "Small-Church Themes and Theology," *The Christian Ministry* 3 (May 1983): 6.

A MATTER OF PACING

Parks also noted the value of the "pause" necessary to young adult mentoring.[44] She rightly observed that when higher education left its roots in monasticism, it neglected to take with it a proper reverence for silence. This is not to suggest that campus ministry must recapture the monastic ethos, though some have attempted and even done rather well at it. The occasional retreat, especially to a monastic center, can provide both pause and conscious conflict since the very experience is alien to the mainline Christian young adult experience. But there are other programmatic dimensions to derive from the value of pause. To expect campus ministry always and everywhere to be "on" and to be visible in high-profile—even frenetic—programs, is to underestimate the potential contribution campus ministry can make by providing the young adult with an unprogrammed time in an otherwise over-programmed life.

Campus ministry is not necessarily called to inactivity. Indeed, the provision of respite for others and the extension of hospitality that asks nothing is both costly and difficult work. Campus ministry that balances activity with hospitality more nearly fulfills the mentoring functions. For example, pause consists not only of meditative silence but also of respite from customary demands. In conversational programs at Brent House, students are invited to dinner—and to bring spouses or friends. Though the substantive discussions of the program are valuable, and the presenting purpose for the students' being there, the students often remark that they particularly enjoyed the mealtime and the opportunity to visit quietly and casually with others. The provision of the meal, and a comfortable and attractive place to share it, are among the more expensive aspects of this campus ministry. But the ministry is in service to a young adult mentoring process that includes pause as an essential component in the mix. The practice of simple hospitality does more than entertain, however. It serves also to inform, to image a way of being in the world.

IMAGINING AND IMAGING

In the "community of imagination" students need *access* "to images (1) that give fitting form to truth, (2) that resonate with their lived experience, (3) that capture the 'ideal,' and (4) that recognize and name the dynamic character of ongoing transformation."[45] Providing such acces-

---

[44] Parks, 145.
[45] Ibid., 147.

sibility, as we have noted, can be particularly difficult in the parish setting. Nor is it necessarily easier in the non-parochial campus ministry. Each of the four requirements of "image," contains seeds for difficulty.

Images that "give fitting form to truth" require that one be open to diverse images and points of view, that one resist the temptation to narrowly define truth, or make exclusive claims for truth. That is not to say that the campus minister or campus ministry community cannot hold an exclusive or particular view in itself, but rather that campus ministries do not serve the young adult in the exploration of a mature faith when they make the choice and deny the young adult that experience. Campus ministries are under obligation to help the young adult explore the myriad images of truth. In that exploration they should be prepared to "witness to the truth that is in us," explaining how and why such images as they hold to be true are forms that accord with their own experience of truth. But the young adult experience may be different, and to that difference one must continue to be open.

Sharing the exploration thus invites the young adult to offer criticism of the faith community's images. The young adult seeks images "resonant" with lived experience. In conversation each learns the relativism of all experience. It is tempting to denigrate the experience of the young as insufficient, when in reality, their experiences are only different. The "truth" of parental affection, and biblical images that characterize God in parental terms, may resonate with my particular experience of mother and father. Yet, even advanced age can be humbled and cowed in the face of young adult (or children's) testimony of contrary experience, experience that reveals the limitations of my experience and opens new images—even unthinkable images—in the truth of parental abuse.

Images that capture the "ideal," then, are of tremendous importance to the young adult. In this regard, campus ministry has the specific gift of particular faith to contribute to the young adult experience. Drawing upon the collective experience of faith communities, campus ministry does offer access to images that capture the ideal—an ideal that is often couched in paradox, as is life itself. Access and admission to a conversation that includes the expanse of the biblical tradition and its witnesses (historical and contemporary) can open the young adult to "the motion of life and its transformations—particularly the dialectic between fear and hope, shipwreck and gladness, death and resurrection, bondage and freedom."[46] Beckoning and welcoming the young adult into that tension

---

[46] Ibid., 155.

is the vocation of campus ministry and constitutes an important part of the young adult's own vocational journey.

The very dialectic of vocation is such that vocational "call" is itself communicated via conversation. We "call" one another. The young adult communicates in many ways the desire to become more and more adult. Response to that desire is not only a response to the young adult, but is also a response to the God who calls the church into relationship with the young adult. In responding to one another we are also responding to God. The delicacy of discernment, however, requires that the church be attentive to the many different voices that call out to it. Thus the process of vocational discernment is also of that paradoxical dialectic.

The "priestly" component of ministry is, then, the establishment and nurture of relationship, the basis for conversation. This ministry traditionally characterized by the priestly, sacramental imposition of baptism and the celebration of the Eucharist, is no longer limited to those functions, important as they are. The "priestly" dimensions of campus ministry invite a daily communion of the baptized in the living of vocation.

The appointment of campus ministry involves the entire community of church and university in conversation. Campus ministry, often described as a ministry "marginal" to both the church and the university, is actually beyond the margins of each. As such, it represents a place apart, within which campus and congregation may share the vocational process, the struggle to be a faithful people.

8

PASTORAL CARE AS STEWARDSHIP

CHALLENGING COMMON ASSUMPTIONS

"You must do lots of counselling." That is a common response to the campus minister's introduction. The assumption that campus ministry devotes much of its energy to private counselling of students, and perhaps faculty, is one that persists in many places, on campus and off. Yet counselling occupies only a portion of the campus ministry agenda, probably no more and frequently less than is true of parochial ministry. American university campuses are replete with counselling resources. Student health facilities are often sophisticated medical units, with counsel available on a wide range of health issues. Student mental health clinics frequently provide in-depth psychoanalysis, as well as group counsel for addiction, abuse, stress, even study skills and dissertation anxiety. Career and placement services offer guidance testing and career counselling. Academic advisors assist in the selection of courses and they, or yet another substratum of professionals, advise students on matters of institutional policy and negotiating the shoals of life on campus.

When Kenneth Underwood described the "pastoral" role of the campus minister in 1969 he realized that the model of "moralistic shepherd" was already defunct. "The question for the future," wrote

Underwood,"has become how to organize the varied skills and historic convictions of individual clergy into an ecumenical ministry that offers respected, recognizable, associated pastoral services in a vast system of personnel workers, counselors, faculty research, student organizations, and continuing and adult education."[1]

The pastoral task of campus ministry, like the priestly task, must be re-appointed for a community of ministry that extends beyond the ordained campus minister. A new ecumenism is called for, but not necessarily limited to an inter-denominational cooperation. A new ecumenism—the root of which literally means "to inhabit"—respects the ministry of all who inhabit the world of campus ministry and, indeed, embraces the whole of creation. That being the case, the pastoral role of campus ministry is one that transcends spiritual direction, counselling, or any of the limited images of pastoralia. The pastoral role of ministry is, fundamentally, a matter of *stewardship*. The transition to a pastoral stewardship demands much more, though, than a change in vocabulary.

The habit of connecting pastoral ministry with human need is hard to break. "Where did we get the modern use of *need*?" asked Steele Martin. "Many clergy and lay leaders, along with our American culture have taken over a marketing mentality and metaphysic....We ask questions like: What are the needs of the church? This is an ambiguous question. Does it mean the church as an institution (more money and more people), or does it mean the physical and psychological needs of church members?"[2] As Martin suggests, the church's professional leadership— and much of its membership—has tended to perceive of ministry in the same way the marketer perceives of the market. Pressed to justify itself in tangible terms, ministry seeks human need to which it can address itself and presumably devote itself to relieving. Failing that, the church—like the manufacturer—is also capable of creating need, urging people to itself. The extreme of this tendency is analyzed in Anne Wilson Schaef's *The Addictive Organization*.[3] Indeed, the classical structure of Protestant preaching is predicated upon establishing the sinful human condition, convincing and convicting the human heart of its need, to which the gospel offers fulfillment.

---

[1] Danforth, v.1, 100.

[2] Steele W. Martin with Priscilla C. Martin, *Blue Collar Ministry: Problems and Opportunities for Mainline "Middle" Congregations* (New York: The Alban Institute, 1989), 40.

[3] Anne Wilson Schaef and Diane Fassel, *The Addictive Organization* (San Francisco: Harper & Row, 1988).

But there is another basis for ministry, rooted in the creation itself. It is the creeds' commitment to a creation that is not only unitive but is also pure gift. Rooted in the origins of human life, the vocation of the human—according to Jewish and Christian perspectives—is a vocation to stewardship. The mercantile bent of modern American Christians tends to limit stewardship to matters of money. Money is certainly a part of stewardship—as are time and talent, each of which is valued in dollars in the current society. But we venture that stewardship is the foundation of pastoral care.

The very word "pastoral" is derived from the vocabulary of animal husbandry, and sheepherding, in particular. The shepherd feeds and tends the flock, though the biblical shepherd never really seems to possess the flock. Moses tended the flock of his father-in-law before being entrusted with God's own flock. The Psalmist knows God to be the shepherd of life (Psalm 23), but Jesus insisted that God was the owner of the flock. Those who tended the flock, including Jesus, were to be ever mindful of the enormous trust invested in their oversight and ministrations. Everything that was done on behalf of the flock, or to the neglect of the flock, measured the stewardship of the shepherd.

Stewards figured prominently in the parables of Jesus. There were wily ones and clever ones, lazy ones and ambitious ones. Even Jesus, though he used the image of financial stewards to illustrate his teachings, seemed especially concerned to impress upon his hearers the reality that life and ministries are to be based in stewardship.

ENLARGING NOTIONS OF STEWARDSHIP

Our research began with a question: Why is campus ministry so little regarded today in the mainline Protestant agenda? We determined to examine, among other things, the financial records of the Methodist, Episcopal, and Presbyterian churches. We were interested in following the ways of their hearts, so we looked to their treasures—on the premise that, as Jesus indicated, where their treasures were, so would their hearts be also. We were interested to see how the stewardship of monies affected campus ministry, for we had heard the frequent and growing lament of campus ministers that funding for this ministry is diminishing. We have discovered that it is for the most part true; campus ministry funding has diminished, at least at the national level of denominational life.

But we also learned that campus ministers' tendency to evaluate relationship on the basis of financing betrays a fundamental insecurity and a lack of self-esteem. Is it not ironic that ministers and ministries that devote copious energies to nurturing and encouraging young adults away from self-evaluations based upon the marketplace, nevertheless succumb to the same dynamics themselves? Campus ministers urge young adults not to value themselves in terms of their earning potential or to gauge their worth on what they can accumulate. Then campus ministers lament that they are undervalued and under-appreciated when the budget is cut.

That is not to exonerate the church or those agencies that still bear responsibility as stewards of the considerable resources God has vested in those who are presently on campus—a large and growing segment of American society. It is to say, however, that campus ministers have perhaps for too long attempted to justify their ministries, especially in the eyes of the institutions and constituencies they serve, by appealing to the institution's or the constituency's *need* of them. Not infrequently, these justifications are rightly identified by the church as self-serving: the implications of these justifications are that the church *needs* ordained, professional campus ministers.

As a steward of life on campus, the church does have a responsibility to extend care to everyone in that arena. But ordained ministry is only one means of achieving that end responsibly. Increasingly, the church is challenged to find new ways to fulfill that responsibility. To break through the anger, hurt, and misunderstanding that attend the campus ministry task today the church needs to reclaim the work of stewardship as its pastoral model. To care for one another, to care about one another, is to exercise a profound stewardship. Just as many people are awakening to a new appreciation for the earth, and developing an ecological theology reflecting greater care for the earth, so that impulse might bear extension. After all, human relations are no less important to the earth's well-being than any other elements of the eco-system. Moreover, a pastoral stewardship is concerned not only with cleaning up the toxic animosities and suspicions that now separate us but is rightly concerned with preventive care for one another. Thus Christians might move beyond a clinical pastoral care based upon the treatment of illness to espouse a stewardship of mutual strength and shared resources.

FROM HURTS TO HEALING

Experience indicates that previous hostilities and hurts in campus ministry have centered largely around budgetary issues. The legendary lore of mainline campus ministry bristles with tales of blood-letting, and some of those tales are true. As this history documents, there were precipitous cuts, especially in national budgets. They were most pronounced for Episcopalians in the late 1960s and early 1970s, and came to Presbyterians and Methodists[4] within the next decade. The cuts made no sense to those laboring in campus ministry because those were among their most prolific years. Students, faculty, and administrators were visibly engaged in many campus ministries. Chaplains were visible and outspoken. Some became articulate leaders in their denominations; a few—like William Sloane Coffin—were even prominent in the national arena. It is true that much of the campus ministry activity of the time was related to the political unrest that was so much a part of the campus scene. Then at the height of this activity the money disappeared.

Campus ministers were not often given a satisfactory explanation for the cutbacks. Or, if they were, they elected not to hear it. At the very least, church administrators must bear the blame for inattention to communication, or, worse, for perpetrating misunderstanding through intentional obfuscation. Lacking any clear rationale for the shift in funding priorities, campus ministers drew their own conclusions. Reverting to the simple equation of cause and effect, they reasoned that there must be a connection between their political activity and activism on campus and the resultant recall of funds from the church. It was a simple and reasonable conclusion. But it was the wrong conclusion; our research indicates that while political sentiments may well have played a minor role in the reallocation of funds throughout the church, other factors were far more important. Three factors, hand in hand, changed the face of the church and, consequently, of campus ministry. One was democratic, the other was demographic, the third was both democratic and demographic. All had economic consequences.

The democratic factor was civil rights. By the late 1960s, the civil rights movement in the United States matured. The issue was engaged, legislative steps were taken to provide legal access to the disenfranchised, and the African-American communities of varied perspectives began to coalesce and assume responsibility for their well-being. What remained, however, was a compelling need for financial resources.

---

4 Though it should be noted that such cuts were least dramatic for Methodists.

Government entitlements opened the door to possibilities but offered little that was tangible. For example, African-Americans could be admitted to schools that had previously been closed to them, but who was to pay tuition? They could move into neighborhoods previously closed, but how could they afford a mortgage? They could develop their own business enterprises, but where would they secure capital? The denominations were pressed to consider these questions. They numbered African-Americans among their own memberships. Prior to the 1960s many had maintained racially exclusive administrations or structures, even separate denominations, but as the decade of the 60s came to a close, the denominations, for the most part, had also been integrated—at least in theory. In local congregations integration was slower in coming. Despite a decade's experience with civil rights, denominations, perhaps of denial, were caught off guard in the late 1960s. When they did respond it was frequently done quickly and out of existing program monies.

But program funds were themselves in short supply. Demographics dealt the church a wild card. By the 1960s, the baby boom crested and the wave of spectacular church growth was subsiding. A more mobile and diverse culture forsook traditional loyalties for new experiences or simple convenience. Birth rates declined, and Sunday Schools began to look like the orchestra for Haydn's "Surprise Symphony": as each finished a part, he or she left the stage until, by the early 1970s there were few little chairs filled on Sunday mornings. Universities, too, faced diminishing enrollments. Those who reallocated funds no doubt considered these demographic realities as they scrambled to address immediate needs.

The third factor, which was both demographic and democratic, had to do with the shape of the church itself. Those who did remain within the church as the sifting of the 1960s progressed were of a different stripe than those who shook out. Those who remained were, in many respects, hardcore. Their dedication and devotion was attested not only in their fidelity to their church membership but in the depth of their commitment to ministry. Sensitized, perhaps by the civil rights movement itself, they were the more aware of how the very structures of denominational administration affected their lives and ministries. As resources grew more scarce they demanded more authority over the disposition of those resources. In the mainline denominations this translated into what was perceived to be increased giving at the local level and lower giving to the national church. While overall giving may well have increased—and would have had to if only to keep pace with rampant inflation—the real story was far less optimistic. In reality the laity were engineering their own reallocation. In mainline churches where lay leadership owns authority for denominational policy the laity opted to retain more funding locally and to exercise their own ministries at the local level.

RESTORING THE PRIMACY OF THE LOCAL

The localization of mainline denominational ministry did, at least in part, reflect the introspective character of the 1970s and was frequently lambasted as such by the hierarchies whose own fortunes were diminished. But the demographic change in the profile of church membership, and that membership's own determination to restore a democratic ministry to the church, changed the economic life of the mainline denominations. Campus ministry, which had not since the 1920s-30s enjoyed close ties to the local church but tended to rely upon regional and national sources for support, overlooked a very important point in this shift: they failed to see that it was not the national or the regional bureaucracy that actually fed them; it was the local church.

Angry and bitter campus ministers harangued conference, synod, diocesan, and national administrators over their reversal of fortune. But the bureaucratic administrators were powerless to change the tide, and still are. They do not control the revenues of the denomination nor do they truly establish the priorities for mission. Increasingly that authority rests with the laity, as it should. The tragic irony, however, is that the laity who possess this authority have not always known the benefits of sound preaching and education or the committed and sustained life of devotion and service through which the gospel's principles are imparted. Those laity who determine budget—which is to say "mission"—priorities may be least equipped to make those decisions, and the ordained leadership who possess the educational and spiritual resources are furthest removed by political constraint from monetary decision. The redistribution of authority has created an impasse characterized by the present tendency toward "survival" as the inadequacies and insecurities of each side conspire to dominate.

At the heart of this issue there lies a fundamental need for reconciliation. This history is not rehearsed in order to assign culpability or to inflame hostilities. While campus ministry has certainly suffered loss of money and morale, campus ministry has some repenting to do to get on with the business of restoring this ministry of the church. At the very least peace must be made with denominational administrations and forgiveness sought for misplaced anger that only compounded their jobs and drove all farther apart. New relationships must be built with colleagues in ministry throughout the church. This much is essential to the stewardship of our lives; to neglect this task is to squander that most precious resource we have in each other.

Every Christian creed professes a common dependency in stating that God has made everything that is. Being of one family—as the baptismal acclamations proclaim, "one Lord, one Spirit, one Baptism"— we "depend," we literally "hang" from this principle. Yet, dependence is hard. It is hard for us individually. It is especially hard for those who know relative autonomy, as campus ministry does. The importance of addressing our dependence, however, has been articulated by Christopher Lasch:

> What makes the modern temper modern...is not that we have lost our childish sense of dependence but that the normal rebellion *against* dependence is more pervasive today than it used to be. But this rebellion is not new, as Flannery O'Connor reminds us when she observes that "there are long periods in the lives of us all...when the truth as revealed by faith is hideous, emotionally disturbing, downright repulsive." If "right now the whole world seems to be going through a dark night of the soul," it is because the normal rebellion against dependence appears to be sanctioned by our scientific control over nature—the same progress of science that has allegedly destroyed religious superstition
>
> Those wonderful machines that science has enabled us to construct have made it possible to imagine ourselves as masters of our fate. In an age that fancies itself as disillusioned, this is the one illusion—the illusion of mastery—that remains as tenacious as ever. But now that we are beginning to grasp the limits of our control over the natural world, the future of this illusion...is very much in doubt—more problematical, certainly, than the future of religion.[5]

A stewardship of one another evinces a dependence that serves as antidote to the pervasive autonomy and antipathy that drive us apart. This kind of stewardship is itself a witness to a different way of being and relating. It extends the Christian vocation into the world and, perhaps more to the immediate point, throughout the church.

---

5 Lasch, 22.

NEW LIVES FOR OLD

Repenting an old life and taking up a new one is hardly ever easy; yet it is the constant work of the church and its members. Lest one think this work outmoded or inconsequential, note that Lynne Cheney, chair of the National Endowment for the Humanities, in 1990 entitled her report to Congress, "Tyrannical Machines: A Report on Educational Practices Gone Wrong and Our Best Hopes for Setting Them Right."[6] Cheney's prescription for educational reform should strike chords of recognition for those in Christian ministry. She acknowledges that while complaints are common, they seldom add anything constructive to the solution. She entitled her report with a phrase coined by William James; "tyrannical machines," maintained James, are the intractable habits and practices that persist, despite their ineffectiveness.[7] Challenging and changing those "tyrannical machines" in the field of education demands "alternate ways."[8]

The "tyrannical machines" that take hold of our lives and dominate were once called "sin" in the Christian vocabulary. Indeed, the apostle Paul would readily recognize Cheney's point. The way Christians have traditionally greeted the darkness includes not only cursing the void, but lighting a candle, as well. Confession is but a part of repentance; seeking a new way—and frequently in the opposite direction—is also required.

Campus ministers should seek reconciliation with churches at the local, regional, and national levels. But what of the churches? What can they do? The most ready answer is "Give more money." But that is not the answer we advocate. We propose something different and, in some ways, something far more difficult than increasing funding. We propose challenging the "tyrannical machines" that hold evangelism, and evangelistic ministries like campus ministry, hostage.

Mainline denominational churches are concerned about their role in the changing face of religion in America. Mainline churches post little or no growth in membership. Intentional programs of evangelism aimed at reversing the tide seem to little avail. In 1989 Wayne Schwab reported to the Episcopal Church:

---

[6] Lynne V. Cheney, "Tyrannical Machines: A Report of Education Practices Gone Wrong and Our Best Hopes for Setting Them Right," reprinted in *The Chronicle of Higher Education* (14 November 1991): A22ff.

[7] Ibid., A22.

[8] Ibid.

We have been working explicitly at evangelism since 1973. Why have we not seen growth? Yes, participation in worship is up 25% since 1974; our giving leads all major denominations; and our retention of members is still the highest. Why then only 2,462,301 Episcopalians as of the end of 1987? Why no more results than these after 14 years?[9]

The question posed by Schwab is echoed in all mainline denominations.

George Gallup and Jim Castelli, in their *The People's Religion: American Faith in the 90's*, confirmed that decline in mainline Protestant church membership is caused primarily by the loss of young adults. Of their members under the age of 30, between 1983 and 1987, the Methodist Church lost 1 percent, the Episcopalians and the Presbyterians each lost 4 percent. In 1988 the proportion of Americans who claimed church or synagogue membership was 65 percent, but that was the lowest figure in the 50 years the Gallup organization had conducted their poll. Of the decline in membership, the polls further indicated that the greatest loss was among college graduates. In 1987, 74 percent of that constituency claimed church membership; by 1988—only one year later—only 64 percent claimed church membership.[10] Yet, as Schwab's computations and Gallup's figures concur, church attendance has remained rather stable.

Campus ministry is fond of defending its place on the church agenda by citing its own contributions to church growth. Al Minor, citing a Gallup Poll, noted that "56% of the members of the Episcopal Church [at the time of the poll] were not 'cradle' Episcopalians..., that 60% of those non-cradle Episcopalians received their first powerful impression of the Episcopal Church from a campus ministry."[11] As Minor adds, that "powerful impression" could have come from a variety of sources, some only peripheral or tangential to the active ministry of the denomination on campus.

A new stewardship might lead to a different conclusion than the one Schwab reported and to a deeper appreciation of genuine care as an instrument of evangelism. Measuring the effectiveness of campus ministry by the number of students, faculty, staff, and administrators that can be accounted for in weekly services of worship reinforces the

---

[9] A. Wayne Schwab, "Orientation to the Decade of Evangelism" report (8 December 1989), 1.

[10] Gallup & Castelli, 26–29.

[11] Al Minor, "Evangelism and the Episcopal Church's Ministries in Higher Education," report n.p., 3–4.

"tyrannical machine" that has driven the church to evaluate itself and its ministry in its ability to *contain* and *retain* members.

READING AND HEEDING EVIDENCES

Gallup and Castelli drew their own conclusions from their data, conclusions that bear examination. They concluded that size of particular denominations was not likely to be an issue in the 1990s; instead, they discerned directional movement as a more important consideration. They saw a trend toward small, conservative, fundamentalist churches on the one hand, and movement out of religion altogether on the other. Secondly, they saw greater interest in religion, despite the reality that the number of unchurched Americans was growing, along with those who chose no religious affiliation at all. Third, they saw stability. They saw the churches as maintaining an even keel, but they saw a rather rough sea in a culture that was increasingly skeptical of religion's relevance in modern society, and whose confidence in organized religion was rapidly waning. In short, they concluded that Americans were drawing ever more distinct lines between organized religion and personal religious behavior.[12]

Interestingly, a similar phenomenon was observed of the Catholic church by Charles Morris. While that communion is not integral to our study, Morris's confirmation of the trends deduced by Gallup and Castelli indicates that the changing shape of American religion portends extensive consequences and implies that these issues are not confined to the mainline Protestant tradition, but pertain to certain structures of American Christianity. Morris notes that "...according to the researches of Father Andrew Greeley, at the National Opinion Research Center, and his associates, Catholicism at the grass roots is flourishing as never before. But yet the official Church is on the verge of collapse—priests and nuns resigning in droves, vanishing vocations, empty collection boxes. The Catholic *religion*...may be separating itself from the hierarchical Catholic *Church*."[13]

---

[12]   Gallup & Castelli, 44.

[13]   Charles R. Morris, "The Three Ages of the Catholic Church," review of *Decrees of the Ecumenical Councils*, ed. Norman P. Tanner, S.J. (London: Sheed & Ward; Washington, D.C.: Georgetown University Press, 1990) 2 vols. *Atlantic Monthly* (July 1991): 112.

In light of these trends—probably more accurately claimed as realities—strategies aimed at encouraging church membership alone are not likely to suffice. If they do, they will appeal only to a limited segment of the population. The dual issues of relevance and confidence, long denied by the churches themselves, cannot be ignored. Those who denigrate relevance and confidence only reveal blindness, or willful ignorance, of Jesus' own ministry. Jesus' ministry was relevant because it was not confined to the synagogue, but went out to people where they were and engaged them at that level (no matter how low or, for that matter, how high). And Jesus' ministry cultivated personal relationship in preference to an institutionalism that was urged upon him from many sides. That he did not "organize" or "mobilize" a movement was a source of consternation to some like Judas. That he might do so was the fear of the religious and political authorities. Within this context, then, campus ministry can offer the church a new way.

Will Hinson, Director of the Charlotte (N.C.) Episcopal Chaplaincy Program, is responsible for campus ministry on several colleges and universities, most of them oriented toward the commuter student. He started keeping a log, largely for his own information, of the people he met in his daily routine. Some meetings were lengthy and of evident substance; others were fleeting—perhaps only a greeting en route and far less easily quantified. The difference in perspective revealed a much more vibrant and vital ministry, one that reached out to a vast number of people when calculated from care instead of containment.

Schwab's report did acknowledge what others have noted of the young adult community, and the baby-boom cohort, in particular: that "when their concerns about job, intimacy and power are taken seriously,"[14] these constituencies are responsive. But what does it mean to take these concerns seriously?

STEWARDS IN COMMUNITY

At the outset, a respectful pastoral concern demands that we listen to one another, and that we honor what we hear. It may be true, for example, that students in the 1970s and 1980s were preoccupied with job concerns and oriented toward self, moving headlong into privatism. Criticism of those student and cultural proclivities was abundant. But as Cheney suggested in her own report, complaint was insufficient to

---

[14] Schwab, 9.

address reform. Few asked or seemed to care to know *why* the concern for jobs and *why* the retreat into privatism. Similarly, when planning programs to address these issues clergy tended to reflect a critical, and often negative, bias.

The University of Chicago is a major research university with an undergraduate college, graduate divisions for humanities and sciences, and four professional schools: law, medicine, business, and divinity. Of the approximately 10,000 students enrolled, about 3,000 are undergraduates, the remaining 7,000 apportioned to the graduate and professional divisions. Students in the professional and graduate divisions are, as one might expect, quite concerned with issues of career. Their work is intense, as are they. They are in a highly competitive environment and graduate into a highly competitive market.

In the autumn of 1985, a new deacon volunteered part-time ministry to the Episcopal campus ministry at Brent House. Cathy Phillips' husband was a student in the medical school pursuing the double doctorate, the M.D. and the Ph.D. A newsletter or journal reporting a program elsewhere entitled "Medicine: The Tragic Profession," piqued our interest. The notion of doctors sharing their perspectives on loss seemed an unusual and interesting topic for pursuit. Cathy conferred with her husband, to ask how he thought medical students would take to the program, and which doctors would be good candidates for the program. His response was encouraging and Cathy arranged for three doctors to share the panel. A member of the board at Brent House, whose own profession was graphic art, designed and donated striking posters that were circulated on campus. On the evening of the program forty students of the approximately 400 enrolled in the medical school showed up. The conversation stimulated by the stated program topic was lively and informative and gave way to conversation that ultimately changed the course of our ministry. The students demanded of the doctors to know why the concerns they addressed in that evening's program were not part of the regular curriculum—why, indeed, such topics seemed forbidden in the classroom.

There was no conclusive answer to the question. But responding to that question with the assistance of the doctors who were present, we determined to address it. Three students at the program volunteered to explore the matter in conversation. The chaplain arranged to meet with them weekly for about eight weeks over a sack lunch. But the tactic taken did not attempt to reform the medical school curriculum. Instead, the chaplain asked the simple question: "If you could talk about anything that you're not talking about now, what would you talk about, and with whom would you like to have the conversation?" A number of questions were elicited and noted, then reduced to six: two programs for each of the three academic quarters. Then doctors and other relevant people were identified who would enlarge the conversation. When asked about practical concerns, the students decided that dinner meetings were feasible "since everyone has to eat, anyway." Program dates were set for the coming academic year on the premise that quality programs, and securing good resource people, demanded a good lead time. Dates were scattered over the calendar, with attention to exams and important conflicts in the medical school routine. The campus ministry offered to coordinate the administrative task of notifying speakers, producing publicity materials, and hosting meals and programs. Vegetarian meals were deemed best for reasons of religious and health dietary restrictions (vegetarian menus allow Jewish students to participate more readily), and because they were economical. A student was hired to prepare the meals on a modest budget, speakers and panelists were invited to donate their time and responded generously, and the graphic artist designed a coordinated brochure detailing the full series and post-card size reminders that were distributed by a student volunteer to the in-house mailbox of each medical student about ten days in advance of each program.

As the series unfolded, volunteers were solicited to plan the following year's series. The routine was always the same: they were invited to attend one, at most two, dinner meetings at which they brainstormed about the topics and speakers they wanted for the coming year, communicated any changes in procedure or calendar that might improve the program, and accepted responsibility for the modest tasks of communication necessary to secure speakers and promote the programs.

Soon thereafter another "pilot" program was tried in the graduate school of business. Robert Payton, then President of the Exxon Education Foundation and an alumnus of the university, came to the chaplain's attention through an interview article in the alumni magazine. He responded to our invitation, flying to Chicago at his own expense, and gave a rousing presentation on "Philanthropy as a Vocation" to about seventy-five students, faculty, and interested members of the university development office and the Chicago philanthropic community. His remarks on philanthropy were provocative and instructive, grounding the history and motivation for philanthropy in the religious heritage that spawned it. His words seemed uniquely suited to stimulating conversation among business school students. Soon we had a committee of business school students exploring programs in their own professional discipline.

When a law student who was active in the local Episcopal parish learned of the initiatives in medicine and business, he asked if we might do something with his professional school. We invited him to gather a few of his like-minded friends and with about six of them around the dinner table, we launched the conversation. After years of wondering how to reach the diverse and dispersed communities of graduate students in the humanities and sciences, it finally occurred to us that most of them would be taking up careers in teaching and/or research. That gave rise to two new initiatives: one for prospective teachers and another for prospective research professionals.

In the autumn of 1989 we invited the undergraduates most active in our worship to come to a dinner with no agenda and to bring their friends with them. Turnout was modest—about 12-15 at most. As we had done with their graduate counterparts, we asked them what we might offer them that they were not at present getting from their life on campus. After several weeks of loose discussion and a zillion ideas, the group agreed that what they really wanted was a drama company. That they already had nearly half a dozen theater groups on campus seemed not to matter to them. They wanted one that was different. They wanted one that would allow them to be directed by a professional director (of which there are hundreds struggling to make their marks in Chicago's theatrical community), and they wanted a chance to use drama as a means of exploring religious and moral themes and issues.

They selected *Godspell* as their first show and put a new spin on this campus musical war-horse by casting an Asian Jesus and a mixed-gender, multi-racial band of apostles. The venture "lost " $900—a pretty reasonable price for undergraduate programming when all was said and done. The following year they were granted $500 from our operating budget. They produced *As Is*, a controversial play about living and dying with AIDS that travelled to city organizations and a suburban parish youth event. Their production of *Cabaret*, chronicling the rise of Nazism and the cost of social collusion, came to campus amidst a season of virulent anti-gay harassment. And they stayed within their budget.

The Episcopal campus ministry at Brent House claims only a modest attendance at weekly worship: about 15-20 at a Sunday evening Eucharist at our main facility; about 15-18 at a mid-week, noon Eucharist on campus in a divinity school chapel. Even factoring the different constituencies of the congregations (there is little overlap), and the varied habits of devotion and schedule that change those weekly congregations, we can only claim to sustain regular contact with 75-100 people through weekly worship.

In the academic year 1989-90, we mounted 36 programs arranged by a total of 58 planning committee members, with 103 guest panelists or speakers. Combined attendance at the programs, the dramatic productions, two continuing education programs for area clergy and seminarians, and one forum on racial justice amounted to 1,710. Changes in our own load, combining of series, and a variety of other factors reduced that number by nearly half the following year, but we still average an outreach—beyond the weekly worship routine—of about 1000 per year.

RESPONSE AND RESPECT

We attribute this accomplishment to a new stewardship that saw the students, the campus, the church, and the community as valuable and valued resources. We respect their vocations—that the students are here to secure an education and that is their rightful priority—and we plan our events accordingly. These meetings are planned over the dinner hour, to last from six to eight o'clock in the evening to allow students and gracious panelists/speakers opportunity to go on to study, family, or other activities. They are episodic programs—not serial, requiring sustained attendance—to encourage varied students to engage at points of personal interest or concern.

We respect the students' desire to make conversation the heart of the experience, thus we put everything else in service to that end. Consequently, we do not expect the students to prepare the meal, secure and set up the meeting place, or attend to details that would otherwise siphon off their energies or detract from the primary purpose of the occasion. Indeed, we have *invited* them here. They are our guests. Often they willingly pitch in, offering to help with publicity, or securing a speaker, or enlisting interest in planning. But it is not required of them; hence, they do not burn out, but tend in some instances to remain quite faithful to the project, as well as to the individual events.

We respect what the students tell us of their concerns and we, in turn, teach that those concerns are inherently religious. They want to know how to balance demanding careers with the personal commitments to marriage and family. They want to know how to relate to clients and patients as human beings. They want to know how to bear the burden of responsibility. They want to know how to relate across the many lines that divide us as a society. And they want to know what resources are there for them to draw upon. These are vocational issues, religious concerns.

But we do not preach to them—not in these settings. We invite members of their own professional community to share these concerns with them. And we dare to be bold in our invitation. As a result, law students have reflected on their profession with former Attorney-General Edward Levi. Business school students have heard William Smithburg, CEO of Quaker Oats, speak personally of ethical responsibility, and have argued ecological reform and employee relations with Ed Rensi, President of McDonald's. Medical school students have heard a dean and noted surgeon speak of his recovery from alcoholism, and listened to a pediatric oncologist tell of the role her faith plays in her daily ministrations to seriously ill children and their families. The response of the speakers and panelists is revealing: though they have donated their time and talent, many thank us for the opportunity to share in this manner.

Because the programs are conversational, we caution guest speakers not to make elaborate preparation: they are being invited because we believe they possess in themselves everything they need to fulfill our invitation. They are encouraged to be casual and open to dialogue with the students. Thus, speakers come relaxed and relate at a different level. Even faculty with whom the students claim familiarity in the classroom will reveal quite different facets of themselves in our living room. Sharing a simple meal, served buffet style, everyone sits casually around the living area, enjoying informal social conversation for half to three-quarters of an hour before the evening's "formal" topic is engaged.

Over coffee and dessert, one of the students from the planning committee—perhaps the one who first suggested the evening's topic—or one of the staff[15] welcomes everyone, says a brief word about the history and purpose of the series, and makes introductions. Speakers are introduced only by name and invited to introduce themselves in whatever manner they wish. Students do not have to remain passive through a long presentation in order to get their own question on the floor. In fact, we make it quite clear that the format for the evening is a reversal of the usual. The questions of the students (and often questions brought in by

---

[15] Staff configurations are variable, the chaplain being the only full-time employee. Associate chaplains (lay and ordained), a part-time administrator, and resident managers all function as host/hostess for functions.

the panelists) are the structure for the occasion. Conversation is always lively and never fails to fill the allotted time to overflowing.

It is true that such discussions rarely venture into complex theology, or only tangentially touch the overtly religious. But the same might be said of Jesus' own parables. This parabolic approach to ministry on campus—replicable elsewhere—is content to meet people where they are, to attempt and perhaps begin a relationship within which the seeds of the gospel may be planted and may grow. We remind those who maintain that ministry demands deep commitment that ministry actually begins with a casual meeting. While deep commitment may be appropriate to any ministry, including those on campus, it is often forgotten that the process toward commitment is gradual.

The first step in that gradual process is important. When a student meets respect for his concern and a willingness to take seriously—even religiously—his questions, when the student is invited not into ritual but a conversation, the student is, indeed, meeting Jesus—and in a spirit that allows the Spirit to make relationship. Honoring the stranger—for everyone we meet is, upon first meeting, a stranger—is a venerable practice of the Christian tradition. Campus ministry, we suggest, is poised to do just that and to do it well.

COLLEGIALITY WITH THE FAMILIAR AND THE FOREIGN

We are also fortunate to be near a parish. But the parish is beyond the campus, in more ways than one. It is too distant for a pedestrian student population. And, as a parish, its life is concerned with different priorities from ours. By collegial agreement, we share our strengths with one another. As a campus ministry, we are ill-equipped to provide church school education or child care. Our chapel is modest and modern, not given to grand liturgy or profound aesthetic experience. We refer many students, especially married graduate students with children, to the parish. And the parish frequently apprises the lone student newcomer on Sunday mornings of the campus ministry. We worship at different times: they on Sunday morning, we on Sunday evening—not for fear of competition, but for pride of service. We are proud to be able to offer such diversity within a single denominational communion.

In some respects, campus ministry shares much in common with, and can learn much from, the more notable independent congregations around the country whose attraction of the unchurched young adult is increasingly visible. It would certainly be more difficult, and arguably less desirable, for parish churches to emulate in every detail these phenomenal new congregations. Anthony B. Robinson profiled the Willow Creek Church in South Barrington, Illinois, (a suburb of Chicago) for *The Christian Century*.[16] Parts of his description of Willow Creek could as easily be applied to campus ministry.

Robinson notes that one of the immediate distinctions of Willow Creek Church is that it is "not like most churches." Not only does the building, which bears no distinctive religious signage, not resemble a church, but it is further different in that it gives the appearance of an extremely "well-run operation that is prepared for guests." While Willow Creek Church resembles a theater, many campus ministry facilities resemble private homes or occupy multi-purpose buildings smaller in scale and different in architecture than the average parish church. The signal importance to this difference, according to Robinson, is that such difference attracts "those who are uncomfortable in most churches and who, by the time they have reached the doors of those churches, have received a number of signals, largely unintended, that they don't belong there."

While congregational participation in liturgy at Willow Creek Church was "non-existent"—not a condition we deem optimal in any worship setting—we propose that campus ministries that engage the unchurched with some program outside the customary tradition of worship effect the same end as Willow Creek, but without violating the fundamental tenet that Christian worship be distinct from passive entertainment. Campus ministry, no less than a Willow Creek Church, can address people's needs, and while we cannot claim to be always "entertaining," we can usually muster up the talent to be engaging. In this regard, campus ministry may actually offer an entry-level experience of greater integrity than that of the congregation that purports to entertain. Indeed, Robinson quotes Wade Clark Roof's argument that young adults "will not just return to church...[they] will pick and choose.... The congregations that attract them provide programs that have integrity and speak to their particular life issues." [17]

---

[16] Anthony B. Robinson, "Learning from Willow Creek Church," *The Christian Century* (23 January 1991): 68–70.

[17] Ibid., 69.

INTEGRITY

The issue of integrity deserves specific attention. It is directly related to the use of Parks' mentoring community in the previous chapter. Stewardship respects limits and practices the appropriate use of resources. Putting a penny in a blown fuse is poor stewardship, for it requires of the wiring more than it was created to bear. Ultimately, it can cost one the whole building—if only for the expenditure of a penny! Stewardship of care means appropriate regard for varied levels of human maturation, experience, and education.

As Robinson points out, "...the more established churches often seem to assume that people's lives and sense of values are coherent and workable. These churches focus on challenging people to get out and serve others. That assumption may be increasingly problematic in a society in which half of all marriages end in divorce and in which addiction is epidemic."[18] This mentality, which urges the sedentary to action and challenges the insular to move out, may well be appropriate to the minority—those who have been thoroughly equipped for ministry but have been sitting in the pews for far too long. But it is inappropriate to the newcomer. It is inappropriate, too, for the church member who, despite years of faithful attendance, nonetheless may have been denied the equipment to minister. Verna Dozier reminds that the church's business is "not soul saving. God has already done that, and nothing can be added to God's almighty work. Not legislating morality. That's shifting sand and lures us away from the Biblical call to repent. Not social service. The need for the church to do social service is eloquent testimony...that we have failed in our business. So what is our business? Ministry."[19]

Those who maintain that students and others need more experience in social action and hands-on ministry are no doubt correct, to a point. In fact, evidence suggests that student volunteerism is on the rise, and national statistics on philanthropy indicate that America is still the most generous nation of all when it comes to financial support in the non-profit sector and in the giving of time to volunteer operations.[20] But

---

[18] Ibid., 70.

[19] Verna Dozier, ed. *The Calling of the Laity* (New York: The Alban Institute, 1988), 117.

[20] The Council on Foundations reported in its August 19, 1991 "Council Columns" newsletter [Vol. 10, No. 13] that Americans gave nearly $123 billion to charity in 1990. Of that amount 83 percent, or $101.8 billion, was in individual donations. Religious organizations received over half of all contributions: $67.76 billion. These figures do

ministry is also needed for those who have not yet reached that point of integration.

Students of our acquaintance evidence, in their choice of conversation topics, a sincere desire to deal with the issues of commitment and integrity that are prerequisite to a life of responsible citizenship in the church, in society, or in both. Inattention to this dimension of stewardship is terribly costly. Soliciting volunteers too hastily and demanding commitment of students or parishioners prematurely is tantamount to replacing the fuse with a penny: it can short-circuit relationship with the church and induce burn-out, ministerial melt-down.

INTEGRATION

Sometimes efforts can be fortuitously combined. When Catholic and Episcopal students at The College of William and Mary launched a combined drama ministry, no one had any notion of what would result. The minimal hope was a decent performance. Three years into the venture, the students mounted a production of *Joseph and the Amazing Technicolor Dreamcoat*. When the professional director resigned for reasons of family health, the students elected to proceed with one of their own as director. Under student leadership (and no coaching from the chaplains), each player was sent into the biblical scriptures to study the story, with particular attention to his or her character. On opening night, the director summoned one of the chaplains with the dire news that the cast was in the dressing room and refused to go on. The greater shock came when the director smiled and told the chaplain the cast refused to go on—until the chaplain came to the dressing room and prayed with them! Eventually, students looked back at six productions over four years—and a profit of over $10,000 that they donated to various charities. They learned much in the exercise, including how to share the tangible and intangible benefits of their own talents and abilities in service to others.

John Leith observed that "...the denominations that appear to be most optimistic about changing the policies of great nations, as well as economic and social systems, seem less concerned and optimistic about the possibility of significant transformation of the life of individuals in the congregations."[21] Those students who participated in the drama ventures at William & Mary in 1977-82 obviously found through that venue a way out of the self-absorption that claimed much of the campus culture in that era. Through those experiences, and the associations with the church and several chaplains they afforded, many of them found a way into the church. Some have stayed, most in active parochial lay leadership, several in ordained ministry. At least three went on to volunteer as lay workers in Latin American missions. Pastoral stewardship, we venture, made the difference.

Still, one ought take seriously Parker Palmer's *caveat* that "...the church is often seen by its members as an extension of private life rather than a bridge into the public."[22] How, then, does campus ministry serve as that bridge that connects the private and the public? Palmer maintained that the church must avoid the image of the church as "extended family," that this image fosters a notion of the church as closed society and encourages what he called the "cult of intimacy." One of the distinctive dimensions of campus ministry is that it can, by careful cultivation, provide a place of belonging without exclusivity. But it can only accomplish this at a cost. That cost is the compromise of traditional images and benefits of containment.

It is here that stewardship is a particularly helpful word. That the church is steward reminds that it is caretaker of that which it does not own, and hence, that over which it has no ultimate control. Campus ministers can be caretakers of students, and faculty, and others, but can make no claims for their loyalty. For they belong to God and not to any other. Campus ministers are caretakers of a community that daily reminds of its transience. As Peter Bunder, Episcopal Chaplain at Purdue University wrote in a newsletter to newcomers:

> Issues of maintenance and the language of ingathering often dominate a parochial venue. Our task here is to carve out a visible presence in a place that is not the church's own. Taking Kierkegaard's advice, we move the religious professionals from center stage, take away from the congregation its role as critic, and make the minister a prompter who gives a line or two to believers who are called to play out their faith on the stage of life...here the ordinary language of "family" and "arrival" is replaced by the language of

---

not include volunteer service, valued by some estimators at $75 billion per year. See Gallup, *Looking Ahead*, 6.

[21] Robinson, 70.

[22] Parker Palmer, "Practicing the Public Life in the Congregation," *Calling of the Laity*, 79.

"friend" or "peer." All here are on pilgrimage to some other place. The image of journey is a powerful one. The communal memory is short

The language of "home" is replaced by the language of "work." Our calendar is neither Julian nor Gregorian but "Purduean." Advent has but two Sundays. Self-worth and self-doubt depend upon the utility of one's field, and the usefulness of one's project within that field. Relationships are contractual, not conventual

This is no "academic village." You live above the store. You eat in your office. You sleep at the plant.... Parishes are often looked to as dependable sources of consolation enjoying some discipline in organization. Here the operative work is "change," "random inquiry," or "experiment."[23]

As stewards of this campus society, it is helpful to remember these realities and to remember, too, that this is not the place for true intimacy.

That is not to say that we shall not make or be friends. But it does set our life together in context. There are campus ministries (and parochial ones) that entice with the promise of intimacy, and they do attract young adults. Indeed, it is a source of consternation and no little jealousy for campus ministers that some fundamentalist and evangelical campus ministries are quite successful at attracting the impressionable first-year student. But the attraction is frequently only temporary and can even ripen into lasting hostility when the student realizes the tyranny of false intimacy and seeks to loose the control of domination. "The quest for intimacy," Palmer said, "leads us into smaller and smaller circles of 'meaningful relations.' It cuts us off from the richness given by relations of various durations, intensity, and depth."[24]

The quest for intimacy is very much a part of the culture, and certainly inherent in the young adult whose wrenching dislocation from family and the familiar may seek immediate assuagement. Indeed, it is particularly acute on campus, where solitude is normal. Study is often isolating and research is frequently an individual pursuit. Graduate students are particularly vulnerable to loneliness, simply because the point of a thesis or dissertation is intended to showcase the individual's work and capabilities.[25]

But campus ministry (and, perhaps, the church) is *not* an appropriate substitute for true intimacy. Thus, one might add to Dozier's assessment

---

[23] Peter Bunder, "Episcopal Campus Ministry," newsletter of The Episcopal Church at Purdue University (Autumn 1988), 15–16.

[24] Palmer, 79.

[25] Henry Rosovsky, *The University: An Owner's Manual* (New York: W.W. Norton & Company, 1990), 154.

of the church's business that it is not intimacy either. If that ministry is, at least in part, bridging and reconciling, then to do ministry on campus may mean denying false intimacy in favor of public life. "The key to public life," maintained Palmer, "is learning to appreciate strangers without having either to reject them or turn them into intimates and friends."[26] That those strangers may become intimates or friends is possible, perhaps even desirable. But our concern is the entertainment of difference and diversity.

We were impressed by the number of correspondents who responded to our request to write us of their campus ministry experiences and spoke not of the lasting friendships or the intimacies secured, but rather remembered and appreciated most the diversity to which they were exposed, and which was tolerated among them. They remarked on their own eccentricities, many of which were confessed somewhat humorously in retrospect. But they were all the more grateful that those differences they brought to the community were not cause for separation. Indeed, some found within those peculiarities the seed to future vocation. For some it was a long-denied sexuality in need of balance and direction; for others it was an arrogant, bullying insecurity that found within the community a new kind of security to temper it and convert it; and for others it was a cloying religiosity that only thinly masked an intense privatism and that found within the community a new piety fit for society and a life with others. What they found in the loose federation of students whose only common bond was participation in even the marginal activities of a diverse campus ministry was something akin to what Derek Bok sought for the university itself: a ministry that linked "individualism and competition with a set of qualities of a very different kind—qualities of a more cooperative and communal nature rooted in a strong sense of personal responsibility toward institutions, communities, and other human beings."[27]

ACCOUNTABILITY

Pastoral stewardship, while critical of both university and church, is nevertheless responsible to both. This stewardship maintains that authority and responsibility extend to institutions as well as individuals.

---

[26] Palmer, 79.

[27] Derek Bok, *Universities and the Future of America* (Durham: Duke University Press, 1990), 55.

Taking care *for* these institutions, however, is not always the same thing as taking care *of* them. The distance that campus ministry enjoys from both church and university frees it from having to take care of these institutions. Campus ministries do not need to defend them; that is their responsibility and to assume otherwise is to deny others their own responsibilities. Thus, as Palmer encourages the acceptance of the differences of others without having to reject them or convert them into intimates, so campus ministry might extend the same principle to institutions.

INNOVATION, IMAGINATION AND MUTUALITY IN MINISTRY

In programming for the graduate divisions at the University of Chicago, we did not excoriate the university for failing to provide these services. Ironically—or perhaps one might say, happily—the medical school and the business school have lately instituted programs that are more than vaguely similar. In fact, on one occasion Brent House mounted a program for medical students on the balance of personal and professional life. That evening, a smaller than usual number of students showed up. One of the doctors and his wife who were invited for the panel arrived breathless and, as they removed their coats, offered apology, asking, "Did you know that this same conversation was the subject of a conversation sponsored by the dean's office this afternoon? That's why we're late! We were invited to participate on both panels!" More recently, we have had to concede the "loss" of student interest in the very programs we pioneered as the professional schools themselves introduced similar programs into their routines. Adhering to the principles we have learned, however, we continue to seek the guidance of students for all our programming. Consequently, the several series with which we began have been transformed into something quite different today.

As interest in the established model waned and momentum slowed, we determined to let the thread play out. Little effort was spent propping up the dying model. Instead, critical energies were engaged as we sought to understand what was happening and why. We were obviously being called to something new and different, but we alone could not determine the shape of that new call. As we pondered the situation, a student came forward with an idea.

Tom Levergood had graduated from the College of the University of Chicago and, after time away in Europe and New York City, he had returned to begin work on a graduate degree. An enthusiastic convert to the Episcopal Church, Tom had had a wonderful experience of the church in New York City at St. Marks in the Bowery and St. Luke's in the Village. He was excited about the possibilities for religious discourse and spiritual formation on campus. He suggested regular gatherings of students and faculty within and across varied academic disciplines for the purpose of religious conversation. In the beginning it was agreed that these gatherings would be modest in size. Tom would issue personal invitation to students, faculty and staff of his acquaintance who shared his interest in a "safe space" for conversation on matters of faith. We would support his program with the provision of a meal and space, and the chaplain's commitment to attend.

These informal programs began with several events gathering twelve to sixteen people for each dinner, with some variation in the guests from event to event. Because we were committed to fulfilling scheduled programs in the professional schools' series, but with diminishing returns, these new programs were greeted as a supplement. They afforded occasions for relaxed conversation that enabled the building of much richer relationships. By the end of the autumn 1991 quarter, the waning series and the fledgling dinners were coexisting nicely.

As the winter quarter began in January 1992 we concurred that the "invitational" nature of the new dinner program, while helpful in maintaining intimacy, promoted an image of exclusivity, despite all attempts to prevent this impression. What would happen, we wondered, if we simply opened these events? The decision was made to open the events, but to confine publicity to the monthly newsletter of the Episcopal campus ministry and word of mouth. Attendance grew to an average of twenty to thirty per event. To facilitate conversation and maintain some semblance of intimacy, we provided additional tables to enable the larger number to divide into smaller groups.

By the beginning of the winter quarter, we had requests from eleven individuals who were interested in an "Inquirers' Class," for instruction preparatory to baptism or confirmation. Some of those who presented the request were among those who had begun attending the informal dinners in the previous quarter. Adapting denominational models for catechumenal preparation, we set up a program that paired each "inquirer" with a "mentor," a person from the community who had been a member of the church for some years. We solicited volunteers for the mentoring function and then paired inquirers and mentors with attention to shared interests, but with some creativity, as well. A young graduate student in theology thus became mentor to the wife of a retired professor; a laywoman serving on our board became mentor to a young woman in the graduate ministry program; a lawyer from the local congregation mentored a student in the law school. Both inquirers and mentors committed to a fifteen-week series that included seven Sunday-afternoon sessions in which the catechism of *The Book of Common Prayer* was used as the outline for group conversation. Outside of these formal gatherings, mentors and inquirers were encouraged to attend a retreat offered by the Episcopal campus ministry and the Provincial (regional) Gathering for Episcopal Students, Faculty, Chaplains and Friends. They also covenanted to attend weekly worship together, to participate in the services of Ash Wednesday and Holy Week, and to meet informally once each week just to share conversation. At the end of the program, eight of the eleven inquirers were presented at the Great Vigil of Easter at the diocesan cathedral. Four were baptized and four were confirmed or received into the church.

As the spring quarter of 1992 ended, we had a clearer notion of where we were being led. Several of those who had completed the inquirers' program became active participants in a new initiative in the local parish designed to continue their exploration of discipleship. While continuing their involvement with the campus ministry, they were making the transition into parish life and serving as important liaisons between the two communities.

With the coming of autumn 1992, we made only one significant change in the program: we officially abandoned the professional school programs in vocational formation as discrete series. The students most active in the new dinner programs constituted a planning group on their own and determined that they wanted to make the dinners a weekly event. Having worked around the scheduled events of the vocational series and having tried different nights of the week, they agreed that Thursday evening represented something of a sabbath time in their routine, an evening that fit the rhythm of their lives and encouraged the relaxation of weekly anxieties and concerns. Regularizing the schedule would make the dinners a part of their routine that could be anticipated each week and would facilitate the building of relationships. There was concern, however, that these very real assets could become liabilities if the weekly event became a gathering of a clique. In time, it would be difficult for newcomers to be integrated and without an intentional design, there could come a time when the incentive to invite newcomers might dwindle.

The chaplain suggested that perhaps one way to address this potential problem, while continuing to serve students who found the former vocational formation series useful, would be to make some of the Thursday evenings more intentionally programmatic. While some Thursday evenings would be devoted only to informal conversation amongst those gathered, at least a portion of the scheduled Thursdays could be given over to a special guest or guests and a specific topic for conversation. Moreover, we could intentionally aim those events at particular students or schools and issue invitation to that group. The idea was accepted and is the current practice.

On one occasion, student volunteers coached by a member of the community who teaches drama did a reading of a short story adaptation with a medical theme. Invitations were distributed to the medical school and on that evening we welcomed about ten students from that sector of the community. On subsequent occasions, two professors in the law school were invited on separate occasions to lead conversation. Invitations were hand delivered to the mailboxes of the law students and on one evening in the winter quarter we welcomed eighty students, on the other in the spring we greeted nearly sixty. With the inclusion of so many visitors, those students who routinely attend the Thursday evening dinners become hosts and advocates, greeting the newcomers and inviting them to come again.

With the current mix of programs, we feel we have achieved a balance again. We offer a full range of experiences prepared to greet the tentative newcomer, nurture the inquirer, sustain the committed, and facilitate the transition into parish life. But we also know that this model, like the last, is only temporary. That is, perhaps, one of the most important points to be made about ministry: that our designs are always temporary, that we must always be ready to change, for a living relationship with a living God demands this of us.

We must be stewards of imagination. By their own initiative, the students, faculty and staff have created in this campus ministry a place where their religious concerns can be engaged and nurtured. Because we did not impose our own program, but rather engaged a discipline of listening and interpreting, of encouraging and enacting, we have helped a community imagine its ministry and to bring that imagination to fruition in action. Where self-consciously religious language was only rarely heard it has now become common. Patience has been rewarded in increased student interest and initiation in spiritual direction, regular retreats, an innovative class for religious "inquirers" mentored by students, faculty, and staff, and a fellowship at table that is more consistent than episodic. Thus, in taking care for the university we have helped it take care of itself.

But the same may be said of the church. In our relations with local congregations and with the diocese, we pursue a distinctive way. Some years ago the issue of inclusive language in our worship arose. At that time there were no authorized forms for such liturgies. Neither had the issue been raised by the chaplain. But when a member of the worshipping community asked, the chaplain invited her to assemble a group of similarly interested students to deal with it. Though she was a Presbyterian laywoman, and this community is Episcopal, she was accorded full responsibility. She was assured that the chaplain would use any liturgy the committee produced, without requiring prior approval. The woman, herself a capable graduate student with a Master of Divinity in her portfolio, was given relevant materials from the Episcopal tradition as a guide, and little more.

Liturgies were tried, evaluated, polished, and in many cases remain in use on a seasonal basis with occasional updating and continued attention to improvement. In this instance the greater problem was not finding someone to take on the responsibility, but assuring the person willing to take the responsibility that her authority would be recognized, that she would not be undercut in carrying out this ministry. Care was certainly taken *for* the church in this instance, in that those charged with this responsibility were equipped to carry it out, not only in their own persons but in the resources made available to them. But there was no need on our part to take care *of* institutional policies and practices. That the local parish and the university chapel did not at that time offer like liturgies only enhanced the importance that we did—not as a matter of competition, but of collegiality. Because we did offer them, made them available to the community, they did not have to. And because they could offer something else—often something in a different way—we encouraged their ministry and shared it.

A stewardship that extends to care for institutions, in our experience, ultimately enriches everyone. In the foregoing examples, the life and ministry of the university was extended and ultimately enriched by our sincere attempt to offer something different. The same has been true of life and ministry in the other local manifestations of ministry on our campus, like the local parish church and the inter-denominational university chapel. Because we try to be good stewards in our care for each other, we offer a greater fullness of each. Our programs enhance the university's and thus expand the fullness of the university and its teaching ministry beyond its current limits. Similarly, because we are free to offer something different in the experience of religion, the definition and experience of "church" on our campus is considerably widened. We do not claim to be better, only different. And in that regard we further undergird the message of our ministry in an integrity that matches what we do to the tenor of what we say about diversity and collegiality.

We have shared detailed particulars of our own experience not because we anticipate or encourage emulation. Indeed, we are very much concerned that distinction be made between the *practices* we have shared and the *principles* we wish to convey. What we have done in the foregoing examples is not nearly so important as the way we went about doing it. Each campus ministry is different and will experience variation. Remaining open to that reality, even struggling to maintain such openness, is some of the most difficult work of any ministry. Encouraging and nurturing imagination is especially difficult when we are preoccupied with a ready-made image, whether it be our own or someone else's. And both are especially difficult in social and ecclesiastical cultures that demand instant answers, quick fixes, and quantifiable results. But this is the task demanded of us.

—⊰ 9 ⊱—

FINANCIAL STEWARDSHIP AS
PASTORAL CARE

THE BOTTOM LINE

But who will pay the bills? What shall be said of money? It is the perennial problem of campus ministries, and likely for simple reason. It is not a pleasant thing to have to admit, but it does seem obvious from the perspective of the campus minister that young adults on campus are given lower priority in the church's agenda because young adults represent a negative on the ledger sheets. Students simply cannot support their own ministry on campus. Not even after graduation can many young adults make significant financial contribution to the church. The cost of higher education in America has risen steeply. Despite generous scholarship aid and parental subsidy, many students now graduate with debts equal to what their parents undertook in their first mortgage. When graduate school expenses are factored into the mix, the total can be staggeringly high. And in most cases repayment of these loans begins only six to nine months after graduation.

Whatever else one may say of campus ministry, when it comes to the matter of financing this work the only appropriate designation for this expenditure is "mission." Arguably, campus ministry is the most prominent field of domestic mission for the American churches. It may be true that the baby boom has passed, but demographic projections indicate no diminishment in college enrollments.[1] Graduate and professional school enrollments are projected to remain relatively constant. Graduate enrollments are projected to increase from 1,617,000 in 1990 to 1,678,000 in 2001. Professional school enrollments will likely decline, but only slightly, from 290,000 in 1990 to a projected 282,000 in 2001. But undergraduate enrollments will continue to grow from 11,651,000 to an expected 12,487,000 in 2001.

The role of higher education in the national agenda is similarly impressive. Federal appropriations for contracts, services, and direct support to campuses in 1989 totalled $15,657,609,000—and that figure does not represent federal investments in guaranteed student loans.[2] State funding in 1991, even in the face of drastic cutbacks, add an additional investment of $40.9 billion. Yet the churches seem not to recognize with comparable commitment the campus as the pivotal arena for engaging young adults in the midst of shaping their own lives and, through their participation with faculty in research, shaping the life of us all. Gallup and Castelli noted that

> the United States is unique because it combines a high degree of education with a high level of religious faith. On many measures of religious belief, commitment decreases as the education level increases. Nevertheless, the level of faith among college-educated Americans remains quite high, and in some key areas—including belief in God and church membership and attendance—there are no significant differences among Americans on the basis of educational background.[3]

Consideration of the "unchurched," which seems to have reached the point of near obsession with many mainline churches, seems oblivious to the reality that of the 72 percent of Americans who are unchurched, the general majority in that category tends to be "young, male, college educated, single or divorced."[4] Fully 30 percent of those aged 18-29 were identified by Gallup and Castelli as unchurched. The reasons cited for this status are rather surprising and do not always correlate with

---

[1] All figures are cited are from the U.S. Department of Education, as reported in *The Chronicle of Higher Education* (13 February 1991): A36.

[2] These figures are as reported by the National Science Foundation in *The Chronicle of Higher Education* (10 April 1991): A24.

[3] Gallup & Castelli, 86.

[4] Ibid., 133.

commonly held notions. The unchurched do not cite their work schedules, their marital status, or their dis-ease with the institutional church as reasons for absenting themselves from the church's life. Instead, they more frequently indicate that they found other (presumably, more interesting, fulfilling, and meaningful) activities; that they started making their own decisions; and/or that they moved to a new community. All three of these factors would likely be present in the experience of the young adult, especially on campus. They do not cite liturgical change, the church's social or political involvement, breadth of teaching or inclusiveness, pastoral inattention, or lax teaching on sex and marriage as their reason for abandonment, but rather just the opposite: that the church is too much concerned for money; that its teachings about beliefs, and sexual and marital morality, are too narrow; that they wanted deeper spiritual meaning than provided by the church; that they left for reason of poor preaching and out of dislike for traditional worship forms.[5] Our experience indicates that these issues are frequently addressed, and responsibly, in many campus ministries. That we cannot seem to reconcile these obvious disconnections results in what can only be deemed a grossly negligent stewardship. How, then, is the gap closed between these disjunctures?

Mainline Protestant denominations (excepting the Lutherans) seem not to have relied heavily upon national structures of funding to finance local campus ministries. A variety of strategies have been deployed. In the immediate post-war period, Presbyterians who pioneered student work on a given campus could then make application to the denomination for funding. The virtue of this partnership model was that incentive was provided to encourage local initiative. Episcopalians, during the same period, took just the opposite tack. The Church Society for College Work provided seed money for the foundation of new ministries, with the expectation that local funding would follow.[6] This design, too, had

---

[5] Ibid., 143–44.

[6] For example, in 1954 the Church Society for College Work distributed $40,000 in grants to 31 college and university ministries, only a portion of which was designated from denominational general missions, the balance supplied by the United Thank Offering—an annual volunteer-giving campaign under the aegis of Episcopal Church Women. *The Church Review* 14 (March 1955): 2.

National church support grew from $22,861 in 1940 to $45,918 in 1945, to $58,294 in 1950, to $142,088 in 1955. *The Church Review* 21 (April 1963): 6. Beginning in 1955, the General Convention assumed greater responsibility for funding, freeing CSCW to become the "research and development" area of college work for the Episcopal Church, funding research for study. *The Church Review* 16 (September, 1958): 3.

merit in that it again provided incentive and, in this case, immediate resources on the front end of the venture. The United Methodist Church tried national funding and saw the dizzying spiral upward as support for Wesley Foundations went from $777,984 in 1956 to $1,844,656 in 1959. By 1960 the Methodist Church had shifted primary funding for its 181 Wesley Foundations to the Annual Conference level. By 1966-67, near the peak of baby-boom expansion on American campuses, total church expenditures for Wesley Foundations amounted to $3,515,750.

In addition to substantial financial support at the local level, the denominations also provided and paid for national administrative support. In the Episcopal Church, denominational funding at the national level supported the work of a staff at national headquarters, with field staff in each of the nine provinces of the church. After 1967 denominational support for local campus ministries was reduced to make allocations elsewhere in the churches' growing list of priorities. As national supports for local ministry were diminished, similar national staff expenses represented much of the Presbyterian, Episcopal and Methodist allocations for campus ministry. Subsequent reductions, therefore, had their most immediate effect in the shape of administrative support at the national level.

MORE THAN MONEY

The perception persists that cuts to national budgets diminished local campus work, even though local campus ministry has, for thirty years or more, been largely independent of such support from the national denominational sources.[7] Perhaps this perception tells us something about the intangibles of support. What did national and regional staff do that was essential to local ministry? National and regional staff provided advocacy, communication, and oversight.

Inclusion of young adult ministry in the regular deliberations of the church, if only at the budget level, at least kept the church mindful of this constituency and provided regular opportunity for its consideration. The

---

National Church support grew in 1960 to $325,366, to $366,607 in 1962, and to $439,546 in 1963. While diocesan figures are not available a conservative estimate of an additional $1 million per year in diocesan support was reported in 1963, indicating that dioceses were "matching" national funds at a rate of 3:1. *The Church Review* 21 (April 1963): 6.

[7] Except for those cases within the Presbyterian Church where national funds supplemented local campus ministers' salaries.

formal inclusion of campus ministry at the national and regional level of deliberation brought with it regular occasion for accountability in the annual, triennial, or quadrennial meetings of the denomination. Representation of higher education ministries at these levels not only provided a "lobby" for these ministries, but quite apart from any political advantage, opened the avenues of communication that served as constant reminder that the young adult constituency—especially those on campus—is part of the church. That may seem obvious, but given the profile of leadership in the mainline churches—which tends to be at least middle-aged, and until recently was predominantly white and male—it is conceivable that younger members of the churches are not always given full consideration, nor their ministries valued.[8]

National and regional staff also serve as a conduit for communication. Within denominations they stimulate those in ministry to look periodically beyond themselves. Through intentional opportunities for regular meeting and enrichment, they promote a collegiality that is increasingly hard to come by in this distracting and isolating world. But beyond denominational collegiality, these staff also provide an important link with others across the denominational lines that distinguish us. With their colleagues and counterparts they can more efficiently transmit the learnings and the leanings of their varied denominational perspectives.

Lastly, staff functioning at the national and regional level provide oversight. Because they function at a different level in the structure, they see from a different vantage. They are better positioned to see the larger picture, to assess larger trends, and to combat the privatism to which institutions, no less than individuals, are prone. Clyde O. Robinson delineated the responsibility of church professionals as three-fold: they are to "articulate a rationale for ministry in higher education that is clear, compelling, and theologically sound"; "describe and accept an enabling role focused on helping congregations undertake ministry in nearby institutions of higher education"; and "identify, describe, and accept the role of prophetic broker, linking the resources of higher education with the priorities of the church in behalf of peace, justice, and the integrity of creation."[9]

These things, then—advocacy, communication, and oversight—were likely the real losses to campus ministry when funding patterns changed. How have we adapted to these losses and how might we replicate these

---

[8] See footnote 67 in Chapter Four for a profile of leadership in the mainline churches.

[9] Robinson, 8.

benefits in a newly structured church? These are the questions that emerge.

As regards advocacy, this is addressed in part by the retention of national staff personnel in all three of the denominations under study. Methodists, Presbyterians, and Episcopalians have had at least one person in their national offices whose primary responsibility is to represent campus ministry in the councils of the churches. In some instances, their functions have been enhanced by the addition of committees of advice. For example, the Episcopal Church's National Advisory Committee on Ministry in Higher Education serves this purpose.

When professional provincial staff officers were eliminated from the Episcopal budget in the 1960s a new system was implemented. Provincial (regional) representatives are now selected from the professional campus ministry community. Each province delegates a campus minister (lay or ordained) to represent them on this committee. In addition to these regional representatives, the national staff officer for ministry in higher education is allowed to appoint additional representation, which privilege allows for balance. The appointive privilege allows for student representation and greater lay representation in this committee. Funding for this committee's work allows it to gather periodically for consultation.

This national entity also assists in the task of communication, since the national office can still route information directly into each of the provinces and count upon a regional representative there to pass the information along in a timely fashion. But because provincial representatives serve without pay and these tasks are additions to their own busy agendas, accountability becomes—as it does in any voluntary association—more difficult to secure. Separated as they are by geography and the concerns of their personal ministries, the task of communicating sometimes only barely gets done and the kind of conversation that is necessary to enrich this ministry is sorely limited to only those one or two annual occasions when the whole committee is gathered to meet.

Voluntary associations, like the Episcopal Society for Ministry in Higher Education, do provide an arena for collegial conversation and collaboration. They also enhance advocacy by representing the church's ministry on campus through the counsels of advice to which they are admitted and through a quarterly journal. But financial support from national denominational budgets for such voluntary associations is frequently lacking. Greater attention to and funding for these voluntary initiatives is one way national and regional funds can improve denominational work on campus.

Lacking these supports, oversight is all but impossible at the national level. One staff person is inadequate to maintain the level of relationship with local ministries sufficient to speak knowledgeably or represent them effectually within the denominational counsels of the church. It is an axiom of ecumenism that churches ought to separate only to do those things which they cannot in good conscience do together. But Avery Dulles suggested that the reverse of that axiom might be more appropriate. Moreover, Dulles' reformulation is the only practicable one within the church at present: we ought to do together only those things which we cannot accomplish separately.[10]

PARTNERS IN VENTURE INVESTMENT

National and regional entities make possible the kind of conversation that is impossible at the local level. Regional young adult gatherings that introduce young adults to larger communities of peers and contemporaries, and that engage them in diversity beyond the campus, and their own age and social group, are essential to health. Regional and national opportunity for young adult participation in the life of denominations is essential to the life and health of the denomination. Likewise, young adult participation in ecumenical and inter-denominational gatherings is important to facilitate communication and collegiality across those divisions.

Such gatherings are expensive. They demand the best efforts of many people, who must be gathered regularly to plan for these events. And the events themselves, because they are only occasionally mounted, deserve greater attention to quality. Good speakers, efficient design and execution, and accessibility are all important. Accessibility is a particularly keen concern. Given that many young adults on campus are financially dependent, regional and national events must be heavily subsidized to make them affordable to students. Additional subsidy may also be necessary to include commuter students, foreign students, and those whose discretionary income and/or parental support cannot allow for their participation in such extracurricular activities.

---

[10]   Avery Dulles, *The Resilient Church* (Garden City, NY: Doubleday and Company, 1977), 182.

Here, too, is a place where private foundations might be moved to support young adult ministries. Assistance in underwriting conference costs, which often include travel and honoraria for speakers and professional consultation for effective educational design, might be supported by private foundations in the same way they support similar endeavors in the educational sector. Even modest foundations can be of tremendous help; a gift of $500-$1000 can often mean the difference in securing a quality resource person.

Foundations can help, also, in the function of oversight by supporting study at the national and regional level. Providing time for campus ministers to gather and to reflect upon experience builds collegiality and enhances ministry while it also informs. Efforts such as this study make it possible for experienced campus ministers to reflect upon their mistakes and their progress and to share that learning more widely.

But what of the funding of local campus ministry? That is a question that remains unanswered. We are inclined toward models of partnership. Early initiatives in the mainline churches began with partnership in one form or another. Given that hierarchical, national structures are giving way in the church to more local autonomy and a horizontal plane of leadership, it is no longer feasible to encourage the national denominational structures to enter into partnership with local campus ministries. As indicated above, there are some provisions these structures can make that are appropriate to the changing structures of relationship within the church. But increasingly, funding for campus ministries is a matter of local concern.

Judicatories and local congregations can benefit from a thorough reassessment of mission priorities that takes into account the reality and the promise of higher education. In most cases a simple inventory of higher education resources in any given area of the United States serves to remind us of how pervasive higher education is in this culture. Few congregations exist that are not within easy proximity to such an institution. The mere ubiquity of such institutions now blinds us to their presence; they are taken for granted because they are endemic. When they are properly identified as a resource for ministry, a new relationship can begin.

At the outset, those undertaking young adult ministry on campus—like all ministry—share a singular responsibility: responsibility to one another. The particular responsibility of ministerial leadership is to see to it that others have the resources they need to conduct their ministries. We do not minister to one another so much as we equip one another to do our own ministries. For example, we do not have it within ourselves to cure the addict. What we can give the addict, however, are those resources she needs to be cured. We can give her respect and new esteem, patience and discipline, and with those resources the addict carries out the ministry to self heretofore lacking.

Within the new relationship, and practicing a new stewardship, the local congregation and the judicatory will find on campus a host of resources for the conduct of its own ministries. Sometimes a most substantial contribution to campus ministry consists of simply inviting or allowing those ministries a place to be exercised. Students who reflected with us on their own experience of campus ministry frequently indicated that parishes that respected their ability and called upon it, as well as campus ministries that deployed their energies and talents, made a significant difference in the way they saw their own lives, discerned their vocations, and shaped their commitments. This kind of support requires no financial outlay.

When money is necessary to support campus ministry, it can be considered venture capital. Money spent, even on existing campus ministries, is always money moving into a new venture, for the constituency is always changing. Thus, to conceive of campus ministry support as "maintenance" is to begin from a false understanding. A venture capitalist is a financial partner in a creative business enterprise. There is risk involved, but the risk is shared. The venture capitalist is prepared to risk and perhaps to lose. The wise venture capitalist will study the prospectus carefully and seek out those investment opportunities that are most promising. In campus ministry this may mean that greater care should be given to the primary expense of campus ministry which is always the professional minister.

WHERE TO INVEST

Whether lay or ordained—volunteer, subsidized, or stipended—the campus minister is usually the greatest expense in providing ministry. Investors expect this person, and those who work with him or her, to be capable and responsible. Are they creative, self-motivated people? Are they committed to this work and do they bring particular gifts to it? Local congregations and judicatories interested in existing or potential campus ministries will want to entrust these ministries to their most capable people and have a right to expect a return on their investment.

Local congregations and judicatories are recalled to an overlooked adage in the life of the church, one that is never overlooked by the good venture capitalist: we get what we pay for. Skimp on the front end and the results will most likely reveal it.

Resources are also needed to train campus ministers and their boards for service in a radically changed structure that places greater responsibility upon local oversight. Both denominational and foundation support might be allocated to this important work. The Lilly Endowment has provided similar support for the nurture of seminary boards of trustees. A like initiative is needed to educate lay boards and their ministry personnel to the demands of governance and financial development. While some board development can be undertaken with simple resources, like directed retreats and work days that encourage and educate, the increasingly complex world of fund-raising, public relations, and communication will require assistance from professional consultants whose services are often beyond the means of religious organizations.[11]

Facilities are also a costly undertaking. Congregational-based campus ministry can work, but it requires not only commitment of people to the enterprise, but commitment of space, as well. When congregational facilities are located within reasonable proximity to campus they can become the center of vibrant activity. It is important for young adults to experience the church in many ways, not just on Sunday morning. Space is very important to students. They have little or no privacy, even in their "homes." They are doubled or tripled in dormitory rooms or share apartments with others. Setting aside space that is for them is one way local congregations can extend hospitality at little cost.

In some instances, a free-standing facility exists or may be purchased. Caution is urged, simply because these earthly treasures invariably rust, moths do corrupt, and thieves do break in and steal—all of which is to say that that one should be prepared for all that such stewardship entails. Whatever property one devotes to campus ministry, however, ought to be of solid construction and good quality. After all, if the church is extending hospitality to students, faculty, staff, and other potential guests, it needs to be mindful of the message that is conveyed by its facilities. To their credit, the United Methodists in their Wesley Foundation structures and the Lutherans in their centers often created the very best of what the

---

[11] A special resource exists in Campus Ministry Advancement, Inc. [128 Clinton Heights Ave., Columbus, OH 43202, (614) 263–3633]. This non-profit philanthropic organization was created "to strengthen and advance Christian ministries in the colleges and universities of the United States."

church can offer on campus. They are, for the most part, attractive and flexible facilities built to house lively ministry and solid contemporary worship. But all such buildings need constant maintenance. Thus caution is recommended before venturing into that investment.

Existing campus ministry facilities could be put to much better use through a more creative strategy for their deployment. Where judicatories have existing facilities, these might be used as the base for extension into other campuses. Existing facilities and established programs might be positioned as "cathedral" centers, central gathering places and resources that use their assets in extension beyond their own campus. A solid Wesley Foundation, Westminster or Canterbury center could take as part of its own mission extension into other campuses. They could be especially useful as links to the commuter schools. Of the several benefits that could be gained from such associations, the commingling of students of varied ages and socio-economic experiences, and the collegial associations of faculty and administrators from different campuses, can enrich everyone's experience of the church's—and society's—diversity.

If the churches expect to have qualified personnel to whom to entrust these crucial posts, intentional planning must be given to adequate recruitment and equipment of ordained and lay professionals. Additionally, where feasible, centers that can afford to support internships or paid staff associates contribute trained, experienced personnel for this important ministry. This, too, is an area where combined resources from national, regional, local and private foundation sources can be directed to advantage.

The Episcopal Church Council at the University of Chicago was awarded a grant in autumn 1992 by the Episcopal Church Foundation in New York for a project to address this issue. The *Campus Ministry Leadership Education Project* provides "Campus Missioners" to train and oversee the leadership of peer ministers on campus, while also offering experiential training in ministry to the lay Campus Missioners themselves. The project does not replace full-time ministers, but rather extends existing campus ministry personnel and resources into new initiatives. The design is one that if successful could be adapted and replicated widely, greatly increasing denominational outreach on campus.

The program places a priority on Chicago-area campuses not presently served by the Episcopal Church. The Campus Missioners are not themselves peer ministers, but are responsible for identifying, training and nurturing a network of peer ministers on the campus to which the missioner is assigned. The program represents one model for new stewardship that uses an existing free-standing denominational campus ministry, in this case, Brent House, as the base for extending the churches' presence on and witness to campus.

The program offers financial, educational and collegial support for two part-time Campus Missioners committed to developing their own ministries through the equipping of others in ministry. The Diocese of Chicago, through its Commission on Campus Ministry, provided funding to add a third Campus Missioner on a campus where full-time ministry had lately been diminished, but where nominal commitment of some students and faculty remained. The Campus Missioners receive a modest stipend and benefits package. It should be noted that all of the grant money supports the missioners; Brent House receives no compensation for its contribution of staff resources to the project.

The Campus Missioners completed a non-residential educational component of 30-days duration in which they studied and worshipped together, read independently and shared in seminars aimed at imparting basic principles of ministry on public and private campuses with volunteer peer ministers. The Campus Missioners continue to participate in a bi-weekly *Case Reflection Seminar* consisting of the Chaplain at Brent House, the Campus Missioners, and others. The focal point of each seminar is the actual experiences of the missioners, sometimes in the form of formal case studies, but more often in informal sharing of accomplishments and frustrations.

By providing an educational orientation to the realties of ministry on campus and an on-going community of colleagues who gather to offer critical and moral support, this project attempts to equip others for ministry leadership. Importantly, it represents a genuine mission initiative of a campus ministry that is seeking to wrest the most out of its resources, giving back to the church a generous return on its investments.

Stewardship, like pastoral care, entails the sharing of strength as well as the sharing of burden. Training peer ministers, mentoring committees of oversight and leadership, and providing workshops for ministry leadership and hospitality for young adults throughout a region, the occasional free-standing campus ministry center can serve a denomination far more broadly than the confines of campus suggest. Campus ministry centers that open themselves—and openly promote themselves—to denominational groups and committees, clergy continuing education functions, and the like are enriching their ministry while accounting to the judicatory for its support.

SOURCES

Funding for campus ministry can come from many sources. It will not likely come from students or their parents (there are rare exceptions, but so rare as to eliminate them categorically). Students and parents are saddled with the immediate expenses of education. Students and their parents can and perhaps ought to be included in any appeal for funds and some will respond, but it is unlikely that this constituency will provide primary budget support. Also, one must ask what values we are inculcating with students when we ask them to direct their limited resources to the support of ministry that directly benefits them. When students are asked to give, their giving should be directed beyond their own welfare.

Alumni will support campus ministry. Indeed, experience indicates that younger alumni—especially with a more recent and memorable experience of campus ministry—are often the most generous supporters. Continuity of program, quality (and often longevity) of leadership count for much in sustaining this kind of support from recent graduates. Establishing and maintaining alumni files is tedious work, but worth the effort. Beyond the obvious benefit of enlarging the pool of potential donors, alumni research can yield a much deeper sense of historical perspective and enhance the story of campus ministry. It is not unusual, for example, to find that some established campus ministries have "graduated" more lay members of the church than the largest seminary of their denomination. Such findings can be helpful in interpreting the work of campus ministry to the church.

Faculty and staff who are actively engaged by campus ministry will frequently give beyond their parochial commitments. Their participation is often key to their support. In many places, they play pivotal roles in building and overseeing ministry in their service on the varied committees and boards that adjudicate our work. Generous with their time, many faculty are pleasantly surprised to find that the church has need of their talents as teachers. Above and beyond what they give of their money, the *pro bono* gifts they can make to a campus ministry program translate into thousands of program dollars saved.

Primary support for campus ministry will and must come from denominational sources: from the synod, conference or diocese, and from local congregations.[12] There is no other source that can reliably fund this ministry. There may be a few campus ministries with sufficient endowment to sustain their entire life and work. But the likelihood that such support will be achieved by any significant number of campus ministries is a foolish dream. Nor is it desirable that endowment be sought as the primary source of support even when attainable. On-going support from denominational sources is essential to the life of both the campus ministries and the other ministries of the church. The church needs to be invested in this important mission work even as the campus needs to be thus connected to the life of the church. Like it or not, money is sacramental and incarnates this relationship. As Jesus himself indicated, where one's treasures are, there will one's heart be also. Where the church invests its financial resources does say something about the sacramental nature of our relationship.

But even as the church observes deliberate care in all other aspects of its sacramental life, so ought it also be vigilant of financial stewardship. Those whose vocation is the management of businesses can teach something in this regard. We have learned that "...a company succeeds because its management balances long-term risk taking with near-term commitment to making small improvements in what works, and ignores tempting opportunities that are peripheral to its core technology."[13] This

---

[12]   As denominations are dismantling the structures and reviving the funding and fundraising practices established over the last 70 years, they would do well to recall the history of what has come to be in order to decide what to do and not to do.

A very helpful text in this regard is Ben Primer, *Protestants and American Business Methods* (Ann Arbor, MI: Research Press, 1979). Primer documents and assesses the bureaucratization of Protestant churches from 1876–1929. One example from his research might illustrate the point of knowing one's history in order not to repeat or recycle dilemmas. Primer shows how centralized funding and fundraising under the auspices of national boards originated in order that local churches would not be deluged by multiple special appeals on an every Sunday basis. If campus ministers and others engaged in ministries beyond the local church were to raise their own budgets through direct appeals to local churches (to whom else can they appeal?), as some denominational executives suggest, local churches would again be overwhelmed by appeals. While we strongly affirm that campus ministers ought to establish and strengthen ties with local churches, we cannot endorse funding of campus ministry primarily through Sunday morning appeals.

[13]   Chris Raymond, "What Makes a Business Successful? A Willingness to Take Risks While Focusing on What Works, Say 2 Management Scholars," *Chronicle of Higher Education* (14 November 1990): A5.

balance has proven quite useful in the stewardship of local ministries, especially when tempted to take flight into an attractive program or idea that, upon closer examination, proved tangential to campus ministry's real vocation. Campus ministries that "work" (and we believe there are many that do) deserve denominational attention especially as the mainline is poised to explore new initiatives for church growth, initiatives that may prove quite tangential in the long run to our vocation as church.

We have also learned that "...the successful company makes investments guided by long-term potential for profit, not by short-term financial equations,...and that if they have to invest in something for strategic purposes, they find a way to do it."[14] This rule has been true of our local experience; this axiom is especially pertinent to campus ministry (perhaps to all Christian ministry), which by its own teachings seeks the long-term potential over the short-term cost. Denominational churches will have to bear the burden of missionary activity on campus if they wish to extend the fullness of their ministry to all God's people. If Methodist, Presbyterian, and Episcopal Christians sincerely desire to have Methodist, Presbyterian and Episcopal ministries represented at the center of the busiest crossroads of young adult life—the more than 3000 institutions of higher education in America—then Methodist, Presbyterian and Episcopal churches will have to pay for that ministry. This is the simple reality of the denominational system.

Denominationalism is not always detrimental to Christian life. Indeed, there is increasing evidence that as our life and world grow more complex Christians need all the more these distinctive ways of being in the world. To pursue a denominational agenda is to be distinct and particular. For this reason, it is impossible to assume that campus ministries bearing denominational identities will find significant financial support in the private philanthropic sector. True, there are private foundations in every state, some of whom will give to specific religious denominational programs and causes, and they should be sought out and approached for support. But most of these foundations are of modest size, and have even more claims upon their resources than the denominations can enumerate. Thus, when they are inclined to give, their gifts are frequently modest and cannot sustain the annual expenses of a concerted ministry on campus. Nearly every foundation capable of such support is bound by its own policies not to grant monies to any sectarian institution, a restriction often cited when denominational

---

[14] Ibid., A12.

ministries venture to apply. Therefore, bearing the name of a denomination on campus is very costly—it costs all the funds one might otherwise secure if these ministries were more broadly non-denominational or purely secular. We do not advocate the non-denominational approach. That work is already being done quite ably by InterVarsity Christian Fellowship and the Campus Crusade for Christ, to name but two. Denominations have something to contribute in themselves, but campus ministries are also painfully aware of the cost of that contribution.

It was noted above that, in general, involvement translates into financial support. Even those who are not particularly active within a congregation will respond to campus ministry if that ministry has provided them a place to share their own ministry. Lawyers, doctors, business people, faculty, administrators and others who contribute their time and energy as guests at programs in the series offered by Brent House have frequently found and/or provided the money necessary to fund those series. Some have made personal gifts and some have solicited funding from their associates or firms, because they see the personal connection between faith and work and they are moved by a church that takes their own vocation seriously.

We can offer no panacea, no ready recipe for funding, but we do bear witness to our experience and our findings that when campus ministry is undertaken as a partnership and a venture it can pay for itself and yield dividends for its investors. The primary concern of campus ministry, then, is not money, but pastoral stewardship. Good stewardship of the human resources on campus and within the church, in our experience, yields the necessary financial resources to do ministry. It may sound simplistic, but is nonetheless fundamentally true, that if believers trust in God, and in one another, all that is needed is provided.

Therefore fund-raising is not the primary concern of campus ministers or campus ministries. Ministry is the primary concern, and when that ministry is being carried out responsibly, the resources necessary to its conduct will be forthcoming. Where our hearts are, there will our treasures be, also. To paraphrase William Rainey Harper, Hebrew scholar and founding President of the University of Chicago, whose own slant on fund-raising remains a helpful watchword for anyone in ministry: "I have never in my life asked anyone for even a single dollar, but I have made it possible for a great many people to express their generosity."

If, then, local judicatories and congregations are willing to invest in creative and dedicated campus ministry that practices pastoral stewardship, willing partners can and will be found. Our task in ministry is to create the possibility for others to express their generosity in every sense. This possibility is born of our own willingness to give, for it is in the giving of self that relationship is initiated and partnership is possible. It is to the dynamics of such relationship that we turn next.

—⚜ 10 ⚜—

THE POLITICS OF MINISTRY
AND THE MINISTRY OF POLITICS

LIFE TOGETHER

Governance is the exercise of power in the structures and loyalties of a society or people; it is rooted in the statutes, functions, and authority of a society's organizations and associations. Thus Christ as King is worshiped in the church when men, already trying to govern humanely, perceive that the model of humanity by which motives and aspirations are to be appraised is love: the building up of the common life so that variety is not sacrificed to harmony or harmony to diversity. The requisite of love here is that fundamental humanity be guaranteed to all and this covenant be built into the major institutions and social processes.[1]

By the late 1960s, the social order exhibited abundant evidence of upheaval in accustomed patterns of governance. All the major battles being waged on many fronts in America shared one element in common: they were struggles "between people who are capable and ready to govern and those who fear vast shifts in balances of power."[2]

---

[1] Danforth, v. 1, 294.

[2] Ibid., 294–95.

Responsible governance called the churches to urge and aid people beyond mere protest to new ways of influence in those institutions and structures that actually govern American life. Underwood's most cogent observation was that "...religious and academic leaders still have not identified where decisions are made and where influence for reform is exerted in the institutions they claim to serve."[3]

The same criticism applies today in systems, attitudes, and institutions that seem only to reinforce a stratification of ministries, and to exacerbate the very problems of modern ministry. Is there, then, another way to shape authority for a whole people and thus make authority and rule inclusive of all?

Any answer to this question leads to the word "politics." This word may need redemption from common abuse to be rightly applied. The church has been especially averse to exploit discussions of politics. The phrase "church politics" conjures up negative images for most church members. Church leaders often cloak deliberations and decisions in theological jargon, but any action undertaken within community is, *de facto*, "political." "Politics" is the only proper word to describe the shared life of people.

It is common to confuse politics with community, though the two are quite distinct. Community means only a common fellowship. It describes, as its root implies, commonality of thought, feeling, space, values, work. What it does not describe is how fellowship is achieved, how such relationship is established and nurtured. Nor does it describe how such relationship is established and nurtured *especially* in those instances when and where commonality is lacking. How do people bridge difference to find a life together? How shall diversity be shared that we might even approach companionship, much less fellowship? That is the role of politics. Every human association is political. As Aristotle maintained, the human animal is a political animal, but not every human association is a community.

Politics is the way human beings corporately govern their lives. In America, and within the church, it is not the avoidance of politics but the lively and responsible practice of politics that orders life. In a democracy the citizens themselves rule. Elected officials are public servants, called and authorized by the citizenry to carry out specific tasks in their behalf, for the good of the commonwealth. So, too, in the church the laity governs the life and order of the whole. Bishops, priests, presbyters, dea-

---

3	Ibid., 295.

cons, elders and other offices or orders are called and authorized by the laity to carry out specific tasks in their behalf and for the good of the community. This political order is a hallmark of the churches spawned by the Protestant Reformation. While details of this structure are disputed within the Protestant denominations and among them, this distinction has long marked a profound difference between these churches and the Roman Catholic system that spawned them. For at least a century, however, the Catholic church, too, has engaged this struggle within its own political structure.

THE CONFUSION OF AUTHORITY

But just as Underwood maintained that *leaders* forget where decisions were made and authority was lodged, so too do others forget. The people "forget" that responsible government (governance) of the American state is a personal responsibility and that responsible governance of the Christian church is, likewise, a personal responsibility. Eschewing "politics," citizens abdicate responsibility to those chosen to be servants. When citizens cease to instruct the servants or default on their responsibility to communicate they unwittingly make the servant their ruler.

In the absence of politics, human associations experience disorder and confusion, or worse, destruction. They lapse into incivility—which is to say, life without politics. The demise of politics and the concomitant rise of incivility on campus engendered a special report of The Carnegie Foundation for the Advancement of Teaching. Published in 1990, *Campus Life: In Search of Community*[4] was the result of a survey of some 380 college presidents.[5] The survey indicated that 75-80 percent of those presidents queried identified campus alcoholism as a problem at their institution; many named racism as a problem; inadequate facilities for campus gatherings were widely cited;[6] 50 percent reported that thefts

---

[4] *Campus Life: In Search of Community*, with a foreword by Ernest L. Boyer (Princeton, NJ: The Carnegie Foundation for the Foundation for the Advancement of Teaching, 1990).

[5] Robin Wilson, "Quality of Life Said to Have Diminished on U. S. Campuses," *The Chronicle of Higher Education* 36 (2 May 1990): A1, A32.

[6] It is particularly important to note that after the student unrest of the late 1960s, many campuses instructed architects to modify existing buildings , and design future ones, to intentionally prevent large gatherings of the type that erupted into massive demonstrations. Thus, on many campuses there may be plenty of buildings, but few or none conducive to socializing events.

were a moderate or major problem on campus; about 45 percent cited problems in serving a rapidly-growing commuter student population; and about 40 percent of the college presidents interviewed felt that just spending more time on their campus would make an important change in the community's life.[7]

Campuses reflect the pluralism of American culture. And, like the culture, the university searches for community in the midst of diversity. Students and faculties have at various times in American history found commonality in shared religious identity (on denominational campuses), shared ethnic or racial identity (on segregated campuses), shared gender identity (on single-sex campuses), and shared socio-economic identity. When schools were rather more narrowly defined as teachers' colleges, or agricultural and mechanical schools, or liberal arts colleges, or fine arts conservatories, or any of the numerous distinctions that unified the mission of a particular institution, students and faculties even shared vocational identity.

Few such institutions remain. Whether private or public, nearly all major universities boast a panoply of options as they attempt to cover every conceivable base. Like the technological explosion that forced a post-World War II America and its institutions to cope with rapid change, the sociological explosion of the Civil Rights Movement—and its many corollaries in varied liberation initiatives—pose a strain upon politics inadequate to the sudden and overwhelming demands of social integration. Attempts to integrate disciplines, races, ages, nationalities, religions and genders often seem like the attempt to unite magnets of the same polarity: the closer they come, the greater the resistance to union. There is no apparent community on such campuses precisely because there is no apparent commonality. The politics of campus, the means by which these differences relate to and with one another, are polarized. "The *ethos* of diversity which is tolerance and mutual respect, is much harder to come by."[8]

Anger and hostility are palpable on campus. Campuses throughout the nation have experienced a steep rise in student and faculty antipathies. Aggressive racism is rampant and not limited to hostility toward African-Americans. New waves of immigration increase

---

[7] Wilson, A32. The last statistic reflects a significant change in campus politics. Changes in the presidential role that remove and/or isolate the executive leadership from campus impose a barrier to communication and thus thwart the effective governance of the community.

[8] George Will, "Curdled Politics on Campus," *Newsweek* (6 May 1991): 28.

antipathies toward Hispanics and Asians. Student publications espousing a "conservative" political bent have led the way, but many students have willingly followed. Students and faculty of divergent ethnic and racial origins have, in some instances, been singled out for particularly abusive attack. Those of varied sexual orientation, too, have been targeted. Gay and lesbian students and faculty have been attacked, some physically and a few quite brutally. Religious and ethno-political diversity marks others for attack, specifically Jews, Arabs, and Palestinians. And those who ally themselves with any side—or even attempt to steer a middle course—are prey, as well.

In the midst of turmoil the search for order eludes easy solution. Some advocate a more aggressive legislation of life. Those who argue the restoration of a curriculum based in Western European sources and those who assert an unimpeded freedom of speech are counterpoised by those who advocate a multi-cultural, de-Westernized curriculum and want civility coerced with legislation prohibiting verbal harassment. But imposing a single viewpoint by law only aggravates the problem. The substitution of legislation for personal responsibility is but another form of abdication. The imposition of law or force does not establish order, it only establishes power.

THE CONFUSION OF ANTIPATHIES

Lacking in many instances is any sympathetic understanding of the natural sources of much of the antipathy. Few seem to appreciate the effects of removing a young adult from the relatively ordered environment of home and community, and the somewhat isolated experience of individual study (often at a computer terminal) and recreation (often in front of a television), and placing that young adult in a dormitory where private space is shared with one or more others who bring their own different experiences and values to that environment. Additionally, this young adult is challenged intellectually and personally in the classroom and outside of it by new ideas and concepts. The cumulative results of so much change in so diverse a setting, with the added burden of restrictions that circumvent the means for expressing fear, doubt, or disagreement, seems as likely a recipe for strife and despair as one can imagine. The incivility of the modern campus is not nearly so surprising as the grace and justice that manage to prevail over such odds. The powers of

persuasion that guide democratic authority, given sufficient encouragement and sympathetic patience, do seem to work.

The university is not the only institution under siege. The churches
are similarly beleaguered. They, too, were once prone to relative homo-
geneity. Members of the Episcopal Church—and its progenitor, the
Anglican communion—could expect at the very least to hear the English
language spoken when they gathered for worship or conference. There
would always be a predictable "Englishness" about it. Yet it is increasingly common to meet Asian, African, and Hispanic "Anglicans."
Prayers and scriptures may be read in several languages at public
worship and when the church gathers internationally the differences are
readily visible in native vestments and multinational leaders.

All churches in America have experienced these and similar phe-
nomena. Diversity in the church extends into many uncharted realms.
Churches now number the divorced, the remarried, and the gay and
lesbian among their members—and many more besides—few of whom
would have been openly recognized or seated in the assembly in other
ages. The strain upon ecclesial civility is especially pronounced.

For example, at the General Convention of the Episcopal Church in
1991, when discussions and deliberations in the House of Bishops turned
to proposed legislation on sexuality and ordination, these ordained
leaders reached the point of personal invective and became so volatile
and hostile that the Presiding Bishop remanded the House to "executive
session." Meeting in private, beyond the scrutiny of the press or outside
observers, the bishops continued their conflict until they reached a
resolution. As an experienced priest of the church opined after the
convention, the meeting was likely one of great consequence not because
of any decision on sexuality or ordination (for there was neither), but
because the bishops learned anew that legislation is not the way to order
the life of the church.

FROM CIVILITY TO COMMUNION

If legislation cannot order our life together, what can? The fundamental weakness of the Carnegie Report was both its appeal to a "higher
standard"—itself an inherently hierarchical appeal that assumes that
somewhere above us there lies a standard that is applicable—and its
failure to articulate one. What the Carnegie report seems to have wanted
to say is that we need a transcendent standard—one that is beyond our

present malaise. But all the Carnegie report could offer was an appeal to civility.

While civility is certainly a standard, it is not "above" us. It is within us, and arises out of relationship, out of our citizenship. What the Carnegie report attempted was a secular standard for community based upon six principles: a community that is purposeful, open, just, disciplined, caring and celebrative.[9] The report failed to articulate the ground of these claims. Such claims could be grounded in civic republicanism. They could also be grounded in civil religion, even one that acknowledges a universal God and the role of the United States in a community or society of nations. In neither of these cases is a denominationally based campus ministry essential to helping the university fulfill its vocation to wholeness, inherent in its very name: *univer*sity. Other vehicles, such as a multicultural core curriculum and legislated civility, reinforced by persuasion, could conceivably assist in that task.

But the values articulated by the Carnegie Report are consonant with the values of the gospel. Thus the values claimed of the report could be grounded in the Christian religion, though the desired consequence of such a grounding—for the Christian—is certainly more than "civility"; it is communion and its correlative, community. As political animals, our life together is based upon the practice of politics. We are more or less (mostly less) reflective about these practices. Denominational campus ministries, as components of the religious community, do have valuable resources to offer the campus in its task of building and being "a community that is purposeful, open, just, disciplined, caring and celebrative."

It is not enough to say, for example, that everyone has a right to free expression. We have proven that abundantly in recent American experience. Free expression can only be tolerated in a people that believes the expression of every person is valuable. Such belief presupposes yet another belief: that every person is valuable. The inalienable rights asserted by our own political system are premised quite consciously upon this immutable assumption. If the rights are abused and abrogated, it may not be the legislation that is at fault, but the absence of those fundamental assumptions—beliefs—upon which everything depends.

The church has a positive contribution to make in any society in its role as a community of believers. What this community holds in "common" is not a specific creed. The sheer diversity of separate

---

9   Boyer, 5.

Christian denominations, the division that distinguishes us from Jews, Muslims, Buddhist and others (and the various distinctions within each of those systems that further distinguish their diversity), makes any claim to "community" based on creed untenable. What we do hold in common is the fundamental assumption that we live by *belief*, that what we believe really does make a difference in the way we live. For example, the first Amendment of the American Constitution guarantees religious *belief*, not practice. Indeed, the practice of religion must be civil by government standards. This proposition may seem so evident as to be laughably simplistic. But documents like the Carnegie report, and abundant evidences out of modern experience, indicate that this common assumption held by the religious communities of the world increasingly distinguishes us from a growing number of people who seem to assume belief unimportant. Those who do not recognize the fundamental power of belief pose a danger to our common welfare. The danger is not just in what they may actually substitute for belief. The greater danger is that they possess neither appreciation or reverence for the importance of belief itself.

In a review of the Carnegie report, President Paul Verkuil of The College of William and Mary noted that "…the critical responsibility in the search for community is to teach people how to be civil during a true exchange of views, not simply how to keep the lid on the campus. In my view, there is more friction on campus today precisely because we are closer to understanding each other than ever before."[10]

Campus ministry has an important role to play especially on the growing number of campuses where civility has deteriorated and where society is threatened in both the aggregate and the individual. If, as Verkuil notes, incivility is not a sign of failure but the result of diversity, proximity, and the ease of modern communication, vocational promptings are discernable within this turmoil. A major part of the university's vocation today is to be "an ideal laboratory for discovering how different people can learn to live together at a critical stage in their lives."[11] As such, conversation—high quality conversation—is critical. But conversation is shaped by politics: the way people relate to each other determines the shape of how people converse.

A political interpretation of campus ministry can lend valuable insights to its role both in the church and on campus. "The problem

---

[10] Paul R. Verkuil, "The University Is Closer to the Ideal of a True and Open Community Than It Ever Has Been," *Chronicle of Higher Education* (25 July 1990): B2.
[11] Ibid., B3.

within which the political interpretation of ministry is set, "wrote ethicist James Gustafson in an essay for the Danforth study, "...is the campus ministries' problem of maintaining identity in the midst of being all things to all [people] that some might be saved. It is the problem of the nurture of a core which forms the perspective from which participation in the world is governed. It is providing a rudder for the vessel that has been castoff from the tranquility of a snug harbor and pointed toward the heavy seas."[12] Gustafson rightly notes that this problem is not just the problem of the campus *minister* but is endemic to campus *ministries*, and to ministry in general. The political task is inherent in all ministry, and thus the responsibility of all the people of God. It is not a vast leap to extrapolate those political features of the ordained minister for the ministering community itself.

Gustafson maintains that, like politicians, clergy must make a case for their work. This is the historic task of evangelism. Yet arguments of utility are no substitute for active, visible service. The model Jesus embraced for ministry, and the only one to which he commended his disciples, was service—not office.

"To stay in office, and yet to be more than the mirrored reflection of those who put and keep one in office, is close to the essence of the political process," maintained Gustafson.[13] But does not a similar tension pertain to all ministers of the church, lay and ordained, who hold their standing as members of a community but are constantly challenged and called to be more than "the mirrored reflection" of the status quo? The ties of relationship are constantly tested by the tension between conflicting expectations and assumptions. Christians may lament this tension, as many do, or capitulate to it. But they cannot escape it. It is the cost of relationship.

RELATIONSHIP

Relationship demands politics, a means for shaping and conducting life together. More than legislation (though legislation constitutes the written codes by which human relationships are ordered), politics entails the full spectrum of manners and morals, protocol and practice. To be political, or to act in a politic fashion, is to live out one's relationship. If, for example, a student comes to the chaplain with a problem arising out

---

[12] James Gustafson, "Political Images of the Ministry," Danforth, v. 2, 250–51.
[13] Ibid., 252.

of conflict with a roommate, the responsible chaplain will encourage the student to consider the perspective of the roommate, perhaps even offering to entertain a meeting with the roommates together. The chaplain will also inquire into other resources the student may (or may not) have consulted over the problem: a resident advisor in the dorm, an academic advisor, student mental health or peer counselor, and/or relevant personnel in the housing office. Failing resolution among the principals, the chaplain may encourage appropriate counsel with those of the aforementioned campus resources. And all of this may be undertaken only to identify the real problem or issue. Once the problem has been identified, the chaplain or some other counselor may assist the aggrieved student to consider a variety of perspectives and to seek out those who can best serve in seeking a solution.

Counsel such as that described in the example above always begins with consideration of all the persons involved, of establishing the responsibility of each and, ultimately, of holding each to accountability. This process lies at the heart of the practice of sacramental confession and extends through the whole of human relations. "Responsibility and accountability are key words from the vocabulary of institutions, and their frequency on the lips of clergy today suggests that we have lapsed into an understanding of the church which emphasizes its primary identity as a complex *organization*."[14] Re-appropriating these words for our own vocabularies is risky but the primary identity of human community is, undeniably, that of *complex organization*. To deny this is to retreat into simple-mindedness.

LIVING WITH THE GIFT OF COMPLEXITY

A complex organization allows and encourages multiple responses at multiple levels. Christianity posits that faith is, itself, response—that humans love because God first loved them. It is of the essence of humanity to be able to respond. Human community is endangered when any person's response is denied or devalued, when any are denied their ability to answer for themselves, to share of their own perspective, or offer their own particular gift. That the other's response may not be the

---

[14] Donald Shockley, "The College and University Chaplaincy: A Theological Perspective," *Invitation to Dialogue: The Theology of College Chaplaincy and Campus Ministry* (New York: Education in the Society, National Council of the Churches of Christ in the USA, 1986): 36.

same as one's own may be frightening, even threatening, but that is the risk with which contemporary persons are called to live both by modern circumstance and by God. It could hardly have been comforting to Jesus that Judas chose to respond as he did to Jesus' gospel and ministry. Still, Jesus' clear directive to Judas to do what he had to do was Jesus' invitation to Judas to exercise his own responsibility—even though it stood in opposition to Jesus himself. Jesus' invitation to Judas, though accounted as impolitic by some, was actually (even literally) a crucially political act. Jesus practiced a politics that acknowledged every perspective, not just the ones that were safe or agreeable, and invited all who would to take responsibility by offering himself to the complexity of their lives. Thus, to be impolitic is not simply to be rude, though that were bad enough; to be impolitic is to be irresponsible.

Leaders have a special responsibility to honor the serious response of every person. Gustafson claimed that certain characteristics were required of ordained leaders on campus. He looked especially at integrity and purposes. "To be an effective leader," maintained Gustafson, "[the ordained leader] needs to have a point of integrity, an integrating purposiveness which gives direction and goals to his various activities. He needs a sense of his office, what it authorizes him to do, what it limits are, what it enables him to lead others to do."[15] Christian purposiveness is supplied in the baptismal covenant. Specific "mission statements" may be helpful, but are not to be confused with the original statement of purpose expressed in baptism. The popularity of mission statements obscured the fundamental mission statement of the church, even as similar mission statements within the universities may have diverted attention away from the fundamental mission of higher education to vocational formation. There has been much confusion in many quarters over "mission statements" that have not served to articulate missions so much as to delineate tasks—and there is a profound difference between the two.

It may be that this confusion has compromised institutional integrity both in the church and on campus. For example, campus ministry that undertakes a program—even a highly creative one—but neglects attention to the relationship between that program and the baptismal mission of the church is not paying due attention to politics.

Integrity, then, involves knowing where one's boundaries are. As Gustafson noted, the clergyperson "needs a sense of his office, what it

---

15   Ibid., 257.

authorizes him to do, what its limits are, what it enables him to lead others to do."[16] Campus ministries and each of us in them, lay and ordained, need also to have some sense of our roles, some sense of our limits, and some sense of our abilities to act and lead. Our programs in campus ministry do not always *appear* to be in service to the mission of the baptismal covenant. This may be in part due to differences that distinguish campus ministry from the only mode the modern churches seem to know or honor as definitive, which is the parochial congregation—a model neither mandated nor perhaps anticipated by Jesus but derived from the politics of the faith community and shaped by the politics of the host culture. This may also be due to the reality that the genuine experience of living within and through that covenant of baptism is severely limited throughout the church, thus constraining imagination.

It is our task, whatever our ministries, to be able to account for the faith that is in us—and to be able to account for the shape of our faith as it issues in ministry. Campus ministry certainly should remain and grow ever more creative. Campus ministry is especially gifted in the diversity of campus life to exercise a far-reaching creativity, as our own ministries have witnessed. But campus ministries do not act alone. They are bound in communion with the Christian church and a specific denominational expression of it. Furthermore, they are set within a university community. They cannot avoid politics; they can only honor them and, sometimes, redeem them.

Campus ministries attempt to practice a politics that honors its constituencies and is faithful to its baptismal vocation by literally asking those constituencies how campus ministry might serve them and attempting to respond out of its resources. But campus ministry also attempts to practice a politics that honors the university by asking constantly how what campus ministry does is related to the mission of the university to educate citizens. Sometimes campus ministry supports the university; at other times, it is in conflict. But nearly always both campus ministry and the university are conscious that in either case both are strengthened for having attended to this question. Two persons do not have to be in agreement to practice mutuality; all that is required is that they be conscious of what they are doing, and why.

Similarly, campus ministry is not always in agreement with the practices of the local congregation or the judicatory. Indeed, in many

---

[16] Ibid.

cases each values this disagreement because it comes out of a conscious inquiry into their respective ministries. For example, Episcopal campus ministry at the University of Chicago values its relationship with local parishes and with the diocese; we are literally dependent upon those relationships. We invite their participation in our life by electing to our council of oversight members from parishes throughout the diocese, thus opening our life not only to their scrutiny but subjecting ourselves to their authority. In setting a course different from the parishes and from the diocese, however, we are not practicing a thoughtless or heedless rebellion. We have, instead, accounted for the ministry that is ours, sharing the reasons for our differences and examining how these differences may be important contributions to a more comprehensive expression of the baptismal covenant.

For example, the baptismal promise to respect the dignity of every human being has led many a campus ministry into the treacherous waters of modern society. Respecting that dignity involved us quite intimately in ministry to persons with AIDS, including one of our own former interns. Similarly, that respect opened us to inclusive-language liturgies, the primary architect of which was a woman from another communion than our own. That respect also led the Episcopal Church Council at the University of Chicago to declare its hospitality to gay men and lesbian women an important facet of its ministry, and earned us a bright blue, spray-painted swastika on our front door. But that same respect encouraged us to respond even to our anonymous vandal(s) with kindness and gentleness, and an expression of gratitude for the obvious pain they had shared in leaving so visible an expression of themselves on our door. These and myriad other differences set us apart but do not separate us from the parishes and diocese we also attempt to serve in our ministry.

THE DEMANDS OF INCLUSIVITY

Inclusive politics means building bridges across diverse constituencies. A primary means of such bridge-building is the art of persuasion. Gustafson argued that "...the clergyperson needs competence in forms of persuasion and in knowledge of his/her fields."[17] Such competence is demanded of the entire ministry community. To persuade does not necessarily mean to cajole, wheedle, or hoodwink. It means only "to

---

[17] Ibid., 258.

advise thoroughly," which in the case of the modern world, frequently means to make articulate appeal to the necessity for an inclusive politics. But inclusive politics also demands that ministers be knowledgeable—a daunting task. How can anyone be responsibly knowledgeable in the midst of so much change and in the presence of so much diversity— except through mutual reliance and respect? Communities of ministries need politics that encourage conversation for the mediation of our respective differences and their reconciliation into creative action.

Inclusive politics is a risky venture, demanding a balance of risk and prudence that issues forth in "wisdom, a sense of the fitting and appropriate action."[18] To be politic does not necessarily mean that one is underhanded or sly in any malicious sense. Jesus adjured his own followers to be wise as serpents, to practice shrewdness and even cunning, and to emulate the innocence of the dove. This instruction seems but an early equivalent of what it means to be politic.

One does entail risk and possible loss when practicing good politics, politics that include everyone and accord all a responsible voice. Indeed, what has earned "politics" a bad name is not politics at all, but is misuse of political office and abuse of public trust. It is not by observing political protocol, but by intentionally circumnavigating it, that injustice is done and crime perpetrated. Bad politics and bad ministry act without consulting others and decide without due deliberation in open process.

Inclusive politics are not born fully mature. They are means of relating that must be nurtured. There are certainly occasions and situations that demand that some persons bear more responsibility than others, or that some be commissioned to decide in the absence of the whole. Centralized leadership may be demanded in a newly established or a severely deteriorated ministry where shared leadership is not yet practicable. No one style of leadership is superior to another; each is appropriate to particular circumstances. But the autocrat is, at least within a politics of the church, a means to an end and not an end in himself or herself. One need only skim the dictations of the apostle Paul to see that leadership demands remarkable flexibility.

The necessity of varieties of ministry, reveal the need of the church to enhance what has been by tradition a parental, paternalistic politics with a politics of partnership. "Parenting and partnership are as ancient as Christianity itself. Both are essential to a faith community. Each is holy.

---

[18] Ibid., 261.

But they describe very different ways to hold one another."[19] Indeed, the most taxing demands of ordained ministry—or any other vocation to leadership—are discerning which style of leadership is demanded of a given situation. Leaders must make the necessary transition within themselves from one style to another and then communicate honestly just what they are doing and why.

With the responsibility of leadership comes also the duty to keep others informed. Communication is essential to a responsible politics, pastoral stewardship and vocational discernment. Churches, universities, and many other American institutions are dominated by hierarchical politics, but they are being challenged—or called—to decentralize, to move toward partnership. The decentralization of most public institutions, such as can be observed, demands more and better communication.

Underwood was particularly concerned to stress the role and importance of communication between chaplains and the institutions they serve. It cannot be overstressed that communication is integral to campus (or any other) ministry. Collegial, horizontal, grass roots leadership is consonant with Christian principles, Reformed ecclesiology, and democratic process. Governance is shared in an inclusive politics, but getting to that end is a process that demands much of us.

Decentralization places more authority for deliberation and decision at the local level, at the center of daily activity. In so doing, decentralization actually encourages—indeed, requires—conversation at the local level. Workers in factories, for example, no longer stand mute on assembly lines tightening the same bolt endlessly; they work in teams, each team assembling an entire item. Collaboration and cooperation is thus replacing the isolation and boredom of mechanical assembly.

Ministry functions best when authority for the day-to-day decisions is left in the hands of those who live and minister at that level. But getting to that goal is not easy, nor does it happen accidentally. The politics of the institution must be structured to achieve that end. The politics—the distribution of gifts and responsibilities, the patterns of communication and relationship—must be deliberately conformed to the goal of shared governance.

---

[19] James D. Whitehead and Evelyn Eaton Whitehead, *The Promise of Partnership: Leadership and Ministry in an Adult Church* (San Francisco: Harper Collins, 1991), 3.

ONE MINISTRY'S EXPERIENCE

The Episcopal Church Council at the University of Chicago struggled for some years with the perplexing question of governance or politics. Established in 1946, its by-laws adequately detailed its structure: elections, length of term, etc. By 1982, the Council had digressed from the design of those by-laws. For example, while the by-laws allowed for diverse membership, office was actually held largely by senior faculty and the ordained pastors of several local parishes. Because they had limited their membership, and could not always find suitable candidates for office, some members had served several successive terms. A rigorous return to the original by-laws opened membership to students, faculty, and staff. In fact, since the only requirement of the by-laws was that nominees be members "of the Anglican communion," membership was gradually extended to a wider variety of people. Ordained membership was restored to largely ex-officio status and included only the chaplain and the Bishops of the diocese.[20]

Since terms of service were set at three years, within a three-year period Council membership was diversified and revitalized. But the by-laws were lacking in one important regard: there was no clear indication of purpose. What was the role of the Episcopal Church Council? Since they only met quarterly, it was improbable that they could effectively oversee an active and growing ministry on such a staggered schedule. Gradually, however, a purpose was revealed—a calling discerned. When the physical facilities, Brent House, demanded attention, the Council determined that they were the appropriate entity to engage the issue with the Bishops and Trustees of the Diocese of Chicago, who hold deed to the property. They began to see their role as stewards of a ministry as they negotiated the renovation of the building and undertook the task of securing funds for the project.

Yet when the restoration project was complete, the question again arose as to what their role should be. The newly elected membership numbered several graduate students, one of whom was particularly adept at group process. With the encouragement of the chaplain, the Council undertook a retreat. They examined their own ministry and undertook to discern their own vocation. The chaplain absented himself from the retreat and, eventually, from many of the Council's meetings, in order that they might move beyond patterns of dependence and experi-

---

[20] Elected membership can and has been held by clergy, but usually those so elected have also been students or faculty at the university.

ence autonomy. The Whiteheads wrote of "the potential of absence" and suggested that the absence of a resident priest often leads a community to a new realization of the abundance they possess in themselves.[21] The potential and practice of absence is an important facet of a politics that seeks to encourage mutuality and interdependence.

From his arrival in 1982, the chaplain wrote two annual reports. One was a report to the Diocese of Chicago detailing the work of the ministry in the previous calendar year. This report was entered into the Journal of Convention, thus making it available to any person in the diocese desirous of knowing about this ministry. In the spring quarter, when the Episcopal Church Council conducted its annual meeting, the chaplain's second report was issued. It was addressed only to the Council and constituted a "state of the chaplaincy" report.

In this report, which reviewed the previous academic year's ministry, the chaplain shared not only his report of activities, but shared the process of vocational discernment. Successes and failures of the previous year were assessed honestly and probed for learning. What did these experiences reveal of the communities we serve? What might we infer from these learnings that can guide us in the coming year? In 1989 the report was written not by the chaplain, but by the co-chairs of the Council, signifying an important change in the life of the ministry as the Council assumed this responsibility. Their report became the annual report to the community and, as such, is mailed in June to everyone on the Episcopal campus ministry mailing list, including all alumni and financial supporters of the ministry.

As stewards of the Episcopal campus ministry at the University of Chicago, the Council now bears responsibility for securing and deploying the resources of the ministry. Funding appeals go out over their signatures; communications and/or negotiations with the diocese or other funders are their responsibility; and care of personnel—including the chaplain—is a ministry they take seriously. Through the chaplain and other staff, and through personal participation, they maintain contact with the active programming of the ministry. On occasion, certain of them preach at worship or take responsibility for leading events.

The chaplain's office serves the communication process necessary to this diverse ministry. The Episcopal catechism describes the ministry of both bishops and priests as "oversight." In a diverse, dispersed community, few can have knowledge of the whole. The role of the ordained

---

[21] Whitehead & Whitehead, 39.

leadership includes this purview, thus the chaplain serves largely to coordinate communications between the several diverse ministries directed largely by a variety of volunteer or stipended, part-time associates and the laity. A monthly newsletter with a detailed calendar apprises the readership (campus and community, faculty, staff, administrators, friends and financial donors) of activities and worship.

THE CAMPUS MINISTER IN A COMMUNITY OF MINISTRY

The person of the campus minister—whether lay or ordained—will likely always be central to campus ministry. But, while in an hierarchical ordering the ordained person stands at the top of a pyramid (at least at the level of the local community of ministry), the understanding proposed here is that the chaplain is at the center point on a continuum, or at the hub of radiating spokes. This is probably true of almost any collaborative administrative structure, but is especially true when working with an undergraduate population. This became quite evident in a personnel review of a campus minister elsewhere who also shared staff responsibilities in a local parish. While everyone seemed quite pleased with the diverse interests and varied contributions of the chaplain both in the parish and the community, there was abiding concern that the undergraduate population seemed consistently under-represented in the ministry. As the review progressed, individuals around the table drew upon reminiscences in describing how the present ministry compared with what they had experienced when they were students. The consultant who was facilitating the conversation suggested that each person who had drawn such a comparison reflect upon his or her actual words. The common thread that united each was the formula by which each had introduced a comparison. When reflecting upon their own experience of campus ministry, each one had begun his or her sentence with some variation of the phrase, "We had a chaplain who..." In that phrase, they had identified that at the center of their experience was a relationship with a particular person who was the chaplain.

This component of personal relationship is especially important to the politics of undergraduate ministry. Like many communities of ministry, undergraduate campus ministry is very time-consuming and person-centered. Personal outreach to and relationship with single young adults at this particular point in their lives is often crucial to them and is certainly important to any ministry. In some instances, this contact will be the work of the chaplain or campus minister. In other instances, this contact may be the responsibility of a lay associate, a volunteer, or a peer minister. But there is no substitute for this personal communication and relationship, and those who would have a ministry among this constituency are advised to plan wisely for this reality. While a campus minister can ably serve as the center for a strong undergraduate ministry, such is likely only in those places where the primary responsibility of the campus minister is focussed on that task and where sufficient support exists to make that feasible. It is likely that others will have to fulfil that role where the campus minister is called to be hub of a more extensive ministry that includes oversight of faculty, staff and administrators, graduate and professional students, and a physical plant.

But in all cases, ministry demands partnership and a politics that honors collegiality. For example, the ministry of the Episcopal Church Council embraces vocation and stewardship. The Council has been well-served in its vocational discernment by respecting the vocations of its members. For example, the contributions of a graphic artist on the Council improved the printed communications of the entire ministry; a lawyer revised the by-laws and greatly simplified them; a financial development professional negotiated the renovation process with the diocese and represented the ministry in conversations with foundations and potential donors; and the grant proposal that made this study of campus ministry possible was written in large measure by two graduate students in their tenure as co-chairs of the Council. In each case, these individuals were encouraged to use their own vocations in service to the campus ministry. In turn, they led the ministry into its own vocation.

PARTNERSHIP

Clyde Robinson, reflecting on the state of campus ministry in the 1990s and its possible future, wrote:

> My experience has taught me that our ministries must be claimed, like it or not, by the bodies that sponsor them...collaboration, interaction, attention to priorities, and accountability are important words in building ownership, and yet sometimes in the campus ministry network we yield to the temptation of the "PR" mentality and resort to that old mushroom strategy, keeping folks in the dark and feeding them an unmentionable food! When that happens campus ministries are not likely to enter significant partnerships with the congregations that we know are critical components of any rational strategy for developing ministries with the community-oriented, non-residential institutions in which more than half of the U. S.

students are presently enrolled. We cannot objectify them as publicity targets and funding sources and expect them to be partners in ministry.[22]

Robinson's point can be pushed further. Campus ministry needs to include not only congregations, but the full range of partners involved in the campus ministry enterprise. This entails not only inviting and involving the ministry of congregations, but of dioceses and other middle judicatories and an increasing number of committed (sometimes baptized and confirmed) believers who are presently unchurched. The inclusion of this latter group not only enhances campus ministry by representing in its leadership one of campus ministry's primary constituencies, but such inclusion also offers the unchurched a place to exercise a ministry that may have been denied in a congregational setting. That this opportunity may re-establish relationship between the unchurched and the churched through partnership in ministry is also a contribution not to be overlooked.

In addition to personal relationship, social relationship is an important component to the politics of campus ministry. "Moral and social responsibility cannot develop through rules and penalties alone. They must grow out of genuine concern for others. The best way of acquiring this concern is to experience situations in which one can appreciate the effects of one's actions on others and understand how one's own interests are affected in return."[23] Such experience is not endemic to the university where competition and solitary study often militate against this end. It is commonly assumed that community service programs are often a good resource for providing these experiences to students. One wonders, however, if even these activities are adequate to provide the "genuine concern" for others and a concomitant mutuality necessary to instill moral and social responsibility not only among young adults, but the larger population as well.

Traditional expressions of altruism beg critical evaluation, especially when they tend to be based upon patterns of relationship that actually undermine mutuality. Without denying the need to help others, one may question those structures that propose to offer help but do not allow for mutuality between those assisting and those being assisted. The politics of altruism in American culture, like other institutions of this culture, tend also to be hierarchical, to the end that even though valuable service

---

[22] Robinson, 5.
[23] Bok, *Universities*, 36.

may be delivered, it is delivered in such a way that dependencies are reinforced.

There are, however, remarkable exceptions. A growing number of opportunities present themselves, such as Habitat for Humanity. This organization, which addresses the need for affordable housing, enlists volunteers to assist potential homeowners by providing "sweat equity." Working side by side with the prospective home-owners, the volunteers do not work *for* others so much as they work *with* them as colleagues in the actual building of a home. All sound ministry possesses this respect for mutuality and campus ministries can, in themselves, be a source for that experience not only in community outreach projects, but in all the daily activities of ministry itself.

If the church is serious about equipping and deploying the ministries of all people, and if the universities are serious about equipping and deploying a company of educated women and men, campus ministry can make a contribution to both by being a locus of experience in genuine concern and mutuality. The work of Gallup and Castelli indicated that Americans want "a wide variety of services, both spiritual and practical, from their churches and synagogues."[24] An examination of those services can be helpful to all ministries in discerning vocation and in assessing the politics of our life.

COMMUNITY

Gallup and Castelli discovered in their surveys that many people desire a sense of community. Gallup and Castelli additionally note that loneliness is a widely experienced reality in modern American life. This finding comes as little surprise to most of us, and both the church and the university have responded in their own ways to this need. Churches now work at "making" or "building" community through a variety of programs and intentional images. "Family" is a word appended to many congregations and congregational events, as though the adjective were a talisman signifying warmth and conviviality. College and university campuses have restructured residence halls to minimize the sometimes overwhelming impact of housing over a thousand students in a single building. By creating "residence colleges" or the equivalent, larger halls or groups of dorms are segmented into smaller units. Frequently these units have designated personnel to oversee their life, providing counsel

---

[24] Gallup & Castelli, 253.

to the students and offering periodic social and educational activities to stimulate a sense of community.

Yet these attempts to create community frequently fail. They are flawed in their basic assumption that community can be "made." In fact, the very attempt to make community can undermine community. The Gallup and Castelli findings were very telling in this regard: "...one dimension of this need for community is the desire for a church life that supports and provides help for families."[25] For all the stress placed upon "family" in congregations, many of the structures—or politics, if you will—of parochial life actually contrive to keep families apart. Many of the activities designed to enhance family life are not centered in the home, but instead demand that families leave home and come to church, where they are segregated by age and urged to take part in "community." Thus the natural community made of blood kinship, already disputed by competing demands upon its members, is disrupted by the invitation to participate in yet another competing community called the church. Continual reference to family was cited by Gallup and Castelli as off-putting to singles, and especially single young adults, who felt excluded because they were not part of a family.

Ministry does not "make" community, God makes community. The church discovers community and celebrates it. The ultimate community for Christians is the community of God's making: the community of the whole created order. This community, whose existence is a matter of faith based upon the first confessional premise of every Christian creed, is the community that shares a common genesis in God, maker of all things. This community, not of human making, is gradually revealed. But that revelation does not come easily, nor is it greeted with uniform enthusiasm. The apostle Paul evidently knew the pain of this revealing process. He seems to have had this process in mind when, in his letter to the Romans, he wrote of a creation that "waits with eager longing for the revealing of the children of God" (Romans 8:19) and groans in labor pains as it awaits the fullness of this revelation.

This revealing comes only in time and through experience. The university does not "automatically" offer these experiences. These experiences are nowhere "automatic"—self-generated—in a people or in institutions instinctively directed toward isolation, competition, independence and autonomy. These experiences, however, are the essence of ministry. Ministry consists of those acts and moments of mediation and

---

[25] Ibid.

reconciliation that encourage and dis-cover (uncover) the fundamental unity that all share in God, the ties that bind all in a common bond.

This revelation is gradual. It comes only in fits and starts. It comes to the infant in the first realization that the universe is larger than the self. It comes to children as they explore through play and accidentally uncover the connections between them. It comes when one falls in love with someone wholly other—even beyond the familiarity of blood kinship. If one is fortunate, it comes in a love for self that is buttressed by respect for one's limitations and confidence in one's gifts. But for the Christian, there can never be any maker of community except God. In the unity between God and humankind revealed in Jesus and manifested in the Holy Spirit, the Christian is reunited with God, the genesis of all life and relationship. In the Spirit that flows out of that living relationship between God and all that God has made (and continues to make), the faithful continually seek and find that unity everywhere, in everything and in everyone.

Thus community is not made, it is discovered. And the search for God and community begins with this recognition. Ministry on campus (or anywhere else) begins with the recognition of existing community. These are the evidences, the clues, that God prodigally scatters to lead us into the revelation of the ultimate community we share in common. Yet, much energy goes into the denial or destruction of community when we assert that Christian community is the only one of God's making and exert our ministry as a competition for loyalty. The campus is made of many communities. Students in a professional school constitute a community: they share goals, classes, experiences, and friends. In a large university, where there are several professional schools, varied graduate divisions, an undergraduate college, faculties, administrators and staff for these separate divisions, the number of communities is manifold. When the many subdivisions within each of these communities are included—the varied loci of commonality that bind smaller groups into distinct communities of Young Republicans, "old boys," Adult Children of Alcoholics, and the many, many others—then the number of communities becomes legion.

Campus ministry, however, is called to be more than a division or subdivision of commonality. And if Gallup and Castelli are correct, more is desired of campus (and all Christian) ministry:

> The spiritual dimension Americans want includes helping them to find meaning in their lives and, for Christians, to deepen their relationships to Jesus Christ. It also includes a strong desire for information about the Bible and its meaning. While Americans want spirituality from their churches,

they also want practical help. They also want their churches to help them learn how to put their faith into practice; to shed light on the important moral issues of the day; to help them learn how to serve others better and to be better parents. Americans understand that for their faith to be meaningful, it must be real and have a real impact on their day-to-day lives.[26]

These learnings are verified in the experience of campus ministries. Those campus ministries that have consistently maintained vitality, especially over the last twenty years, have been those that took seriously to heart these stated needs and placed them, if not ahead of, at least in relationship to the agenda of churches that tend to define community more narrowly as exclusive loyalty and thus live out of a competitive politics. Such ministries, on campus and elsewhere, take seriously the desire for practical integration of faith and life and provide the tools and opportunities for this reconciling work.

Ministry devoted to reconciling fragmented lives is ministry not to a few, but to all modern people. American society in the 1990s is divided across many lines, the most prominent of which may be "the cultural right," "the cultural left," and "the cultural middle."[27] Using the rather common socio-political connotations of those three groups, those on the left are characterized as highly educated, socially mobile, and politically liberal. Those on the right tend to be less well-educated, more socially rooted, and politically conservative. Those in the middle tend to be divided within themselves and thus prone to the tensions of maintaining balance, especially in career and commitments.

The "chasm" between these divisions may explain, at least in part, the tension between campus ministries and mainline churches. Higher education continues to be held in high esteem in the American culture, but not for its own sake. The association of education with social prestige and earning power, with technological advance and increased productivity revalued higher education. Education, except for a relatively small elite and for educators themselves, is not so much an end in itself as it is a means to an end. The leadership of mainline Protestant churches has tended to be dominated by university-educated educators, including the clergy.

The church may have made "an awesome mistake by trying to legitimate efforts in the direction of liberation, justice, and peace by using

---

[26] Ibid.

[27] Tex Sample, *Lifestyles and Mainline Churches: A Key to Reaching People in the 90's* (Louisville, KY: Westminster/John Knox Press, 1990).

a rationale that may be compelling to the university-trained—at least some of them—but leaves a chasm between professional church leaders and cultural-right people."[28] The cultural right, which includes but is not limited to Jerry Falwell's "moral majority," might also be characterized by Martin Marty's informed definition: all those who have been left out by everyone else's liberation movements. Increasingly, we all tend to define ourselves by these images of exclusion.

What is important here is not a detailed analysis of the division, but rather how this division likely has shaped the politics of campus ministry. That Americans tend to characterize themselves by the images of exclusion premises their lives on fear. Both Parker Palmer and the Whiteheads wrote of the way this perspective contributes to fears of scarcity and blinds one to God's abundance. A politics of scarcity makes people suspicious of one another and exacerbates divisions. As the Whiteheads have astutely noted, this fear is particularly virulent in notions of power. People caught up in political restructurings may be especially fearful that power is in scarce supply and that what little they might possess is in danger of being taken from them.

At the very least, this distinction has factionalized the churches. One need look no farther than the Episcopal, Methodist, and Presbyterian struggles among their own memberships. Each of these denominations, struggling with many of the same or similar issues, will readily recognize within itself this great divide. Partisanship is so pronounced that even if one succeeds in securing a new member to the denomination, that member must then decide which is the "true evangel" among the many competing voices that vie for the new member's allegiance.

Students who arrive on campus with lively experience of a parish behind them often bring this partisanship with them. They may visit the campus ministry, but abandon it when it is revealed to be "of the opposition." Their campus experience is, for many students (and for an increasing number of adult students, faculty, and others), an introduction to pluralism. And their campus *ministry* experience is, for many, an introduction to the pluralistic diversity of their own denomination and of the Christian religion.

If the politics of the church are partisan, is the gospel truly proclaimed? No easy answer is presumed; this is a dilemma that confronts all Christians. But, in one sense Christian campus ministry may deliberately and purposefully choose to be partisan: in insisting upon an

---

[28] Ibid., 69.

inclusive—even prodigal—politics, campus ministry may effect a partisan stance that distinguishes it. In order to minister to any people, one must begin where those people are.

Further, one must respect and honor people precisely where and as they are. This is what it means to recognize community. Each person brings his or her community with them, in the shape of family, in the constellation of personal values derived from home and those communities that have nurtured them. And they bring with them their fears— fears that are intensely personal and fears born of their own communities. Respect for each person, and for each person's fears, is difficult in a politics of exclusion and competition, for each person must then either hide the truth of himself or herself, repudiate all prior community, and conform to the demands of the new community or each must suffer denigration, rejection of all previous community, and exclusion from the new community.

FAITHFULNESS

Campus ministries are under particular pressure to mediate remarkable differences. It is no wonder that so many fail; it is great wonder that any excel. The campus minister and the community of any campus ministry are called to love at the crossroads of difference. It is difficult to respect the stiff-backed student who will not receive communion at the hands of a female pastor and the hurt, angry student who insists that God cannot be called "Father." It is difficult to love and respect the denomination when it refuses funding and difficult to love the university when it denies access. It is difficult to make room for the gay student and for the one whose fervor for a literal interpretation of the scriptures admits no tolerance. It is difficult to work both sides of the divide and remain faithful to the God of all creation.

Faithfulness to this God would seem to entail inclusive politics. An inclusive politics eschews "membership" as a criterion and assumes "membership" as God's gift. While it is true that young adults (and older ones, too) seek out and benefit from a sense of belonging, belonging does not necessarily entail exclusivity. The predominant theme of the letters we received from former students and others connected by experience to campus ministries was that their sense of belonging was almost always immediate, and often precisely because there were no requirements for membership in the campus ministries they encountered.

Such inclusive politics are, no doubt, a frustration to some. They are especially problematic for those who evaluate campus ministry by the number of members retained. And they are anathema to those who demand doctrinal purity as a measure of orthodoxy. Yet the conversion Christianity seeks is not one of denominational loyalty, but rather one of reunion with the ultimate community of origin—life in and with God.

Still, campus ministry laments its own perceived powerlessness. Campus ministers are no less competitive and no less fearful than any other. Fear has often separated them from the churches and, as frequently, from the universities they serve. They have too often practiced their own politics of fear, locked in combat fearful of losing their potency. Campus ministers have not been nearly so critical of institutions and others as hateful of them.

That campus ministry is considered *marginal* to both the church and to the university is perceived by some campus ministers (and by churches and universities) to be evidence of powerlessness. But in this regard, marginality is more blessing than bane. Indeed, it is the hallmark of Christian ministry. For any ministry that is called to be mediating and reconciling must of necessity be somewhat beyond the edges of the estranged. If the mission of campus ministry is to reunite the fragmented lives and institutions this ministry is called to serve, campus ministry can be in no other place than on the edge.

Yet this paradox is commendable: the campus ministry that excels is not only marginal, it is also integral. Campus ministry—like all ministry undertaken in God's name—*is* the church. There is no gradation of ministries in the Christian church; whatever is done in God's name—no matter by whom, to whom, or with whom—constitutes ministry.

And campus ministry *is* the university. It is integral to the life and experience of the university. Without it the university would not, and could not be what its name implies—it could not be *whole*. In some shape or other ministry must be present on campus, or the university is incomplete.

Within this paradox, then, there is abundance of resource and opportunity. In order to realize both, however, campus ministry needs an appropriate politics, a politics not of scarcity, but of abundance; not of fear, but of faith. Campus ministry demands a politics that meets individuals and institutions where they are and honors the value each brings, as the politics of a new community that is the oldest community of all—the one of God's own making. In the next, and final, chapter we turn our attention to process and the product of vocational ministry, pastoral stewardship, and this politics of faith.

11

LEADERSHIP: A PROPHETIC MINISTRY

LIKE A SHEPHERD

What constitutes the prophetic expression of ministry on the modern campus? The prophetic role of Christian ministry is classically embodied in the Johannine image of the shepherd, one of "serving, selfless leadership who guides and safeguards the lives of those entrusted to his care."[1] The Johannine shepherd provides two dominant images: leadership and servanthood. The image of the shepherd is especially appropriate, if considered from the biblical experience of shepherding—a perspective not widely understood in an American society with limited experience of sheep. The American experience tends toward cattle and the celebrated cowboy. The gritty action of cattle-herding, the stubborn, brute force of cattle-wrangling, seem more characteristic of the American style of leadership than the patient, meditative care of the shepherd.

The shepherd of the biblical metaphor is often ahead of the flock, seeking out green pastureland, lest the sheep overgraze and thus destroy their own food source. Sheep, unlike cows, will tend to stay in one place, grazing the same spot. They will eat the tender leaf of the grass, then the shank, and then the roots themselves, ripping the grass from the earth

---

[1] Underwood, vol. 1, 84.

and leaving barren ground. Thus the responsible shepherd goes just ahead of the flock, in search of food. When food is found, the shepherd leads by calling. The sheep, responding to the shepherd's voice, follow in confidence that the greener pastures, the sustaining waters, and the sheltered resting places necessary to life are where the shepherd is.

The leadership embodied in the shepherd is a particularly apt metaphor of the vocational model of priestly ministry, the stewardship of pastoral ministry, and the politics of ministry. Leadership based in the search for sustaining pastures and the response to call suggests a prophetic mode that is consonant with the priestly mode of vocation. For the children of Israel, there was only one true shepherd: the God of Abraham and Sarah, of Isaac and Rebekah, of Jacob, Rachel and Leah. God was the shepherd who led Moses, Miriam and the people of Israel out of bondage and into a new life. God was the shepherd that led Jesus into the waters of the Jordan, through the wilderness, and into his own vocation. Jesus, who embodied the fullness of human vocation, became for those who succeeded him the very incarnation of a leadership that dared to live in response to faith in God the shepherd. The role of the shepherd, then, is bound up in vocation itself. The seeking of pastureland, water, and safe haven is a process of discernment as the shepherd moves abroad in search of resources provided by God out of the abundance of creation itself.

Seeking these resources is bound up in a pastoral stewardship that matches care for the sheep with equal care for the resources provided. To care only for the short-term welfare of sheep might allow them to eat only once of a grazing ground; if allowed to eat their fill and overgraze, they could ultimately destroy any future opportunity to return to the pasture and eat again. Yet, overzealous conservation of the pasture might encourage the shepherd to lead the sheep elsewhere, or lead them into starvation itself, lest a blade be disturbed by their hunger.

The delicate balance of care in the practice of sound stewardship gives rise to a politics that includes both the sheep and the creation in the shepherd's purview. Habits and structures, routes and routines are devised whereby the shepherd can lead the sheep safely to graze, while also honoring the available resources—and the possibility of other shepherds and sheep dependent upon the same. Such politics require of the shepherd a gentle patience that respects the pace of the sheep, that knows when to rest them and when to encourage them on. It is a politics that reminds the shepherd that shepherd and sheep constitute a partnership in themselves, that they are mutually interdependent. The sheep depend upon the shepherd to realize the fullness of their vocation, which is provision of wool, food, milk, and the promise of new flocks in the birth of lambs. The shepherd, in turn, depends upon the sheep for clothing, sustenance, and livelihood.

A LANGUAGE FOR LEADERSHIP

The shepherd as prophet understands the prophet as one who tells forth. The derivation of the English word "prophet" is Greek and means "to speak before."[2] But the language of leadership, like the language of prophecy, is not necessarily verbal. "Forth-telling" is sometimes less effectively accomplished with words than with actions. The prophetic mode of campus ministry tends to be non-verbal. It tends to use the language of activity and example. Indeed, there are few places within either the church or the university where campus ministry can claim the power of voice. Lacking an "audience," campus ministry—and increasingly, all Christian ministry—must become fluent in the language of incarnation, that quiet but forceful language that, according to the familiar aphorism, speaks louder than words.

The language of Christian witness, and the language of prophetic leadership, is incarnate action. The poverty of words alone is the very premise of Jesus' own incarnation. That the words of the prophets, themselves a gifted company of mature spirituality and integrity, failed to move humanity fully to faithful relationship with God is the premise for the gift of God's incarnate Word in the person of Jesus. The flesh and fabric of human existence and human experience is the universal language that binds all God's people in relationship. So it was that Jesus left little behind in the way of recorded utterances, and nothing inscribed in his own hand, save an enigmatic scribbling in the sand. What he is recorded to have said is based upon memory, and that memory almost always buttressed by concrete action and example. The words never truly stand alone, but are always couched in context, and that context always of the rich human experience of touching, healing, feeding and teaching.

The true prophetic leaders—the ones that remain after history's withering scrutiny strips away all pretense and ruse—are those of genuine integrity, those who practice what they preach. This is the

---

[2] <OF *prophete* < LL *propheta* <Gk. *prophetes* < *pro-* before + *phanai* to speak. *The Standard College Dictionary*, 1080.

power of the Incarnation, the potency of Jesus, whose charismatic gifts found affinity with the deepest needs of people at all levels of his own society—including a good many women and men of political and economic standing whose characters in our own generation have been overshadowed by a preoccupation with the extremely poor and outcast. It is disingenuous to gloss over the likes of Joseph of Arimethea, Nicodemus, Matthew, Saul of Tarsus, the four Evangelists and others who obviously enjoyed the benefits of education and political position. Indeed, one might well ponder what would have become of the Christian event and story but for those whose gifts of intellect and influence preserved and protected the gospel through quite difficult times. The triumph of our religious history is that it exists only because of the unlikely coalition of diversity that found communion in the leadership of Jesus and thus handed the heritage on to any equally diverse company in every successive generation.

But the power of the Incarnation, the potency of Jesus, is also that power of all leadership, which is sometimes reduced to the simple principle: never ask anyone to do anything you are unwilling to do yourself. The most effective and genuine way to communicate one's integrity is to be seen actually doing that which one expects to be done.

One of the most striking biblical instances of this principle is the Johannine version of what Jesus did on the evening of his arrest (John 13:1-15.) In the midst of a dispute over primacy and preference, words were ineffectual. Jesus, probably exhausted and not a little desperate, employed the only language that could communicate to the disciples the attributes of leadership in God's realm. He got up from his place, girded himself with a towel, took up a basin and silently proceeded to wash the feet of the contentious, fractious disciples—presumably including the one who would later betray him. The sum of his teaching was reduced to the simple verbal instruction, "You are to do as I have done for you."[3] The only chronicle of the footwashing, tellingly, is that of the gospel of John—the account given to the greatest reliance upon words and abstractions in the telling of Jesus' story. Those who compiled that account, to judge by the richness of physical detail and action in the narrative, understood full well the necessity of incarnation as a medium of communication and employed it skillfully as a balance to the abstractions of language upon which their narrative relied.

---

[3] John 13:15, NEB.

The forth-telling of God's word, then, in the Christian experience is accomplished in both word and deed. Word without deed becomes empty posturing and abstract idealism. Action without a word that grounds the action in God leaves action at the level of humanitarianism (or "secular humanism")—which can be laudable, even holy, *behavior* but does not acknowledge God as the source and the substance of all *being*. The synthesis of abstraction and example are revealed in Jesus and gradually transform (or more accurately, restore) forth-telling—or witness—to a dynamism that is lacking when either word or action is imbalanced. The dynamism of Christian witness—this wedding of word and deed—is the substance of Christian prophetic leadership.

After Jesus, at least in the Christian experience, there are no prophets, as such. True, there are saints and holy figures by whose lives and examples God's word and will are communicated. But the notion of prophecy, after Jesus, takes on a different character. One can see within his leading of his few disciples the basis of a different kind of forth-telling. It is a forth-telling which evidences experience. It is witness—an Old English word (*witnes*) for knowledge. But it is witness with specific purpose. It is witness the purpose of which is to mediate God with humanity. It is witness not so much to prove a point as to introduce. As such, this witness—like that of the prophets—constitutes leadership.

A PURPOSE FOR LEADERSHIP

The word "lead," derived from Old English, means "to cause to go." As distinct from ordering, leadership has a compelling, persuasive quality about it. Thus the prophets presumed no power or right to order the nation of Israel to particular relationship with God, but rather spoke forcefully and persuasively of why and how Israel should and could restore right relationship with God. Christian leadership has as its ultimate object the reunion of all God's creatures—specifically God's human creatures—with God. This witness, which is frequently characterized in very personal terms, is a communal activity. While personal witness is, indeed, a legitimate and valued component of Christian evangelism, Christian witness is never a solitary activity. Even Jesus' witness is surrounded by and dependent upon a host of characters, both historical and contemporary.

John W. Gardner, former president of the Carnegie Corporation and the Carnegie Foundation for the Advancement of Teaching, wrote a series of insightful "Leadership Papers" that are helpful to this consideration of prophetic leadership. Gardner's observations seem particularly helpful in contemplating modern Christian witness, witness in a context of diversity and division—a witness of the church dispersed.

The image of the church dispersed is more helpful than that of the church as divided and fragmented. While the latter images are probably accurate and helpful in calling the church to the ever-present need for continued reconciliation, one can ask with equal sincerity if the present differentiation of the church—quite apart from its expression in fragmentation—is not also an expression of God's will and word. Are the people of God dispersed in many denominations, and these divided into factions, for a holy reason? Are the people of God sent and set to their respective tasks, bounded by the limitations of their contexts, to some purposeful end?

Gardner maintained that the dispersion of leadership through the varied segments of society (government, professions, minority communities, universities, social agencies, etc.) and through the several levels of social functioning (presidential, managerial, labor, etc.) is necessary to the American "system," which was conceived to function not as a hierarchy—like the monarchies—but as an interdependent democracy. Thus one cannot determine the constituency of the team by studying the organizational charts. The leadership team of an organization may consist of only a few of the members of the governing board, one person from the management sector, and perhaps none of the executives. Even persons not formally associated with the organization may be included in the leadership team.[4] The same seems to pertain to the church and the university. The true leaders—the ones whose lives and actions cause the organization to go—are often a disparate lot, drawn from all over the map, that changes with what seems a rapid turnover.

This has certainly been true of campus ministries. They are set in highly transient surroundings and populated by an eclectic assortment of people with a sometimes breathtakingly odd commingling of talents and interests. Yet they do occasionally take off and even lead. When they do, it is never a single person, but the team that actually leads. That it has happened may in some instances have been happenstance and the work of the Holy Spirit. That it can happen, and should, is the prophetic task of campus ministry.

---

4 John W. Gardner, "The Nature of Leadership: Introductory Considerations," Leadership Papers/1 (Washington, D.C.: Independent Sector, January 1986), 16.

This task, like that of the biblical prophets, is not undertaken easily or welcomed wholeheartedly. There is especially in America and particularly in the present era, a palpable hostility toward the very concept of leadership. Leadership is suspected because of its associations with hierarchy, and rightfully so. We overestimate the role of leaders and we underestimate the "systemic and external considerations" that comprise the interaction of leadership and constituencies.[5] These mis-estimations are the source of those tensions, suspicions, and hostilities that arose between those campus ministers of the 1960s and 1970s who steadfastly believed themselves "prophetic" and those of both the church and the university communities who, with equal conviction, believed those campus ministers to be off-the-wall, or worse, irresponsible.

> As the society becomes increasingly fragmented it needs more than ever leaders who can bind together the fragments. There are systems that can survive for considerable periods without leadership, but our pluralistic society is not one of them. Broadly dispersed initiative and power of decision produce a greater need for leaders who will help citizens pursue their common purposes.[6]

The greater danger in American organizational life may be the peer pressure that can be "more relentless than any leader."[7] Campus ministers who fail to take seriously the need to be a binding, reconciling force in the midst of the turmoil that upended and continues to reshape American life, not only abandon the principles of leadership; they abandon the mandate of the Christian gospel and Christian leadership that is the vocation to reconciliation.

A PASSION AND PATIENCE FOR LEADERSHIP

The work of binding and reconciling is cruciform in shape. Holding fast the polarities is far more dangerous and exhausting than retreat into the extremes. Yet campus ministry professes to know that this is our call: to share Jesus' cross and death as we share Jesus' resurrected life.

It is this reality that positions campus ministry at the margins. Campus ministry decries its marginal status, even as our ancestors in

---

[5] John W. Gardner, "Leadership and Power," Leadership Papers/4 (Washington, D.C.: Independent Sector, October 1986), 17ff.

[6] Ibid., 19.

[7] Ibid.

faith cursed the wilderness and looked with longing behind them to the relative comfort of ordered existence under Pharaoh or looked with anticipation ahead of them to the ease of an endowment paying dividends in milk and honey. Yet it is this very marginality that verifies the vocation to reconciliation. In order to reconcile, one has to be between. Thus was Jesus pinioned, gripping in one hand his abiding love of God and in the other his abiding love for all humankind. Stretched taut between those extremes, he lived and died.

Nor was Jesus' death a quick one. The path to reconciliation, like the path to resurrection, is not instantaneous—a particularly difficult reality for moderns to grasp, much less appreciate. There are constraints and frustrations in interdependence.[8] The revolutionary movements of the 1960s and 1970s were unquestionably necessary; the turning of time does sometimes require considerable force. But once set in motion, the movement of something so cumbersome as human society demands a steady pace. There was, for good and sufficient reason, a forceful impatience among those who participated in those revolutionary events of the 1960s and 1970s.

Revolution requires impatience, but interdependence demands a profound patience, which for moderns is likely as close as we shall get to the passion of Jesus in our own experience. This patience comes under particular duress just now as the church and the world appropriate the fruits of the most recent revolutions in our society—revolutions that have set in motion a new order of interdependence in which those who were on top of the wheel descend and those who were beneath the wheel ascend, the natural and expected order of things as the wheel turns. The fear that grips us is that the wheel will reach stasis again, and that those who were on top will be permanently crushed beneath—or that the wheel will by gravity's force roll backward and those who were beneath will too quickly be crushed again. Patience is necessary to a leadership that mediates between these real and potent fears and the natural impulse to act hastily upon them.

Campus ministers know, at least in some respect, the value of patience, for they frequently have occasion to counsel more of it in their work with young adults. But in their own circumstances, patience is harder come by. In these days, as the institutions within which campus ministers work and live struggle to effect greater interdependence, it is

---

[8] John W. Gardner, "Attributes and Context" Leadership Papers/6 (Washington, D.C.: Independent Sector, April 1987), 7.

especially difficult to be patient with these processes. It is hard to find that patience when budget re-allocations threaten their livelihood. Edgy and angry defensiveness often prevails over calm reason and faithful patience. Energies that go into defense drain resources from the patient work of conversation by which the importance of our ministry is mediated with equally important work elsewhere in the growing complexity of church and society.

Leadership in campus ministry is particularly challenged just now to find a counterpoise to the deadly partnership born of our premium upon largeness and our fears of scarcity. As indicated earlier in this study, American institutions—and the church in particular—are literally fascinated by images of scarcity. They are held spellbound in terror and awe by the possibilities of want. Whether one is of the generation that still vividly remembers the experience of the Great Depression, or of the generation that has tasted of unparalleled abundance made possible only by the illusions of unregulated credit consumerism, Americans are paralytically aware of the possibility of want.

Leadership is painfully difficult in a climate of fear. It is practically impossible when that fear extends to the leaders themselves. Campus ministers have little confidence of abundance, and what little confidence they possess is threatened in church settings that are equally fearful and give witness to that fear in expansive gestures aimed at institutional (and financial) growth. The urgency with which American mainline Protestant churches embrace church growth tactics and programs does not communicate gospel or good news at all. It only betrays the panic of scarcity that underlies the urgency.

Steadfast faith and ineffable patience are necessary to proclaim in word and deed the abundance that is ours in a climate where people persist in seeing the cup as half-empty and leaking fast. The power of modernity to enthrall, and the difficulty of breaking that paralysis, is exemplified in the experience of a gathering of lay and ordained leaders attending a judicatory meeting where the presenter was a noted university futurologist. The futurologist did an excellent job of informing these leaders of the current capabilities of computer technology and of its probable potential for practical application. He spoke of the computer's usefulness as an analytical and communicative tool, of how American education was being transformed at all levels by the use of interactive machines. Children would begin from their earliest years to learn on these machines and thus, between computers and television, would spend the vast majority of their developmental lives into adulthood, in conversation with video screens.

The excitement mounted as the speaker continued. When the conversation was opened, participants shared with a fevered mix of anxiety and enthusiasm ideas for deploying these technologies in the church. They spoke excitedly of computerized networks for church communication, and of the need for interactive resources to communicate the church's message and its programs. They were energetic and animated as they spoke of the need and potential for developing television resources, for utilizing the medium for their work. They wondered aloud at the cost of mounting such marvelous networks. And they gradually sank into depression at the daunting prospect of financing such ventures.

No one seemed to see that there was another side to the futurologist's scenario. They seemed oblivious to the image of a world of children and adults bereft of family interaction and human socialization. They were so captivated by the notion of reaching thousands, even millions, of people that they seemed not to contemplate the solitary loneliness of the individual tied to the world only by an electric impulse and a plastic keyboard. In their fears of a church by-passed by technologies, and their visions of a church equipped to meet the future on its own technological terms, they overlooked completely the gift of present resources.

It occurred to one (a campus minister) that the world described by the futurologist was one ideally suited to the gifts of the church for gathering people, for nurturing relationship, for encouraging and sustaining intimacy. What the futurologist was revealing was that the future (which was and is very much present) had specific need of what the church has to contribute and that, perhaps, those gifts of the church would become all the more unique as the future unfolded. That revelation, when shared, registered genuine surprise—and not a little outright resistance.

A PLACE FOR LEADERSHIP

In considering pastoral stewardship it was noted above that campus ministries that make careful, responsible stewardship of their human and spiritual resources an immediate priority frequently find that financial and other physical resources are forthcoming. If the essence of leadership is "to cause to go," then campus ministry is among those ministries of the church that can call the church and society away from the paralyzing preoccupation with the need for more and the fear of less, into the abundance of life.

When developing leadership, one encounters the paradox of the bigger-is-better phenomenon: "...large organizations and communities have a suppressive effect on the incidence of leaders in the system....The number of *significant functions per individual* tends to be greater in small social units than in large."[9] The vast complexity of American institutional life discourages leadership development: "Our young people are born into a society that is huge, impersonal and intricately organized. Far from calling them to leadership, it appears totally indifferent. It does not seem to need them at all. Far from creating the confidence that young leaders require, it is apt to create puzzlement and a sense of powerlessness. It is very hard for young people today to believe that any action on their part will affect the vast processes of their society."[10]

While one cannot always alter the fundamental realities of size and complexity, new methods of organization can be devised that mitigate their ill effects. Thus, the church may provide in some of its oldest methods of organization the very antidote that is needed to encourage and develop leaders. This is an especially important role for campus ministry and one that is frequently overlooked by churches that measure campus ministry solely in terms of the numbers of warm bodies it gathers and contributes to the whole.

The mainline churches did appreciate this reality in those times when campus ministry was considered an essential recruiting ground for ordained leadership. But when the need for ordained leadership tapered off, campus ministry was seen as less valuable to the institution. There seems to be little appreciation that the mainline Protestant churches have consistently maintained the highest-educated memberships in America— that significant portions (in some denominations, a majority) of churched mainline-Protestants possess college degrees—and that campus ministry is as essential today to the recruiting and development of *lay* leadership for the mainline churches as it once was for ordained leadership. It seems an ironic twist of clericalism that experience that was once deemed desirable for attracting ordained leadership should be denied the laity.

Yet campus ministry in many places continues to supply the church with leadership by offering sound experiential education for leadership in models that are often at odds with what the church deems appropri-

9 John W. Gardner, "Leadership Development," *Leadership Papers*/7 (Washington, D.C.: Independent Sector, January 1986), 5.
10 Ibid., 6.

ate. Providing small, compact organizations is an essential component to the development of leadership. Leaders benefit from opportunity to actually practise leadership and this practise is denied in large structural organizations.

But to develop leaders it is increasingly necessary to urge movement away from narrow specialization. "Leaders have always been general-ists....Tomorrow's leaders will very likely have begun life as trained specialists, but to mature as leaders they must sooner or later climb out of the trenches of specialization and rise above the boundaries that sepa-rate the various segments of society. Only as generalists can they cope with the diversity of problems and multiple constituencies that contem-porary leaders face."[11] Campus ministries that are compact in size, but diverse in constituency, offer and reinforce this call to generalization. Campus ministries that are bound too narrowly to images of protective containment ultimately deny young adults this experience and render them less capable of meeting the complexities faithfully. This reality is exemplified in those fundamentalist campus ministries that cultivate student dependencies and, for a while, may be successful in terms of numbers but eventually lose young adults who can no longer tolerate the tension between the ordered control of a tightly bounded community and the demands of daily life in a complex culture. Some of those students are lost to other denominations more tolerant of diversity and ambiguity; some are lost to the church forever; and some are lost to madness or suicide when the tension proves unbearable.

Further, the university prepares leaders by providing sound liberal arts curricula, equipping students to live in a world of unceasing change. But the church and campus ministry also have an important role to play in this regard, especially when the university itself is overwhelmed by the forces of specialization that prevail in the minds of students despite every available opportunity to countermand them. Through contact with the liturgical cycle, through preaching and worship, in counsel and activity, and through other expressions of campus ministry, young adults often learn how to to mediate between constant change and eternal values.

Connection with the religious history of God's people is absolutely essential, for as Gardner noted of the young adult leader, "They cannot know what they want to preserve against the buffeting of change, or what source of strength they can draw on to channel change, unless they

---

[11] Ibid., 7.

know the path already traveled.[12] Leaders must understand a cultural history that is largely latent. For Americans the religious component of culture is latent, and in danger of sustained dormancy, fewer and fewer persons are, in church or society, connected to its history through the reading of scripture. Reading itself is a diminishing facility.

Campus ministry contributes to the self-knowledge that is important to the development of leaders.[13] Self-knowledge proceeds out of experience in communities where intimacy and relationship encourage honest conversation. Self-knowledge is a particular "fruit of the Spirit" in the Christian experience, the gift that comes of personal relationship with God in the experience of Jesus and in the communion of the church. The church, through its ministry with young adults on campus, has nurtured generations of women and men who come to their experiences of themselves in the company of people who believe themselves in relationship with God, and thus related to all that God has created. Such a sense of oneself gives rise not only to a sense of one's own wellness, but also of one's role in the continuing welfare of creation through kinship with it.

The role of communication, as noted earlier, only grows more important to all facets of life and ministry. Communication is the "single, all-purpose instrument of leadership."[14] While particularly charismatic leadership will possess special gifts for communication, much of communication can be taught. Facility in writing and speaking one's own language is essential, and given global interdependence, a working knowledge of a second language is increasingly essential.

PARISHES AND OTHER PARTNERS

But leadership in the church requires still more. A working knowledge of the language of the religious community, including the history of its derivation, is required of those who would lead in the church. Here the educational task of the church becomes most evident and its recent failures most pronounced. The mainline Protestant churches do not always rightly comprehend the truths evidenced by their critics, especially when those critics are within. The charismatic Pentecostalists of the denominational churches rightly called attention to the imbalance of a Christianity that allowed form to overpower spirit. In their extrem-

---

[12] Ibid., 11–12.
[13] Ibid., 13.
[14] Ibid.

ism, they urged a corrective that eventually gave rise to a renewed spirituality in the churches—sometimes (as can be the case in any extremism) swinging the balance off-kilter in the opposing direction.

But similarly, the fundamentalists and biblicists rightly wage a renewed consideration for the story upon which faith is based, and upon the necessity to impart that story intact to successive generations. Biblical illiteracy is more than an embarrassment and a nuisance; it is irresponsible. One of the best ways the churches can support young adult ministry on campus is to pay increased attention to the educating of children. No campus ministry can effectively do its job with young adults without sound Christian education in the churches. At the least, poor Christian education in the parishes saddles campus ministry with the task of providing remedial education instead of the vocational education to which it is called. At the worst, poor Christian education in the parishes renders the task of campus ministry impossible by denying succeeding generations of young adults the one point of communion they have with the church on campus, which is their story and its vocabulary.

On campus, the presence and program of denominational campus ministries provide access to the Christian story and, importantly, within the context of other religious stories, not the least of which are the American cultural stories, which syncretically hitch a ride on the Christian story, diffusing and confusing its message and its power, or constitute outright rivals to the Christian narrative and experience. Religious pluralism is not an academic course; religious pluralism is the way people live their lives, and always have. The story of Christianity (and Judaism) is replete with evidence that believers have always wavered and shifted among a variety of religious options, that the dynamic of faith is just that—a dynamic, and not fixed.

Whether ordained or lay, leaders in campus ministry must be fluent in the language of Christianity and be competent apologists for it. Theological apologetics is not a particularly popular vocation today. The defense and explanation of the Christian faith depends upon story, and fluency in the language and images of both the Bible and modern culture. Apologists G. K. Chesterton and C. S. Lewis continue to enjoy wide readership, especially among young adults, testimony to their facility in translating the Biblical and ecclesial experiences of the historic faith community into modern images. Their images, however, belong now to a rapidly outdated sense of modernity. They were exponents of the industrial revolution; their images have since been eclipsed by those of the technological revolution and will soon be completely obsolete and inaccessible to generations for whom industrialism is as foreign as agrarianism is now to the majority of American children. The church needs articulate post-modern apologists.

At the heart of sound campus ministry are the gifted apologists, lay and ordained, who through teaching and preaching, by word and example, impart the stories of Christian faith through contemporary images and experiences that make them real and present to the lives of a new generation. Consistently, the responses of former students who reflected upon their campus ministry experiences for this study indicated that sermons and worship-related experience were among the most important. One student wrote of the preaching and provocative educational conversation experienced in campus ministry:

> By matching the intellectual rigor of the University…and surpassing it by providing a coherent and sensible framework of belief, [campus] ministry gave me a firm foundation upon which to build my life.
> I remember clearly a number of sermons there about salvation and what saved people should be like. The important part of the message was the latter. The Church does a good job explaining how one is saved, but guidance on the latter is difficult. Salvation comes once; living with it is a daily task.[15]

On assignment with the Peace Corps in the Philippines some years later, the same former student earned the trust and respect of the native people. He married a Philippine woman and, only days later, was taken hostage and held for political reasons.

> When I was held hostage the faith I'd built up was tried beyond anything I would have believed. Utterly helpless and nearly alone, I had nothing else to hang onto sometimes. God was my best resort and I turned to Him often, silently, in whispers, sobs and screams. Simple faith helped hold me together. It would not have worked if I had not built up such a solidly founded faith that makes sense. Brent House more than anything else, helped me build that foundation.[16]

Another graduate of a different campus ministry wrote: "The Holy Scriptures began to speak to me in college through dialogue and sharing in community, and, in subsequent years, God's Word in Scripture continues to speak through shared communication with sisters and brothers in Christ rather than through any private, personal experience

---

[15] Tim Swanson to Sam Portaro, LS, 14 July 1991, 2.
[16] Ibid.

of revelation." Now an ordained Episcopal priest himself, this same graduate reflected on the sermons he heard as a student active in campus ministry,

> sermons which are still among the most inspiring and stimulating messages I have heard in Christ's fellowship, [that] provided me with a witness to prophetic Christian ministry which I am still trying to follow in my own life and vocation. Before the rise of the "men's movement" you showed me what it was like to be vulnerable and open to pain and feelings; before the acceptance of the gay rights movement into the mainstream dialogue of the Church, you challenged me and other students, at great risk, to rethink our deep sexual prejudice, and reach out to sisters and brothers who had been marginalized in Christian parishes because of their sexual preference and expression. When I was struggling with academic and professional accomplishment and "success," your words enabled me to understand the Gospel call to a life of integrity, authenticity, and of the work of peace and social justice. When I was tempted to look for easy answers in the depths of spiritual void, your words and example always offered me the opportunity to see the power and merit in the Anglican way of paradox and ambiguity. When the temptation to search for meaning in the dead ends of orthodoxy came my way, I had your example of the life-giving ways in the challenge of the conventional and the status-quo.[17]

But in addition to the preaching and teaching provided by the formal, liturgical sharing of the Christian story is the imparting of the story via shared experience with a people committed to living the story. It is in this regard that parish or congregationally based campus ministries have much to offer and free-standing campus ministries have much for which to compensate. Those former students who wrote of their experience in parish-based campus ministries often cited the connection with the congregation as an essential component in their own faith development.

But what they found was more than a replacement for the congregation left behind when they came to college. As one, now himself an Episcopal priest, expressed it: "...I found a new Church, for it brought me into the Episcopal Church at a time when I was spiritually searching for answers and directions."[18] Another alumnus of the same campus ministry noted that the fact that the parish housed and contributed substantially to the campus ministry communicated "a concerted effort on their part to make collegians feel a part of their church. As a result,

---

[17] Hugh E. Brown III to Sam Portaro, LS, 9 July 1991.
[18] Roger Schellenberg to Sam Portaro, LS,1991, 2.

there were students, like me, who became part of two parish families [the campus ministry community and the parish itself]. Had I chosen not to be active in [the campus ministry] I would have still felt the presence of campus ministry and had opportunities to become involved in the life of the parish."[19]

"Programs that bring a number of young leaders together for a shared experience," wrote Gardner, "have an impact over and above the nature of the particular program."[20] Among the benefits of such experience, he lists the following:

> —Opportunities for students to test their judgment under pressure, in the face of opposition, and in the fluid and swiftly-changing circumstances so characteristic of action
> —Opportunities to exercise responsibility and perhaps to try out one or another of the skills required for leadership
> —Opportunities for students to test and sharpen their intuitive gifts, and to judge their impact on others
> —Exposure to new "constituencies."
> —Exposure to the untidy world, where decisions must be made on inadequate information and the soundest argument doesn't always win, where problems do not get fully solved or, if solved, surface anew in another form.[21]

Moreover, the best of these learning opportunities afford the student instruction, counsel, or feedback that encourages and enables the young adult to actually comprehend the experience and appropriate it as learning.

THE PROPHETIC LEADERSHIP OF IMAGINING AND IMAGING

What distinguishes campus ministry from many extracurricular and off-campus experiences, and qualifies it (using Gardner's estimation) as a superior opportunity, is the guiding—and abiding—presence of the mentor, the campus minister. As the evidence supports, the story of campus ministry most often begins, "We had a chaplain (or campus minister) who..." "There is much about leadership that is best learned

---

[19] John McGee to Sam Portaro, LS, 19 July 1991.

[20] John W. Gardner, "Leadership Development," Leadership Papers/7 (Washington, D.C.: Independent Sector, January 1986), 15.

[21] Ibid., 16.

from living examples."[22] The role of the mentor, or mentoring community, in developing leadership thus demands that the mentor or mentoring community practice the same qualities it hopes to instill. The Christian community encourages vocational integrity in the practice of vocational integrity; it models a caring pastoral stewardship in the practice of the same; it envisions a politics of equality and even prodigal love and respect by incarnating those politics in its daily living and its structures; and it speaks the prophetic forth-telling of God's word and will by actively incarnating that word and that will in the company of those young adults it seeks to inspire.

Taking a leaf from Maria Harris, whose *Teaching and Religious Imagination: An Essay in the Theology of Teaching* frames for teachers some of the same issues considered here for campus ministers and ministries:

> The heart of teaching is imagination, which in Paul Ricoeur's words, "has a prospective and explorative function in regard to the inherent possibilities of human beings." For Ricoeur, "the imagination is par excellence, the instituting and constituting of what is humanly possible; in imagining possibilities, human beings act as prophets of their own existence."[23]

Prophetic leadership, therefore, consists in the active imagining—the incarnating—of possibility. The mainline Protestant churches, especially those inclined to measure all ministries—and especially campus ministry—against purely utilitarian indices, are like the society they criticize. Ministry and the life of the church, or lack thereof, are approached as problems to be solved. That the churches have too few members and too few dollars are seen as problems that can be solved by the application of technique—the ultimate expression of which is the church-growth movement.

The academy, facing similar "problems," seeks in vain for the proper techniques to achieve its own ends. Wanting, however, is a vision that draws on religious imagination:

> I am convinced that our society desperately needs a philosophy of teaching that explores the dimension of depth in teaching, a philosophy that begins not with technique, but with the majesty and the mystery involved in teaching....I want to move away from teaching seen as a problem, to a view that assumes it is far more appropriate to see teaching as a mystery. With

---

[22] Ibid., 17.

[23] Maria Harris, *Teaching and Religious Imagination: An Essay in the Technology of Teaching* (San Francisco: Harper & Row, 1987), 3.

William Walsh, I believe that "all too many of the problems of education are mysteries made shabby by the absence of reverence."[24]

The prophetic task may not directly answer problems, but instead, reverences mystery. In the night in which he was betrayed, Jesus had a profound problem on his hands. His life was drawing to a close and his disciples had obviously not appropriated what he longed to teach them. He did not address the problem; he reverenced the mystery in the reverential act of service. With the basin and towel, kneeling at their feet, one by one, Jesus invited the disciples into that mystery. They followed.

A PROGNOSIS FOR CAMPUS MINISTRY LEADERS

In the long run, however, there remains the most daunting and compelling demand of leadership: "It is one of the tasks of leaders to ensure the continuous renewal of the systems over which they preside."[25] Campus ministry, like every other facet of the church's ministry, is challenged to this task of renewal. There is no evidence that campus ministry will ever again know the priority status it enjoyed, if only briefly, in the mainline Protestant tradition. Lamenting the loss of that status, mounting accusatory denunciations, and hurling dire threats of future membership decline is not prophecy; it is the bitter complaining that looks longingly back at Pharaoh. Such backward-oriented glances, like those Lot's wife cast upon the cities of the plain, only render campus ministry a pillar of bitter salt; such a ministry can have a predictably emetic effect upon those who are literally sick of hearing its complaints.

Prophetic leadership in campus ministry has tended to lament, forgetting that prophetic leadership can also charm. The vision of a renewed church begins in Sunday schools and in campus ministries. When students gathered for InterVarsity's Global Issues Conference during the Urbana missions convention in 1990, one group was challenged to envision what kind of leaders the world and the church would need in the near future. One student summarized the experience:

> ...we had to re-examine our expectations of leadership—you know, that we are all going to change the world, doing all these great things for God. Instead, we affirmed that we are called to lead moral and ethical lives daily,

---

[24] Ibid., 24–25.
[25] John W. Gardner, "Renewing: The Leader's Creative Task," *Leadership Papers*/10 (Washington, D.C.: Independent Sector, March 1988), 3.

in every little thing that we do. Then we looked at what words come to mind when we think of leadership: money, power, position, manipulation, high profile. We realized that the world's definitions have nothing to do with the servant leadership that Jesus modeled. Leadership is what real Christians do as they stand out as examples of moral and ethical living

We see a trend in the church toward a team model of interdependence. Leadership is shared in community, not something we try to control and manipulate toward our own ends. At the turn of the century we will need some strong, visionary people, no doubt, but they will not be on top of a pyramid. They'll be part of a community of accountability where the practical personal balances out the visionary rather than just being squashed, and vice versa. Styles of leadership are as diverse as people themselves, and God has called people from every ethnic, cultural, and socioeconomic background into leadership.[26]

The prophetic leadership of campus ministry is evident in this student's vision of the church, a vision increasingly incarnate in imaginative campus ministry. But the churches lack a complementary imagination. One woman shared in correspondence her own experience of the disparity between campus ministry and parish life:

There are...ways campus ministry contributed to my life which could broadly be categorized as preparation for life in the wider church. My campus ministry experience gave me the opportunity to learn to lead as well as to follow, to begin to discover ways of taking responsibility for the life of the organization, and to practice the hard lessons of living in community. In that way, campus ministry provided me with a model for life and leadership in the church, one which, I am sad to say, the "real" church has often not lived up to.[27]

Another wrote that her "only regret for having been involved in campus ministry is that I thought that I could easily find another community like it!...God and I are still on good terms, but I don't enjoy going to a church that's all nicely boxed and wrapped up and which doesn't challenge its members to think!....I had such a good experience with campus ministry..., I've got high standards!"[28]

One clergyman opined that those who depended upon campus ministry were spoiled ever after for parish life. There is some truth to that accusation, but in reality, culpability for the spoilage lies on both

---

[26] William Long, "Global Issues: Student Responses to Worldwide Crises" *Student Leadership Journal* 3, no. 3 (Spring 1991): 5–9.

[27] Tara Kee to Sam Portaro, LS, 1991, 2.

[28] Jennifer DeNapoli to Sam Portaro, LS, 25 May 1991, 3–4.

sides of the issue. Campus ministry that does not work exceedingly hard at the task of mediating young adult religious experience with ecclesiastical realities is irresponsible campus ministry. Despite best efforts (or perhaps because of them), as the student indicated, young adult standards are changed by the experience of sound campus ministry. It is possible, in some instances, that the standards of the young adult represent a call to the church to be faithful to its own vocation—a prophetic leadership. As one student mused, "Ideally all congregations are to be open and supportive organizations and perhaps the church as a whole should take a lesson from its 'foster-child,' campus ministry, on what a congregation is really all about."[29]

Students like the one at the InterVarsity conference, having imagined a church of servanthood, carry that image with them and it becomes the standard. For some it becomes the judgment of the recalcitrant congregation or denomination. For others, it becomes the transformation of life and the expression of the gospel in the witness of the church dispersed. One student wrote of her experience in United Methodist campus ministry: "Ever since I left Chapel Hill, I have been searching for...another Wesley Foundation group."[30] Chronicling her search, she went on to say that she didn't find it in graduate school, nor in her early work with the Equal Employment Opportunity Commission. A close approximation grew briefly out of the association she and her husband enjoyed with half a dozen other newly wed couples who supervised a youth group for a large Baptist congregation. But five years into their marriages wrought the predictable changes of children, home-ownership, and career demands.

Where has she most closely and most recently found the "intimacy, the passion, the purposefulness, and the sense of *call*" that were nurtured by her campus ministry experience? She has found them in political service, as a county commissioner and in service to a hard-fought U. S. Senate campaign. Her vision continues to guide, sometimes bringing her into the communion of the church, if only to sustain her and strengthen her for "mission" elsewhere—a kind of ministry that the church may have to take more seriously, but for which it will find abundant evidence in its own early life.

The story of the early church is not only the story of congregation, but the tale of travel and dispersal. Whatever the truth behind the stories

[29] John Burton to Sam Portaro, LS, 1991, 2.
[30] Susan Green to Sam Portaro, LS, 9 July 1991, 7.

of the apostles' deaths, the tradition that places their ends at remote places, far from their original source and separated from one another, may for many become a sustaining image of life in Christ. If the experience of this woman be expressive of others, campus and similarly evocative young adult ministries may prove ever more important to the life of the faith community as the last opportunity in their educational and developmental progression where the church can effectively meet them as a gathered community.

Still, the church continues to be strengthened and sustained by campus ministry. Correspondence from former students and faculty who were inspired by campus ministry to seek ordination have been cited. But the response of the laity indicated comparable benefit. "Working with a student vestry, and with several chaplains and ministers opened my eyes to the demands put on church administrators. I now have more realistic expectations of the clergy and feel more comfortable around them,"[31] wrote one former student. Another offered that "...practical experiences offered by campus ministry, such as election to a working student vestry, gave me considerable insight into lay leadership. I developed many of the skills I needed to be involved in parish, community and professional projects. I learned how to be accountable and how to hold others accountable."[32] The same correspondent has since assumed responsibility for a campus ministry in his hometown. "The design and shape of this ministry will be different from the one I knew," he wrote, " but it is my hope that it might achieve the same end—bringing members of the college community closer to Christ and each other."[33]

Among the more powerful reflections were those of former students who identified what for them was a singular distinction of campus ministry and why it cannot be organized or structured like other student organizations. A laywoman wrote:

> As I look back, I can remember going to Wren Chapel and worshiping with members of sororities and fraternities, non-Greek students, gay students, straight students, fundamentalists, liberals, recovering alcoholics, partyers, tee-totalers, black and white, men and women, old and young, students and community members. In my sorority we wore our Greek letters to show our unity, but in Canterbury we had a common bond that was much more sincere, stronger and much more long-lasting: The Holy Spirit. I felt like Canterbury was my home and when I would return to my sorority house

---

[31]   Emily Clark to Sam Portaro, LS, 1991, 1.
[32]   John McGee to Sam Portaro, LS, 19 July 1991, 2.
[33]   Ibid.

and see my sisters socializing, I often felt like there was something missing, like *they* were missing something. I can't say that working with the people in Canterbury was always easy—it was often very difficult! That difficulty was the price I willingly paid to know that I shared campus ministry with a refreshing assortment of people.[34]

Another, now ordained, shared a similar perspective:

Here's the important point for me. I believe one of the great potentials for the Episcopal Church lies in how college students who are searching for spiritual nurture may be brought into the Church, and brought closer to God. If a Canterbury Association were only one more campus activity, it would have only a limited effect. But it is not. It's not a religious fraternity or an alternative to the sorority scene; it doesn't take the place of my dormitory or my team or being part of student government. Those all ended when I left college. None of them had the power to give me life and hope. They were diversions and entertainment. It's funny to remember how my fraternity brothers would chant "Not four years but a lifetime" to suggest our ties to one another would last longer than our college careers. But they were wrong. The thing that has lasted beyond graduation has been my relationship with God and my membership in the Episcopal Church. I have Canterbury to thank for it.[35]

In conclusion, the prophetic leadership of campus ministry—leadership that incarnates vocation, practices a stewardship of care, honors the politics of diversity and inclusion, and reverences the mystery in a profound servanthood is perhaps most powerfully, and appropriately, conveyed in a story. It is not the story of any one person's achievement or accomplishment, nor the story of an exemplary model or program. It is a story of failure and triumph, of death and resurrection, of sin and redemption. And it is the story of a community.

It is the story of an event that took place over a winter holiday. Episcopal students, chaplains, faculty, and friends gave up several precious days of their Christmas/New Year recess to gather at the YMCA of the Rockies in Estes Park, Colorado. The gathering of so many, and of such diversity, was not a familiar experience. The protective boundaries of tradition did not pertain for this community whose brief life together was bound up only by a shared commitment to the Christian faith and the Episcopal expression of it.

---

[34] Jennifer DeNapoli to Sam Portaro, LS, 25 May 1991.
[35] Roger Schellenberg to Sam Portaro, LS, July 1991.

Throughout the conference those gathered shared the stimulation of provocative keynote addresses that challenged perceived notions of truth and authority, opening vistas into other cultural experiences and social realities. Small groups gathered for conversation on theology, addiction, sexuality, intimacy, and a widely ranging menu of topics relevant to young adult and academic experience in the church. Worship offered not only the forth-telling of the word in the reading of scripture and in thoughtful preaching, but in movement and music. The tensions of so much diversity gathered for such a short time, at such a high physical and spiritual altitude, were evidenced in spirited debate and high-spirited frivolity.

On New Year's Eve the assembly gathered for a party. It was a rousing event and lasted well into the morning hours. Sometime in the pre-dawn dark, after many had retired, a few hangers-on kept the vigil with dance and legally, if not wisely, consumed alcohol. A brief dispute erupted over the selection of music for a dance. Tempers flared, a racial epithet was hurled, then followed by physical blows as the tensions of a whole community were exacted in the bodies of a few. The local police were summoned and quelled the altercation, the whole event all but unknown to the vast number exhausted in their beds.

The next morning, New Year's Day, a palpable dis-ease spread through the assembly as word circulated—as word will—of the early-morning events. No one seemed to know exactly what had happened, but everyone seemed to know that something was wrong. Immediately after breakfast, the assembly was to convene for its final event: a closing celebration of the Eucharist celebrating the new year, and the theme of the conference itself, "A Naming of Darkness, A Calling to Light."

As the community gathered in the amphitheater auditorium that served the several functions of study and worship throughout the five-day conference, the setting was familiar. Musicians were on stage, poised to commence. The eucharistic table was set, its candles lighted and inviting a quiet hush that was laced with a palpable foreboding. The entrance rite seemed about to begin when the presider walked alone to the center of the altar and waited in silence for a quiet that was quick in coming. In his office as national staff officer for Ministry in Higher Education, Mark Harris evinced a low-key, casual leadership style. In his characteristically calm voice, he began rather simply, but directly.

He informed the assembled congregation that in the early-morning hours the life of the community had been fractured by violence, verbal and physical. The community, he announced, was broken. He made no attempt to specify who had broken the community, nor how. But he continued, saying that the Eucharist was a celebration of reconciliation and that this Eucharist would not begin, would not be celebrated, until we had been reconciled. Then very simply, but very deliberately, he extinguished the two candles on the altar and took his seat in the presider's chair.

There followed an interminable silence. The only sound memorable to this author was that of his own heart, pounding in his ears so loudly it seemed as though the whole room pulsed with nervous anxiety. This was worship totally out of control, beyond the safe and predictable bounds of written corporate confession and rote absolution. It was literally nerve-wracking, and heart-wrenching.

After what seemed an eternity, a young man rose to his feet in the far upper corner of the tiered seats. In a quiet but audible voice he identified himself as the person who, only a few hours earlier, had become angry and in his anger had called another "a black bitch." He asked her now, if she would stand to signify her acceptance of his sincere apology. In the lower reaches of the seats, almost at the opposite pole of the room's compass from her attacker, she stood and offered her acceptance, and her forgiveness.

But it did not end there. Slowly, others stood and, one at a time, confessed their own contributions to the community's brokenness. One young man confessed that he had knowingly and willingly shared a particularly scurrilous anti-gay joke in the presence of those he knew to be homosexual. He asked their forgiveness, and others stood to grant it. On and on it went, like a living re-enactment of the Pauline catalogue of human sin, each one tumbling out in search of forgiveness, each one met with absolution.

There is not much more to remember or to tell. There were tears, so many tears. But somewhere in the crying, the eyes were cleared and a new vision became apparent: this is what it means to be the church, this was a living incarnation of our story. This was why and how Christians have survived the centuries. We who were present and privileged to see it somehow knew that we were in the very presence of God. We stood, if only for a moment, in the mystery.

The Eucharist that followed felt not like the culmination of our life together, but only its commencement. It was not a moment of false camaraderie or manufactured community; it was far too gritty and real and ugly, and yet more embraceable and tangible and beautiful. It seemed then, and remains, a powerful image of prophetic leadership—the living witness of a community of young adults struggling through their diversity to find union in God. And God did not disappoint.